LIFE IN THE COUNTRY THROUGH THE EYES OF A KID

The Good Ole Days (1942—1956)

Life on the farm can be tough and uncertain but without them the world population would be a whole lot tougher!

Ken Willingham

KEN WILLINGHAM

ISBN 978-1-64300-100-5 (Paperback)
ISBN 978-1-64300-101-2 (Digital)

Covenant Books, Inc.
11661 Hwy 707
Murrells Inlet, SC 29576
www.covenantbooks.com

Contents

Memorable Moments Flashback..7
Preface..9
Introduction...17

First Memories of J Highway...19
Farm and House We Moved To...23
Winter Cold and Fun..33
Salt River Ice Break Through..42
Grinding Feed in the Grain Shed 47
Axe Cut and Bloody Leg 50
Slopping the Hogs..54
Funny Drunk Pigs..57
Log Cabin and Groundhog Burn Out..................................59
Journey to the Fishing Hole 69
Fishing before the Bus Arrives 71
End of Winter and Last Wood Cutting 74
Elementary School Formal Education 77
First Bike Ride to Santa Fe 96
Santa Fe People and Places 103
Fun at Scott Holland's..117
Lela Williams and the Rug Loom 127
Nighttime Entertainment and Consequences 130
Saturday Night Entertainment and Visiting the Ballpark.........133
Mrs. Blaker and Brother Jim's Warts...................................137
Change of Season 140
Best of Springtime in the Country.......................................142

Uncle Jody and the Bobcat 151

Uncle Jody at Simmons's Stable 153

Larry and the Dead Rooster 157

Uncle John and the Skunk..159

Fishing with Grandpa Burl 169

Farm Kids Eat the Best 173

Community Butchering and Fresh Meat 179

Lost Sheep and Newborn Baby Lamb..................................186

Christmas Tree Search with Brother Jim's Help.................190

Christmas Pageant Night before Christmas 195

Dad's Fly Rod and the Kids with the Hornets' Nest............199

Smells of the Farm and Trapping the Skunk 205

Saturday Morning in Mexico..210

Blackberry Picking with Mom and Helen Sharp..............220

Dangerous Farm Animals and Race with Bull...................222

Dumb Move: Climbing the Bluff 227

Second Dumb Move: Retrieving the Arrow.......................231

Jim and Kennie: The Cowboys...235

Working Team of Horses...243

Black-and-White Pony 246

Quail Hunting with Dad and the Uncles............................254

Bird Dogs and Rabbits at Helen Sharp's House 259

Fun on the Farm 263

Going to the Movies at Perry and Mexico..........................266

Clothing for Kids: Then and Now.......................................271

Washday on the Farm...274

Attempted Murder in the Neighborhood............................278

Member and Activities of 4-H Chapter 282

4-H Contest on the Radio...284

First Moneymaking Schemes 291

Jim and the Outhouse Pit...299

Childhood Medical Problems...303

Hospital Visit and Tonsils...309

Kids and Their Toys 315

Mom Dressing Chickens to Fry...323

Kids' Annual River Campout 327

Big Day in History on the Farm: The Day the TV Arrived 332
First Full-time Farm Job with Otti Roth 341
The Day We Moved to a New Home 350
Second Farm Job with Kendrick Brothers 358
Back at the Main Farm 365
Short Description of the Kendrick Clan 374

Memorable Moments Flashback

You will find scattered throughout the articles a variety of short one-paragraph stories that popped into my head as I was sitting in front of the computer. They mostly consist of ideas that came to me while thinking back to yesteryear. They are not in any special order or sequence. They are true and did happen but did not seem as important in my life as the complete stories. These memories consist of mostly very short thoughts that took me back to my very early years and came alive in short spurts.

Brother Jim and the Killer Turkey
Searching for Petrified Wood
Searching for Guinea Nest
The Day I Learned to Read
Children Then Compared to Today
Lessons Learned the Hard Way
Charlotte Davis's Winter Weekend Visit
Jim and His First Chew
Gee Dunlap and His First Smoke
Gee Dunlap Remembers His First Smoke
Seining Salt River
Putting Up Hay at Russ Scobee's Farm
Community Hay Baling
Uncle Ronald's Yellow Fishing Boat
Rotten Egg Battle
Feeding and Breeding Rabbit Colony
Terrible Home Health Remedies

The Day Dad Got Sheep from Wyoming
Annie, Annie Over the House
Snow Ice Cream
School and 4-H Field Trips to Mexico
Dinner at Aunt Hattie's House
Uncle Billie and the First Pizza Parlor
Electric Fence and a Hog's Memory
Price of Products during the Late Forties
Grandpa Burl and the Fox Hunt
Rites of Manhood: Owning a BB Gun

Preface

This entire book started when my grandpa, Burl Willingham, moved into a nursing home many years ago. I swore that I would spend time with him and listen to and write about tales of his youth being raised around the late nineteenth century. I planned to write them down for future generations to learn about their roots. He died at age eighty-four, and I had done nothing to keep his life and legends alive. When my dad turned ninety, I swore that I would work with him while he was alive and document his legends and tributes over the years. I never got around to that either. When he died, I realized that I had lost some of the most important moments in my family history that was now gone forever. While sitting in my office at the real estate agency where I worked since retirement, I began thinking about the wonderful life I had led since birth into the Willingham clan. It suddenly dawned on me that now I was the senior family member and would probably be the next to leave planet earth in the very near future. I decided to put my memories on paper, and if anyone was interested in what my life had been, then so much to the good. As I began writing chapters of being a country boy, I found that my memory was near perfect and that the early years of my youth was very easy to relive. It was almost as if my return to age seven, eight, and nine happened recently and not almost seventy years ago. I ran off several copies that I gave to my few remaining older relatives. I began hearing that maybe some younger persons would be interested in what yesteryear was about, and maybe a book would sell a few copies. This brings us to the period in my life where the writing of my thoughts has run into many pages. Having run out of new ideas, we will now see if anyone is interested in a poor country boy's raising back in the good ole days.

Mom and Dad 50th Anniversary taken in 1996

Same day picture taken at Mary's house. Always felt really tall when standing next to sister Mary. Jim and I in our thinner days, 1996

Papa Clyde with his record rod and reel catch. Flathead Catfish weighed 27 pounds and was caught below the water supply dam that provided water for the City of Paris North Fork west of Paris.

Mama Olive with her prize geranium hanging basket. Spruce Tree in background was planted by Papa Clyde as a seeding.
Mother's Day basket 1995.

KLW probably a lot less than two years old with Mary's dog Phoochie

KLW almost two years old
with one of Phoochie's pups

KLW either taking the weekly
bath or could be just enjoying a
dip in the kiddie pool of the day.
Would be in trouble with the law
if this was taken during the 2000s.

KW 5 years driving Mable and Dollie from field to barn. Dad was standing just outside of the picture.

Mary 8 years, KW years on new swing set just made Ice House in the background.

KW 6 years. First day of school. First Grade.

Jim 5 years, KW 9 years with Blondie. Chicken house in background. Same time as the Christmas Tree chapter.

KW 2nd Birthday 1944

KW 1st Birthday 1943

KW 3rd Birthday 1945

KW 5th Birthday 1947

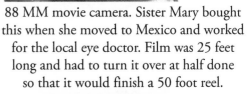

If ever there was a memorable moment to behold, Momma Olive would have her trusty camera along to capture on film the action for eternity. The cameras shown here are samples of what she had available to work with up to and including the 60,s. We still have these cameras in our collection.

The Kodak Instamatic, small but efficient and would fit in her purse. Used flash cubes for 4 rapid shots without changing cubes.

88 MM movie camera. Sister Mary bought this when she moved to Mexico and worked for the local eye doctor. Film was 25 feet long and had to turn it over at half done so that it would finish a 50 foot reel.

First and oldest camera I can remember. Kodak Box Camera and have no idea how far back this went.

Brownie Target Box Camera could look into the glass prism and actually see what you were taking. Pictures could be vertical or horizontal.

Brownie Hawkeye Camera Great camera was one of the first with flashbulb so could take pictures inside. Bulbs came dozen in a pack and lasted forever.

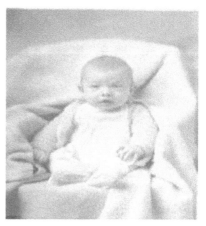

KLW at about 3 months of age, first official baby picture about Sept. 1942

Mama Olive taken May 1942 about one month before KLW was born

KLW approx. 10 months of age.

KLW two years old feeding one of the many stinking sheep that was always around. Living on J Hwy outside of Mexico.

Introduction

On June 29, 1942, a son was born in Audrain County located in north Missouri. The parents were Clyde and Olive Willingham who were sharecroppers living north of Mexico, Missouri approximately two miles on J Highway. They named their son Kenneth Lee Willingham after Dad's younger sister, Naomi Lee. Both parents were factory workers in Mexico during the days, and Clyde worked the farm during his off hours. Farming was done with a team of horses and along with several hogs, cattle, and sheep we eked out a living. At harvest, half of the money produced by the farm was given as rent to the landowner, and in turn, the family had a house to live in until the next harvest. I have tried to explain in detail what it was like to be raised on a farm during the midforties. Times they were tough; we were poor as church mice. We did not know what poor meant because we spent our waking hours working to meet our everyday needs. When we moved to a larger farm in the spring of 1946 and began sharecropping for the landowner, Ralph Bridgford, everything started to fall into place. This is where the majority of my stories and adventures took place. Every memory I have written about is 100 percent factual; there is absolutely no fiction in this entire book. Reading this, you can live my life through the years and see what being called a country boy really means. Keep in mind that this was written by a product of the country and in no way does it fit the correct grammar of a professional author. I can however tell a lot of stories about being a kid, and everything you read here did actually happen in real life.

First Memories of J Highway

A problem arises when thinking about where to start when remembering the times and trials of your youth due to the author having seventy-five years to look back upon. If you look back to all the good times that you were blessed with while growing up, it would take nearly an entire lifetime to bring up on the memory screen everything that you remember, that you think you remember, and everything that made you what you are today. As Dolly Parton said in her song, "We had no money, but we were rich as we could be." There is little doubt that what you are today is a direct response to your parents, your culture, your teachings, and your beliefs. Everything that we are is directly linked to dear ole Mom and dear ole Dad. If everything goes according to plan, you will be for your children almost identical to what your parents were to you. No time, culture, outside forces, or sleeping under a power line will change you from your upbringing. You may turn a curve and get off track, but eventually, you will still have that genetic makeup that puts you back into the state of being for what and who you will become. I can shut my eyes and see, hear, smell, and bring back to life the things that did not seem all that important to me as a kid. It now ties into my roots and thoughts and is of the utmost importance. My goal is that, somewhere in this short passage of memories, I can bring alive in those that read it some long-forgotten memory that brings back feelings of our youth. With this, I hope to convey to the readers the fact that of the millions and millions of parents that have been and that are presently well and strong in America, my parents were the finest, most honest, and most loyal hardworking people that could ever walk the face of the earth. I cannot imagine what my life would have become if I had been born to any couple in this world other than my own mom and dad. As old as I am today, I still want to be just like them when I grow up.

Born in the year of 1942, my first real vivid recollection was the spring of 1944. Those moments are somewhat vague but still very much a part of my thoughts and remembrances. One thought that flashes into my mind is that of feeding baby lambs with a bottle through the woven wire fence and them knocking it out of my hands by nudging the nipple, trying to make the milk rush out faster. Living on the farm, there was always some baby animal that needed to be looked after at one time or the other, and there was no shortage of times that Dad was seen working day and night to keep things going around the farm. Gardening was a way of life during the spring and summer and was never completely done. There was always something that demanded the family to pull together to work the dirt. It must be done so that the seeds could become a plant and then become something that would eventually end up on the dinner table. With the gardening being so successful, there was never a time in our lives that we did not have all we could eat and some leftovers. There was always plenty for feeding to the animals, be it the dogs, the cats, or the pigs. Everything got their fair share, and never at any time did we ever go to bed the least bit hungry. So was the life on the farm where blessings were ample and many.

Another memory is that of my granny Edwards being ill and living with us for a period of time. One did not ask why she was there; it was expected to be to take care of the sick family members. And no matter how long they were sick, they were always welcome. Sitting on the edge of the bed and listening to my granny read to us was a memory that keeps coming back to me. I can also remember the day that I was taken to the neighbor's house down the road to visit a family by the name of Pat Mudd. I played with little iron toys that his son had outgrown. Seems when I got home late that afternoon, there was another newborn animal in the house. They named it Little Brother Jim, which was formally James Clyde Willingham.

My memory of smells from the farm is an item that is most vivid. One smell that rushes back to me is the smell of newly plowed soil in the garden in the early spring that Dad worked up with the team of horses. The team went round and round the enclosed area until every last square foot of dirt was turned over. Last year's stems and stalks were turned under to eventually rot and add to the growing power of the jet-black earth. It was even a greater memory that before the plowing began, there was the really terrible smell of whatever Dad brought from the barn and spread over the garden in a thin layer just before the turning under took place. It was a welcome change from a vile stench to a mellow odor soon as the added layer disappeared from sight. One would also wonder how food items could come from that smelly layer of mixture and not taste or smell to some degree of what it had grown around. Today we still garden but not like the good ole days. The size of the food plot turned under back then was close to an acre or more, and today, if we plant a fifty-by-fifty-feet garden, we think we have done a bean. Planting back then was kid stuff. Dad marked off the rows and dug a slight trench. Mom kept the kids loaded with seeds, and our chore was to listen to instructions and place the seeds in the trench at just the right distance apart. Planting potatoes seems to really stick with me as it seemed that we planted at least twenty-five rows of potato eyes. One would think that we would never get done in time to be ready for supper that evening, but we always did finish before dark. To this day, it never fails to amaze me that we grew veggies without commercial fertilizer; we never sprayed plants for insects, and we never once watered the garden once planted. Every time summer turned around, there was enough produce from that patch of dirt to fill the fruit cellar from floor to ceiling. Once the canning was complete, there was little chance that this farm family would ever know a hungry winter day. In fact, one of the first moneymaking ventures I ever got into was picking green beans after the family had enough in the cellar. I took leftover beans to Mexico and sold door-to-door to the city folks. At the end of a Saturday of sales, it was not uncommon for me to have as much as two dollars in my pocket. Now for a seven-year farm boy to have that much money in his pocket was nearly unimaginable.

On the entire trip home, this country boy was thinking about how many fireworks this much cash would buy.

Spring planting also reminds me of the thought that chickens would be placed in the brooder house about this time of year. Coming home from Blacks Feed Store in Mexico, we would bring one-hundred- to two-hundred-day-old chicks and place them under the kerosene heater. It seemed almost forever before they were close to big enough to eat, but finally, Mom would dress two of them, and we had the first fried chicken of the year. Now that chicken—along with mashed potatoes, milk gravy, green beans, and corn bread—was the closest thing to the taste of heaven you could imagine. The drumsticks (some called them chicken legs) were so little you almost had to use your imagination to find enough meat to fill up on. It was totally worth the wait to fill the dreams of fresh fried chicken on the farm. You also knew in the back of your head that each day that went by, the next fried chicken dinner would be coming sooner, and each day, the drumsticks and thighs were getting bigger and better.

Farm and House We Moved To

The day we moved to our new home from the homeplace along J Highway, we found a house that was totally unique and would provide days and weeks of getting used to if you were a kid. Standing on the front porch, you could see open pasture before you that had a single road or driveway that led to the county road. This was about the length of a football field and was dug down about a foot below the soil surface on each side. Problem with this arrangement was that in the wintertime when a snow fell, no matter how deep, the wind would blow the snow across the flat level pasture and deposit it in the ditch that contained the road. It was great for kids playing in the snow, but it was terrible when trying to get the car from the county road to the house; in fact, it totally stopped all four wheels the moment Dad turned into the driveway. Dad would break a trail with the tractor, but that failed to make any improvement as did putting on chains at the bottom of the hill due to the depth of the snow that would pack under and around the wheels. The solution was to leave the car at the end of the driveway and walk to the house, which was not that big a problem unless you had groceries or a kid to carry and then that driveway got to be a lot longer.

Thinking back to the day, we left the house on J Highway and first turned into the driveway of our new home; one must realize that it was right at seventy years ago. I was standing in the back seat looking out the front window when a two-story house appeared in my vision. Jim was really little at that time, and I can remember very distinctly that he was sitting on his mother's lap and was screaming at the top of his lungs and really getting on everyone's nerves. It seemed to be a huge house, two stories and a fenced-in yard with dozens of trees that needed to be pruned and cut back drastically. It had a porch that nearly covered the front and a door above the porch that seemed to lead to nowhere. Entering the house for the first time, I noticed a set of stairs that seemed to reach into the uppermost floors of the house. To the left was the living room; to the right was the master bedroom, and to the left of the living room was the kitchen. The kids' bedroom was in the back of the house just off the master. Strange thing that we found out the first year there was that the kitchen was located on the north side of the house, and when the temperature got below forty-five degrees, that room was totally unbearable. To solve this problem when it became nigh on to winter, we all pitched in and moved the entire kitchen to the south side of the house so that it was then the master bedroom and the kitchen combination. It remained this way until the last frost, and then it was moved back to the north side. The empty room was utilized as a workroom and storage, especially when the butchering was completed. I really dreaded the time when Dad would hang the beef halves and the hog halves on each side of the room and take the hogs' heads and put them on the floor until he had time to work them up. To get to the outside door, you had to go directly in front of the hogs' heads, and if you looked at them, you would see the glassy dead eyes staring directly back at you. Had to run fast to get to the outside door. I could not look at that cold dead stare. What a relief when Dad took them outside and processed the heads into what most folks considered a delicacy called hogs headcheese. That, along with fried brains and mountain oysters (hog testicles), was one of the few foods that I did not then and do not now partake of when available.

Another section in the house that was very interesting was the screened-in porch on the back side of the house. This was where the milk separator and clothes washing facilities were located. Mom had every Monday scheduled as washday, and that day was used for scrubbing clothes for as long as my memory served me. It started out with a tub and washboard but later was replaced with a machine that was run by a small one-cylinder gas engine. Later, this went to an electric motor when we got electricity on the farm. On the east edge of the covered porch was a door on the floor that swung up when a rope was pulled. Under the door was a set of steps made of huge flat stones that led down into a hole in the ground that they called a root cellar. It was about the size of a moderate room and had one little window about ground level, and from this little bit of light, you could see that there were shelves around the entire room. On these shelves were dozens and dozens of fruit jars full of every food imaginable. The walls were lined with flat rocks stacked very carefully so that it held up the wall and kept the temperature in the cellar a very cool degree year-round. When Mom was ready to prepare a meal, she would tell one of us to go to the cellar and get a jar of whatever and bring it to her. A little flashlight was all that was available, and that put out a very pitiful amount of light, so it was not an easy task to locate the desired product. Another problem that arose frequently was the fact that this area was very much sought-after in the summertime by snakes, snakes of every size and color. About every third trip down, a person would find a huge black snake lying along the shelves or coiled up under the rocks on the side. If you did not see a snake, you nearly always saw several huge snakeskins that had been shed and left behind so that you would not forget that they for sure had been there.

The screened-in porch was really a great place in the summertime when the heat was hanging on. There was a door that came out of the living room, a door that came out of the big bedroom, and a door that came out of Mary's tiny personal domain. So nearly at all times, there was a breeze moving through the house and through the screened-in porch. The porch was also the room that held the community commode that everyone but Mom and Dad used if needed during the night. Personally, I found it better to open the back door of the porch a crack and shoot a stream alongside the house. However, if I got caught doing this, the parents said not to do that as it was causing a stink outside the door. That did make sense, so I did not do that again until the need arose in the future.

Just outside the summer kitchen on the north side of the house was a back porch that housed the hand-pump water well. This was where the drinking water came from, the washing water, and in the summertime the shower water. I was the only one that did it on a daily basis. About dark, I would draw a bucket of water, stand on the end of the porch, pour a dipper of water over my head, and then soap up. After dipping, the remaining water over my head and body had accomplished almost what could have been called an evening shower. When winter arrived, it meant that the outside shower could not be used, so the bath was moved into the kitchen behind the woodstove. When a kettle of water began boiling on the woodstove, Mom would pour it into a metal tub placed behind the stove, and all three kids took turns soaping up and then rinsing off. This sufficed as being a weekly bath, which cleaned about as much as could be expected. Often during the week, we would take a sponge bath by using a small pan of hot water and washing off with a washcloth. Very little water was wasted on bathing, but no one really thought much about it as being a real problem. Seeing as how we did not get electricity until the early fifties and as the water heater had not even been invented as far as we were concerned, the practice of daily bathing was way in the future.

I can readily remember the new additions that were introduced into our home that made life so much more pleasant and enjoyable. First heat we had when arriving at our new home was two woodburning heaters. One was in the living room, and the cooking stove in the kitchen was also a wood burner. The kitchen stove did have a water tank on the side so that, if it was kept filled with water, it provided hot water if and whenever it was needed. Later, a new cookstove that was fueled by coal oil or what today is classified as kerosene was added. This was a great improvement over the woodstove as it had an oven and could be turned on when needed. It did not have to heat all the time, which made it a very important asset when cooking in the summer. Heat in the living room was still wood, and the heat in the winter kitchen was wood, but the living room heater was replaced with a potbellied coal stove. This really produced a better and hotter heat than anything we had used before. All other stoves remained the same until the day Dad brought in an oil heater for the living room. No more dirty coal soot and no more carrying in the coal and out the clinkers. Just pour the oil into the reservoir about every two days, and the heat kept coming out. Each time a new source of heat arrived at the farm, the better the lifestyle prevailed. Made one wonder just how much better could life get what with all the high-efficiency tools we had acquired. Entering each of these phases was very trivial to the arrival of the first electric line strung from the chicken yard to the house. This one item ushered in a total life-changing moment that would affect us for the rest of our lives.

This is a pot bellied coal stove which is pretty close to being like the one we had in the living room when first moving to Santa Fe

Wood burning cook stove like this one mom cooked on daily plus kept the kitchen warm in the winter time. Was not nearly as fancy as this one as well as I can remember.

Free standing wood burning that was used in the kitchern when dad bought in the new kerosene cook stove that replaced the wood cook stove. This thing was fired up at the first frost and was not cooled off until the last frost in the spring.

When dad bought this kerosene cook stove home it automatically cut mom's work in half. Only heated when needed for cooking so did away with constantly stoking it with wood and was much cooler in the kitchen during the summer.

If you looked to the right of the porch a few steps, you saw a fence that may or may not have been a fence as it was pretty much rundown. As it did not keep anything in or out of the yard, it really did not make much difference if it was there or not. The gate was another thirty steps to the right, but people usually just stepped over the fence. Being short, we kids were not able to step over. So by climbing over it, the weight of each person tended to bring it down a little more.

On the other side of the fence was a huge building they called the icehouse. It had a sloping roof that covered a huge room in the center and a lean-to-type shed on each end. On the east end, the coal was stored for winter heating so that it was out of the weather and remained dry so that it would burn cleaner and produce the most heat. They delivered the coal in a huge truck and dumped it through a huge opening in the rear of the shed. Some of the coal was busted into pieces that you could easily put in a bucket and carry into the house, but most often, they dumped a lump of coal the size of a hay wagon. This made it necessary to bust it up with a mallet or sledge hammer into pieces about the size of a football or smaller. This task was generally given to the middle child to be certain that there were at least three buckets of coal waiting in the storeroom to be used to stoke the fire when it began to die down. On the other end of the shed was an open area that usually housed turkeys or old hens and occasionally capon roosters that were destined to be Sunday dinner sometime in the future. In the center of the shed was a huge open room that was about twenty feet high and had no windows and only one doorway to enter. The walls were built with two walls side by side with a space between them of about a foot. At one time, the walls were filled with sawdust from top to bottom, which served as an early form of insulation. It was many years before my time, but the reason for the building was to store ice, which had been cut from the ponds during the dead of winter in huge chunks, drug by horses to the building, and stacked until the entire room was full of ice from top to bottom. When the entire room was filled, they placed a thick layer of straw over the top of the pile to provide more insulation. When the thaw of spring came around, the entire community would come to the building and chop out chunks of ice and use it for ice boxes or to have a cold drink during the hot summer months. This story was told to me by Minnie Bell Bridgford's father who would occasionally drop by our place to sit and visit and tell us kids about things that were going on when he was a kid. His purpose in life at this time was to carry a bucket of seeds from last year's watermelons, cantaloupes, and pumpkins and to walk over the entire neighborhood looking for old and rotted hay stacks. He planted seeds in and around the stack and then moved on to another one on down the road. He was certainly like Johnny Appleseed, and because of him, the entire community had tons of melons to eat and preserve for the next winter season. It was said that Mr. Grimes, his name was Avery Grimes, had thousands of seeds planted every year all over the county and surrounding farms. It was during one of his visits as we were sitting on a bench beside the shed that he asked if we had any idea of what this big building was all about. He explained in detail about the folks sawing ice from the river and ponds with crosscut saws and about how many days and weeks it took to fill the huge space. When summer came around, the people really appreciated having free ice during the hot and dry summer.

As the building was not needed for ice storage, Dad did make use of the space by opening up one wall on the inside of the lean-to and placed a chicken wire fence across the opening. In this space, he housed a flock of pheasants that consisted of about fifteen hens and a rooster. The idea was to produce eggs and then incubate them with bantam hens, raise the chicks to maturity, and sell the dressed birds for the meat market. Each day the hens would lay an egg, we the kids picked them off the floor and carefully placed them in the kitchen pantry until there was enough to set a half-dozen hatches. It actually seemed to work well until we had forty or fifty dressed birds and found that people really did not care to buy them as much as they wanted ordinary chickens. This left us with a large number of dressed pheasants. So to say the least, we ate many birds prepared many different ways. Can only remember doing the pheasants for one year as we arrived home one afternoon and found that the hogs had gotten into the yard and were trying to get to the chicken feed inside the pens. In so doing, turned over the runs, and pheasants were scattered all over the place. Some we caught by running them down, but they quickly found that they were free and with a little practice discovered that running was not nearly as efficient as flying. The ones that we could not catch were scattered far and wide, and the ones that Dad didn't shoot headed across country. We got calls for days from people around the county telling Dad that they had birds in their yard. Dad finally told them to just shoot them and have a good meal with his compliments. Farthest one reported was when Stanley Poage called and said that he had one on his pond bank about three miles from our place. After that, it seemed that they just kind of disappeared.

On past the icehouse was my favorite building, which was the granary shed. This was by far the most interesting place as it was where grain from the previous harvest was stored. It had a concrete floor, a big sliding door on each end, and on the east side was four separate bins that ran up the entire side. Each had a door in it with wooden slates that could be tacked up or removed as the bins were being filled or emptied during the year. All the tools were hanging on the west wall, which was the shop area, and the back part of the building was stacked with bales of hay for the horses to feed during the winter months. This was also the area where the corn sheller was fastened to the floor and was the implement that Jim and I were expected to run ears of corn through until the basket under it was filled for the next hog feeding.

As you're standing on the front porch of the house and looking to the left facing due west, you would see the livestock barn. It was two stories with a hallway in the center with an open area on each side with the back of the barn facing west and the open ends facing east. On the north side of the barn stood a hay mow that opened to the barn loft so the hay could be stacked the entire length for storage to be used during the winter months. A person could break a bale from above and drop the hay sections—they are called a leaf of hay—into the mow. This was a big help as the worker never had to get out of the loft to feed the cattle. The loft held approximately five hundred bales that—with an average winter—would last the entire cold season. Behind the barn was a well that utilized a hand-operated pump that was used to bring water to the surface and provide water to the cattle or hogs held in the pens. One side with the opening toward the east was the pig birthing area. As the sows were bred year-round, they invariably would have a litter of pigs some time during the coldest part of the year. The life expectancy of a newborn pig when the temperature was halfway toward zero was several minutes unless we were there at the moment they arrived and covered them with straw. When the temperature was really severe, Dad would put them all in a box and take them to the house and place them behind the woodstove for a couple of hours and then take them back to the barn and place them next to the sow. Nearly always, the babies would begin nursing and immediately afterward burrow beneath the hay and pile together for warmth and protection from the frigid air. This was the way things were before electricity, but once we had a line to the barn, then it became much easier to hang a heat bulb about two feet above the delivering sow and kept the temperature inside the delivery pen a balmy forty-five degrees. The heat bulb was a great improvement, and the live birth to one-week-old ratio jumped dramatically. There would be about six sows delivered at one time, but very seldom did more than two happen at the same time. When the baby pigs were able to take the cold, they were moved from the heat lamp, and the next mama pig moved into the birthing pen. During my early years, I was not required to make the nightly trips to the barn during the cold times, but no telling how many times Dad went out in the dead of the night and assisted with the hog birthing. I did go along to supervise when I turned ten or so and can attest that zero nights are really uncomfortable.

Behind the barn was the hog fattening and weaning area. When the pigs were two or three weeks old, the sow and babies were moved to the back lots that had several moveable hog sheds. This was where they stayed until weaning age of about three months. When weaned, they moved to the feedlots in front of the livestock barn. This was their living quarters until they reached anywhere from two hundred to two hundred twenty-five pounds. When they reached this stage of weight and age, Dad would call either Shennie Davis or Russ (Fat) Bishop, the local livestock haulers. Depending on which one was going to St. Louis stockyards the next day, a time would be set to load the hogs out early the next morning. When they arrived, we moved a portable loading chute beside the barn; truck would back up to the chute, and we would drive the shoats into the barn and up the chute into the double-tiered truck. Driver would close the gate and give Dad a paper with the number of hogs that had been loaded, and away they went to the market. The check from the buyers was usually in the mailbox in about three or four days, so it was then time to pay off bills and debts that had been owed. We then started to get ready for the next set of hogs. When they arrived, the process started all over again. Occasionally, such as Christmastime and just before school started in the fall, Dad would load up one or two market-sized hogs and take them to the sale barn in Mexico. This would supplement Dad's check from the hammer mill when extra money was needed. If a hog was not ready to go, then there usually was a fat steer that made the trip to Mexico. Kind of rolling over a 401K today, but then was rolling over an eight-hundred-pound steer or a two-hundred-twenty-five-pound shoat.

Winter Cold and Fun

If you would stop and think back to your childhood days, I would wonder if memories of winter months and snowstorms would come to the surface. To me, winter was a time of really great times. Deep snow was a blessing, and there was never a degree of cold too severe to get out and play. I do think of a time in later life when Dad gave us chores to do each day, and then some of the fun ended, and winter took on a complete new meaning. I guess I'm getting a bit ahead of myself though as my first memories of snow and ice had nothing but fun memories, and when the adults talked about the dreadful winter of 1948, it really did not have the same meaning to me. We looked forward to lots and lots of snow, and the more that fell, the better the start of the day. It has to be true that the older you get, the more the cold affects you. For many is the time that as a child, the cold in our house was bone-chilling, but I never really paid that much attention to it.

Thinking back the house we lived in has a lot to do with us being uncomfortable during the winter months. The house we moved into was a two-story farmhouse that was built in the late nineteenth century. When we moved in about 1945, insulation was not one of the materials used to elevate the level of comfort. The lower floor consisted of a living room, two bedrooms, a kitchen on the north end, and a storage room right off the screened-in porch with the root cellar under the floor. The kitchen was a seasonal room due to the fact that it was on the north end of the house. When the winter season rolled around, it revolved into a storage room for the winter months and then changed back to the kitchen after the last freeze of the year. With the coming of cold weather, the family all worked together to move the kitchen into the south bedroom. Whatever the temperature outside, the north room was the same inside during the cold months of winter. One would wonder what kept the pipes from freezing in the house when no heat was available. The answer was very simple; there were no pipes in the kitchen. Running water was only there when one of the kids ran out to the pump and drew a bucket of water and ran with it back into the kitchen where the woodstove was putting out slim British thermal units. There was, in the living room, a huge cast iron stove that we called a potbelly stove. And when really low on fuel, it would hold two buckets of coal. When this stove was at its best, you could hear a dull roar, which let you know that you better close the damper as meltdown was to begin in the next few minutes. The roar, along with a cherry red flu pipe, let you know that no matter how cold it was outside, inside the living room, everyone would be snug and warm. Heated by a coal stove, it produced warmth in many different ways. Number one was how warm you became when breaking up the massive chunk of coal the truck delivered as it was about the size of a small farm wagon. It had to be broken down into pieces the size of a football or smaller so that it could be transported into the house and dumped into the stove in the living room. The warmth came from the burning coal, which led then to the warmth generated from having to dig out the clinkers and carry them out to the ash pile in the chicken yard. A person never had a chance to get cold if all steps were carried out in a timely fashion. Heat was also available in the kitchen where you could find a woodstove that provided warmth, hot water from a tea kettle, and steam to provide moisture in the air so your nose did not get so terribly dry because of the dry heat we produced to stay alive. What with the ten-foot ceilings in most of the house and the ten-foot ceilings in our bedroom, no one complained of being hot during the months of November, December, January, February, and March. Sleeping was about the only time the entire body was warm, which brings me to my next thoughts of being young down on the farm and sleeping in a room with no heat. While temperature on the outside was in the single digits, the inside was seldom more than ten degrees warmer in rooms that had no stoves. This was due to noninsulated walls and single-pane windows that did not fit snug enough to keep ole man winter from entering the bedroom. The first procedure to keep warm was that of using goose-down mattresses, mattresses so thick that you could almost fully immerse yourself in them. On top of that were the flannel blankets, which in turn were covered with no less than two quilts. On very cold nights, Dad would gather the throw rugs from the floor and place them over our legs. When you got in bed for the night, you made certain that you went to the bathroom before the covers were being placed and that you were in a really comfortable position. Once all covers were in place, there was really no way that you flopped and turned over to find any other position. Fact is you were doing good to breathe, let alone move around.

We found early on that there were things that could be done to hasten the warming of the blankets using more than body heat to reach a comfort level. You always had flannel PJs and a pair of thick socks to wear to bed. One trick used nightly was to back up to the coal stove and let the flannel heat up until it was just at the verge of burning the skin on your back. You would reach around with both hands and wrap the material into a ball, hold on tight, and run like crazy to the bedroom so that as much heat as possible would transfer to the cold sheets before hypothermia set in. It is truly amazing as I cannot remember ever having a runny nose or bad cold back in those days. We never woke up in the morning other than fully rested and rearing to get myself beside the warm stove in the kitchen. I can almost hear you thinking that it could not have been that cold in the bedroom or someone would have died from the croup or pneumonia. To justify the cold bedrooms ever so often, one of us kids would forget to get a drink before being loaded down with covers. Good ole Dad would bring us a glass of water, which we all shared, and what was left over was placed on the table between the two beds. The next morning, the water left in the glass was frozen solid and had to be placed on the shelf behind the kitchen stove to thaw out. Another sign of it being rather nippy in the bedroom was the presence of ice forming on the windows on the inside. The mound of snow found on each and every windowsill when it snowed and drifted toward the south side of the house was a dead giveaway. There was always little finger of frozen precipitation pointing toward the center of the bedroom from every corner of each window. As well as memory serves me, there were four windows in that one room that had fresh air entering at all times. The woodstove was forever a welcome and highly used area in the house during the winter months and, in fact, was the hub of activity and the main meeting place for family gatherings. It was held in high respect by all who entered as being the place that would forever be warm and toasty and could be depended upon to help rid aching fingers, pain from toes that were just a few minutes away from frostbite. It was also a place to dry out gloves that was nearly frozen to a person's hands. It was often used as the lifesaving area for the many tiny farm animals that were unlucky enough to be born in the middle of a really cold winter snap. Often, they were bought into the kitchen in a cardboard box and seemed to not have a drop of life left in them. It was nothing short of a miracle to watch a newborn pig lying lifeless and not seeming to breathe make a complete recovery in a matter of minutes when the warm air hit them. The moment they are born, they have an inborn instinct to begin searching for the utter of their dame and, even in the coldest grips of winter, can live and thrive after getting the first milk that Mother Nature has provided. When the outside temperature is below and oftentimes way below freezing, the only saving grace they have is to get a belly full of milk and burrow deep into the pile of baby pigs or bed of straw. One instance I witnessed was many years after leaving the farm and returning to establish a herd of miniature cows after my retirement. It was in the middle of January, and Missouri was going through a record-breaking cold snap with temperatures hovering around zero mark and slightly below. As I stepped out the north door of the garage, which was sitting on a hilltop facing north, I felt the cold sting of zero weather slap me across the face, looked at the thermometer hanging on the side of the house, and saw it read minus five degrees. Headed toward the barn as rapidly as a short-legged man dressed in set of jeans, insulated coveralls, insulated boots, insulated coat, and two pairs of insulated gloves could rapidly move. When the cold air is going through that many layers of insulation, you just got to believe that this is one terribly cold morning. Stepped into the barn and saw a single solitary cow standing by herself in the middle of the alleyway. In front of her was a mound of red fur rolled into a ball and was covered with frozen afterbirth, which meant she had not cleaned it off the minute it hit the ground. This also means that the life expectancy of her offspring would be approximately five minutes, give or take a minute in either direction. Rolled a wheelbarrow up to the frozen mound and prepared to remove it to the boneyard for the coyotes. Picked it up by the head, and could you believe it, the little frozen mound opened one eye and looked at me. It was for all purposes frozen solid on the outside, but somewhere on the inside, there was a tiny spark of life still smoldering. Quickly laid it on a mound of hay, threw more hay on top of it, and ran to the shop for a lamp and heat bulb. Arrived at the barn a few seconds later, plugged in the heat lamp, held it about a foot above the supposedly dead calf, and within a few minutes, the wet hide started steaming and thawing out. Several minutes later, the calf raised its head, opened both eyes, and let out a very weak but still alive bawl. I made a dash to the house and mixed up a half cup of milk, half a beat-up egg, teaspoon of sugar, and about two ounces of coffee. Warmed the mixture, found the bottle I had used last year on a baby bottle, filled it with the concoction, wrapped it with one of Judy's tea towels, and quickly headed back to the baby calf. It was almost holding its head up, so with a little coaxing and nipple in its mouth, it got nearly half of the warm serum down its tiny throat. All the time, the old cow was standing in the same spot taking it all in. In about ten minutes, the calf was trying to get up, so with a little help, it was standing by itself. Wiped it dry with bunches of hay and, if you can believe it or not, placed the baby next to its dame, and within a few minutes, it had found the udder and was nursing with vigor. That baby had gone from a frozen mound of fur to a very lively bull calf in less than forty-five minutes, had gone to the very brink of death, and—with a little assistance—came back to live a full life as a miniature Hereford bull. Last I heard, he was a herd sire somewhere in the state of Michigan. This was by far a great moment of triumph over death, but when we were in the barn alongside the old house outside of Santa Fe, not all stories ended with such a high note. Many nights, Dad and I would wrap up against the bitter cold of winter and wait patiently for an old sow to deliver a litter of pigs. For the most part, Dad was successful in getting them past the first twelve hours of life so they could help the Willingham family pay their bills and buy what supplies was needed in the coming months. We seemed to be successful most of the time but sad it was when the ones that came to the stove heat just did not have that little bit left in them to come back from the death of cold that comes with the months of old man winter.

Winter and youth—combined with frozen rivers and ponds, snow-covered hills, and deep drift—always spells fun and entertainment. Long before the commercials called for travel to the slopes of Colorado for the best in winter sports, we had it all right here in Missouri. Well, maybe we didn't have the ski lifts and the downhill runs, but we did have the hill on the back of the farm that was a lot better than having to travel to faraway places. One such hill was behind the government pond, one we called "the Big Pond" because it was the largest one on the farm. This hill was on the highest elevation on the farm and had a dirt road that went down between two fields. It had two slight curves on it and then finished off with a long flat area that was totally free of any dangerous trees, ditches, or articles that made one stop quickly upon impact. This more or less was pretty much danger free, but at the same time, when there was a thin layer of sleet or ice on the run, you could get the "silver streak" sled going at an unbelievable speed before flipping over on one of the curves or bottoming out at the end of the run. If you prepared the runners correctly with steel wool before starting out, there was no telling just how many miles per hour you could attain. With the wind whipping you in the face until tears came to your eyes, you could almost feel that you were flying and maybe even leaving the ground occasionally. With the two tractor tracks going down the hillside, it was all too natural that two persons would race down to (1) see who could get down the fastest and (2) who could go the farthest at the end before coming to a stop. Of course, brother Jim had a little sled that could, on most occasions, get to the bottom a little ahead of the much bigger sled, and if you were anywhere close to going past him, he would most certainly go across the grass median and cause a pileup, which in turn there was no clear-cut winner. Brother Jim really did not lose many races if he could help it.

The best place for long sleigh rides was on the blacktop that went down the hill between the stores and garages in Santa Fe. Early evening, when the snow and ice was just right, we begged Mom and Dad to take us and our sleds to Santa Fe so that we could join the no less than twenty other kids in the neighborhood for a sleigh party. The slope was just steep enough to really get a head of steam up and went on for at least a quarter mile so the ride was fast and long. You had to get there at just the right time as the county road crew would eventually get around to driving the cinder truck up the hill and throw out shovels of black and nasty cinders and clinkers from the back of the truck. Until the time that they made it up the hill, it was really slick. When cars drove on the newly fallen snow, it would pack down to a perfect layer of ice. When you started in front of James and Mac's grocery store, held the sled in front of you with both hands, run as fast as your legs would carry, you then flop down on the sled, hold on for dear life, and hope that a car not come around the curve at the bottom and ruin the wild and exciting ride. Close to the bottom of the hill was a curve that took off to the left, and straight ahead was the driveway of Stanley Poage. The objective was to go the distance of the hill and end up in Stanley's front yard. This was not a problem unless the cinder truck had been by and it not only stopped you from getting down the hill but would, in fact, stop you from getting away from the top of the hill. It was great fun on the downhill run, but it sure was a long hard drag pulling the sled all the way back to the top. And if your legs were as short as mine, then it took forever to get back to the starting point.

This brings us to another topic of winter fun, that of ice skating on the Big Pond. When Dad chopped down into the ice and found that there was three inches or more thickness of ice, then it was deemed safe to play on. When I was about nine and brother Jim was four years younger, we both received a pair of ice skates for Christmas. My skates were a pair of really neat hockey skates, and

Jim, being younger, got a pair of shoe skates with double-runners. While I was trying to learn how to maneuver the single runner and spending nine out of every ten minutes on my rear, Jim was going around me like I was sitting still of which I usually was. Hate to admit it, but he was really good for such a pipsqueak but would not have admitted it at the time. After a period of time, my ankles did condition themselves to some degree, and this is when the will to win took over. First, we started having races across the Big Pond and then graduated into turning corners and going laps around the Big Pond, and then as that grew old, we decided that we really needed to have hockey equipment to play with. Not having any money to buy such equipment, we went into the woods with our trusty cross-cut saw and looked for just the right tree limb that would make a Mother Nature's ready-made hockey stick. By the way, going to look for something to cut down with brother Jim, I made certain we started out early in the morning and on a warm day, not to let myself ever again be put into the same predicament as with the cutting of the Christmas tree. Nonetheless, after finding two hockey sticks, we looked for just the right-sized maple sprout that, when cut down, would produce a fair number of hockey pucks by making the second cut about two inches above the first cut. All in all, this turned out much better than I thought it would as the equipment was almost as good as manufactured sticks even if the looks did leave a lot to be desired. Putting two coffee cans at each end of the pond, we were ready to let the games begin. To brag a little, when we first started out, I was by far the better of the two what with running down the court with the hockey puck out front heading for the goal. As you would know it, brother Jim was not to let anyone get ahead of him, let alone the older brother. So here he came on double-runners fly-ing like a streak across the ice behind me. I for one was not going to let him get around and was dead set on letting that happen. Jim, coming alongside, acted like he was trying to get the puck, but in all reality, he was lining up a shot at my legs, and that was just what happened. He drew back and slammed a shot just above my skate tops and hit dead center on the shin bone that made a loud thud and shot pain clear up into my hip area. When the tears cleared from my eyes, all I could see was Jim going the other way heading for the goal pushing the native Missouri puck before him. Not only did I have the agony of defeat, I had the agony of the shin bone as well. That taught brother Jim a real lesson. No matter how much we played ice hockey, every time I got going toward the goal, his favorite move was to whack his opponent across the shin at just the right angle, and the game turned around really quick. Forget about trying to run him down and get a whack at his legs as there has not ever been a professional skater that could catch up to him as long as he had on that pair of double-runner skates.

Salt River Ice Break Through

I f you're reading this chapter today and if you're over sixty years old, then you know firsthand what I'm talking about when I say that as kids we were outside nearly the entire day. If it was snowing or had snowed a half foot of white fluffy and you had been playing in it for at least an hour, then it was a basic fact that your feet were so cold you could not feel them if you wiggled your toes. That time was before the days of insulated rubber boots and before the days of fleece-lined leather hiking boots. Actually, we were lucky to have a pair of four buckle overshoes that did not leak, let alone boots that were insulated. Three pairs of wool socks worn inside a pair of boots that were two sizes too big were about the best we had to offer. It did seem though that when you were young and having a ball throwing, lying in, rolling in, and building with snow, it didn't really hurt that bad until you backed up against the stove in the kitchen to thaw out occasionally. For the most part, wet gloves, wet feet, and wet up to your waist were to be expected. If you can remember back to a time that you were under ten years old and can remember being cold at any one particular time, then you can bet your allowance that you had been only a few degrees from hypothermia setting in. One such memory was when a group of us kids were boot scooting on the Salt River ice just outside of Santa Fe. Dad always said that if we were going to play on the ice on the river, to watch carefully for running water or riffles that tended to keep the ice from getting thick. If you came upon such a place, get off the ice and walk the bank around it. Happened to be real good advice I soon found out as we were scooting along and came to an area that looked solid but

had the makings of a riffle flowing under the ice. After studying it
for a long time, maybe ten seconds, we all pretty much dismissed the
idea that there was running water anywhere close to this particular
spot, so scooting along I did go. As usual, there was always a kid
who wanted to be out front to act as a leader and also to show others
they could be in charge. In this instance, it happened to be me
ahead to make sure that no one else would be first in line.
there was a loud crack and a sinking sensation on my part
needed to move back and move back quickly. Needless
turned to retreat, the ice at that very moment gave way,
there was liquid where a moment ago had been solid
second, I was up to my privates in water that was so
been older than my present nine years would most
given me a heart attack. As luck would have it, the
this spot was only about two feet deep, but to a four-
plenty deep enough to have most of the body sub-
merged. Getting out of the water and onto the bank was not all that
big a deal, but once standing upright, it was evident that there was a
slight breeze coming down the river that ordinarily would not have
been noticed. When it hit two pant legs of wet jeans and two boots
full of water, the freeze factor was tremendous. I started to become
very uncomfortable in a very short period of time. My choices were
few. One, I could try to run the half mile home and get out of these
wet clothes. Two, I could light a fire and dry off, but all my friends
were too young to carry matches. Three, I could run up the hill and
go inside James and Mac's grocery store. Or four, stand in this same
spot and freeze to death in the next several minutes. Seemed the logic
thing to do was head for the grocery store as it was the closest warm
place compared to where we were standing. Took out up the steep
hill as fast as my wet water-filled boots would carry me, and about
halfway up, I suddenly felt that my feet were becoming lumps of ice
and my pants were quickly freezing to my legs. What seemed like
an eternity, I rounded the corner of the store and instantly realized
that they were closed on Sunday afternoon, and for sure, this was
well into that afternoon. Moment of panic but quickly realized that
Grandma Burl's house was only two blocks north of the square, so

with what little bit of strength I could muster, I went hobbling down Main Street. I could see the house ahead, but the next two blocks seemed like the longest race of my life, and if I had been any farther from the house, it may have been my last. Stumbled through the door and got beside the nearest woodstove I could find. It took me about eight seconds to be standing in the middle of the living room floor with nothing on but my half-frozen skin.

Backed my nearly frozen backside to within three inches of the stove and felt instant relief over my entire body. I suddenly realized that life was beginning to be a whole lot more comfortable than it was five minutes ago. I'll never forget Grandma putting quilts around me and smiling that smile that only a grandmother can smile. I knew that everything was going to be just fine until Dad heard the story of how his son had not heeded the warnings and nearly paid for it with his toes and almost his life. All in all, there was a valuable lesson learned that day that was carried into adulthood. The meaning of cold and the meaning of frostbite and the dangers of being caught out in the elements could easily cost the person or their family some dire consequences. To this day, there are provisions of food, water, and blankets provided in my automobiles when traveling during the months of winter.

First car that I can remember the day we bought
it home. 1938 Chevy purchased used from Dad's
cousin Jimmy Creed about the year 1947.

Was not the only car we owned but cannot remember any others between the 38 Chevy and this one. This was a 1952 Chevy purchased about the year 1957.

Only truck we used on the farm. 1952 Chevy purchased around 1958 and the set of wheels Brother Jim drove to school when he got his drivers permit. Cannot imagine how many miles he put on this one but was thousands.

Memorable Moments Flashback
Brother Jim and the Killer Turkey

To get to the brooder or the chicken house or if one wanted to go to the big barn, a person had to open the gate into the chicken yard and proceed directly due east. This seldom was a problem until Dad decided to raise a flock of turkeys and came home one day with four hens and a Tom. The hens paid little or no mind to anything or anybody entering into or being inside the chicken yard. Not so with the Tom Turkey as we found this out quickly the day they arrived. Jim and I were going to get some feathers from the chicken house to make a corncob missile by sticking four feathers into the end of a cob. When the cob was thrown, it would catch the wind and whirl like a helicopter. Jim had not gone ten steps until there appeared a very angry male turkey that came at us with wings flapping and feathers puffed up until it made him look about the size of a charging bull. He was making a noise like a screech owl, and his feet seemed barely to be touching the ground. For the longest moment, we were unable to move, and by the time Jim realized, we were about to be attacked by a killer turkey; he was almost upon us. Jim went past me like I was standing still when suddenly I realized I was standing still and first in line to meet the huge bird head-on. Jim got to the gate first and, being little, leaped through the crack in the gate, which left me the only target for a killer turkey to go after. He hit me in the rear with wings and claws and placed at least two sharp pointed beaks about halfway up my backside about where my bare back began. Grabbed the gate latch and cleared the gate with one huge leap. Ole Tom Turkey stood on the other side of the gate with tail fanned and wings drooping and kept making clucking noises that pretty well told us that we were no longer welcome in his domain. This was the way it remained until Dad got enough eggs to make a hatching, and Mom baked him for Sunday dinner. Up to that point, we never did argue with that killer Tom Turkey as to who really owned the chicken yard.

Grinding Feed in the Grain Shed

Any time there was grain in the bins, you could know that we would be feeding a huge number of mice and rats. The corn bin was by far the favorite location to provide housing for dozens of mice. When it was full of ear corn, one could only imagine how many hundreds of rodents were located there. For certain, this was the place that most of the cats chose to hang out day and night to take advantage of a mouse lunch if one would unwisely venture farther than a few inches from the bin.

The building is the granary that stood to the left of our old two storey house and just behind the ice shed. The little fish pond was just a few feet left of the lean-to on the left. This shed faced south and was one of my favorite places to spend most hours of the day back in the late forties and most of the fifties. This is how it looks today but the pond has been filled in and gone many years ago.

About twice a month, Dad would bring the hammer mill to the farm to grind corn for the fattening steers. They would back the machine up until the loading chute was just beside the bin with the corn, start the huge engine, kick it into gear, and then start scooping ear corn into the grain auger. This then took it into the grinder where it was broken down from a complete ear of corn to a ready-to-feed ground-up corn and cob base and at the same time mixed it with black strap molasses. The mouse part came when the bin was about half empty and the scoop taking the ears from the level floor, which caused the pile of corn to slide down to floor level. At any one time, there could be as many as ten or twelve mice running in all directions. Ever so often, one would find its way up the leg of the man doing the scooping, which would cause that person to stop what he was doing and begin a dance that was a lot like what the Indians did when ready to go on a war party. Just occasionally, there would be a rat's nest, but they were much wiser than a mouse and would climb straight up the two-by-four board in the back of the bin and disappear along the roofline. The cats always looked forward to the moment they heard the mill start up as they knew that in the very near future there would be a mass migration of mice away from their hiding place. Bad part of the mill grinding was the eardrum bursting roar that the grinder put out from the moment it started until the very end. It was so loud that you could see the person beside you through the layer of dust that was hanging in the air, and you could see their mouth moving, but there was no sound to be heard. This probably was the reason that Dad could not hear very well the last twenty-five years of his life as his ears were still roaring from the sound he worked with every day for fifteen years. It would have been good to have worn ear protectors, but back in the late forties or early fifties, no one paid any attention to what the problem would be years later. The same day they did the corn, they also ground up a two weeks' supply of hay for the sheep, but that was done at another location in the corral of the big barn next to where the sheep were fed. Here, the hay could be taken directly from the barn and put on the augers on the back of the mill. It seemed there was a lot more molasses used on the hay, which in turn tended to lessen the amount of dust produced. This also made the ground-up hay warm to the touch and produced a smell that was not unlike the molasses cookies Mom made in the kitchen. When the mill was finished and the motor shut down, the men placed a huge sheet of tin over the wagon to keep the feed dry and fresh until fed out. It was now ready for me as my job each evening was to head directly to the big barn and scoop enough ground hay from the wagon to fill each of three troughs, which had about three dozen sheep waiting for my appearance. Did I mention that Jim was supposed to go along and help feed the sheep? He most generally did follow me to the barn, but his contribution was to swing on the Tarzan ropes until all the work was done. Actually, the work involved with putting the hay in feeders was really not all that a big deal, but when there was a half foot of snow on the ground, getting to the barn and back was a bit of a tiring task. When the wind was blowing directly out of the north as it was nearly all winter, it was to say the least a cold trip to get the feeding done. Most days, I found myself yelling for Jim to get his clothes on and get out and help me, but many was the time that I waited for him to show up at "the Big Barn" but found to be by myself generally. The Big Pond was directly behind the Big Barn, and the ice had to be chopped twice daily so that the cows and sheep could get a drink. I was not allowed to use the chopping axe as it was razor-sharp and could easily chop off a toe or a foot if you made a mistake of where it landed. It also tended to become even sharper when the ice hit the blade, so after a few weeks of ice cutting, the bit became extremely sharp.

Axe Cut and Bloody Leg

Cutting ice in the wintertime was a twice daily job, and you cannot imagine how sharp a two-edged chopping axe can become. I found this out the moment I fell off the concrete step out back of Grandpa Burl's house one winter Sunday afternoon. Strange how a person can remember so much in detail as this seems it happened last year. It happened when I was actually seven years old. It was midafternoon in the middle of winter, and all the families had gathered at Grandma's house for lunch. About midafternoon, nature called, and as the two hollers were way out back and being ice covered and very cold, the logical thing to do was stand on the back step and take care of business as quickly as possible. Just about halfway through the procedure, two old coon hounds, of which there were no less than half a dozen, got into a discussion on which was going to lay on the rug beside the door. As they began growling and causing a loud scene, they bumped into me and knocked me off the ledge where I was standing. The fall was not all that much of a problem, but it just so happened Grandpa Burl had leaned the two-bit axe against the step, and as bad luck would have it, it was directly under my downward journey. The front blade caught my jeans just below the right knee and sliced through the jeans and my leg like it was hot butter. By the time I got back into the house, blood was running down my leg and making a solid stream of red clear across the kitchen floor. As it did not really hurt, I kind of wondered what all the screaming and hands grabbing me were all about. Aunt Mildred jerked my jeans off and found just below my right knee about a half inch was a very severe gash in my leg. It was then that the not hurting went away, and the really did hurt started. As we were about twenty minutes from Mexico and the only doctor available on Sunday afternoon was Audrain Hospital, they quickly wrapped my leg in a towel and headed for town. After the visit to the hospital, we returned to Grandma's house, and as well as I can remember, the wound was not nearly as bad for me as it was for all the aunts and uncles as they all looked like they had seen a ghost. Mom did say that the doctor told them that if the cut had been just a tad higher, I probably would have bled to death or that the knee would have been unable to bend for the rest of my life. Today the scar is right where it all happened some seventy years ago, and the leg bends just as well as the left one, so I guess everything turned out OK.

Memorable Moments Flashback
Searching for Petrified Wood

Here it is fall again and the rains are falling almost on a daily basis. When we go down the road driving toward town, it is readily apparent that the ground has reached the point of saturation, and nearly every drop that falls joins millions of other drops. It all heads downhill to form a puddle or better yet cover a ditch or branch that is flowing, freely seeking its own level. As a little kid looking for adventure and free entertainment, the water reaching from bank to bank on the branches and rivers was a sight to behold. If the temperature was above sixty degrees and the rain was a steady downpour, this was the time to grab your walking stick and wade down the center of the rushing water. It was a great adventure to seek where all that water was going to end up. Many were the time on a Sunday afternoon after lunch at Grandma and Grandpa Burl's house and it looked like the sky had opened up. It was soaking the earth for miles around. Now was the time for the kids to head off below the barn to where the creek was rolling and a booming. Usually, it was Minnie, Ginny, and I that made up the exploring pact due to the fact that the younger kids were too little to be turned loose in the woods without adult supervision. The older kids were far enough along to not find exploring woods and creeks of any great importance. We would start at the road where the driveway began, crawl under the wooden water crossing, and wade up to our knees in rushing water that disappeared into the woods about twenty-five yards from the bridge. The creek meandered back and forth through the woods and down the hillside for about a quarter mile where it dumped into Young's Creek. This was far enough to wear out a kid that was fighting to stand up and walk with the current for about an hour or more. As with Missouri weather, the rains usually came up fast and dumped many gallons of water in a short period of time, which caused the creeks to fill up fast. In the same instance, it would cease entirely minutes later. In a matter of minutes, the creek would go from a semiraging body of water to a babbling brook and then return to a dry rocky creek bed. The three of us would retrace our steps slowly back toward the starting point and, along the way, look long and hard for any rock that had been shaped, polished, and uncovered by the running water. The most sought-after piece of collectable rock was chunks of petrified wood. This was often found along a particular section of this very creek and seemed not be found anywhere else in the area. It was a rock formation but was about the size of a small thick board, flat with straight lines across the top. It seemed to have wood grains like a split log would have. It was explained to us that centuries ago a tree had fallen in the woods and then become covered with sand, dirt, and silt.

No air could reach the fibers and start the rotting process. It turned into rock and stayed covered with dirt until rainwater washed it off and made it visible to kids that were walking along the creek a long, long time later. Many of the bigger pieces were taken home and kept around the house to be looked at and wondered about. Some were used as a doorstop if big enough to keep a door from going shut. So goes the glory of searching for petrified wood by kids back in the good ole days.

Slopping the Hogs

Directly north of the house was about twenty-five acres that was usually planted in sorghum milo or legume hay. On the back side of the farm were two more plots of about thirty acres each that was the soybean or corn ground, depending on which year it was as the corn ground and soybean ground was planted in alternating years. The beans were supposed to leave behind nitrogen from when they were growing so that the corn could use the mineral next year to grow better. The field north of the house was usually planted in milo as this was known at the time to be one of the best hog feeds available to finish out a bunch of fattening hogs. This crop was also a plant that grew fast and matured a little earlier than corn, so Dad could go into the edge of the field and cut off heads of the plants that had begun to mature. This was fed to the shoats that were destined to become ham and bacon in the very near future. By using the milo heads to help feed them out before the corn was ready tended to keep down the cost of having to buy feed. When it was mature and the moisture was at a low percentage, Dad would combine the entire field and put the milo grain in one of the bins of the granary. We had several ways that feed was provided to the pen of fattening hogs. One method was to mix ground corn and water in a fifty-gallon wooden barrel each night. This would sit in the sun during the hot summer day, and the powdered corn would soak for twenty-four hours, which produced what we termed as "slop." Depending on how hot the water became during the day, the slop would be slightly fermented and gave off a sour odor that drove the hogs crazy at feeding time. On the other side of the fence, Dad had connected three or four hog troughs end to end with one end removed so that it became one really long slop trough. As he dipped a five-gallon bucket into the barrel, the hogs realized that in the next few seconds they were going to find supper going down the trough from end to end. When he began pouring into the nearest end, the hogs would nearly go crazy trying to get their share and more. By moving rapidly from barrel to trough, Dad actually got the mixture to cover the entire distance. If it took him three minutes to empty the barrel, the hogs would have it devoured in three minutes, so supper was delivered and consumed very rapidly. There was usually fifteen to thirty heads of pigs eating at the trough at any one time, so you can imagine the squealing and pushing that took place during the slopping. After the barrel was empty, it was then time to carry three or four five-gallon buckets of ground corn and dump it into the barrel. Dad's tractor was parked below the pond dam up the slop from the pig pen beside the granary. Attached to the power takeoff on the tractor was a water pump with an inlet hose in the pond and a long outlet hose that ended up by the slop barrel. I held the end of the hose, and when Dad started the tractor and turned on the power takeoff, the pump would turn, and water would pour from the hose into the barrel. In a few minutes, the barrel was full; a paddle was dipped into the concoction and stirred around. The mixture took on the consistency of mush. If there was no ground corn to make the mixture, then we made do with using shelled corn by putting corn kernels in the barrel and filling it the rest of the way to about three-fourth full with water. The reason you only put enough water in the barrel until about three-fourth full was that the corn would swell up to twice the original size, ferment, and make a frothy foam that ran down the side of the barrel. By the time feeding time arrived the next day, the corn had swollen. Outside shell burst, so—with the heat of the day—it had become another version of slop to be fed to the waiting hogs. After working with this concoction on many an occasion and seeing and smelling the by-product of this barrel, it is of little doubt why having hominy on the table for dinner really did not appeal to me and to this day does not.

On the other hand, the real slop was produced in the kitchen. There was a five-gallon bucket with a board top on it that received any or all scraps from the cooking or leftovers from any of the three meals that were eaten during the day. When this bucket became full, it was replaced with an empty bucket, and the full one was taken out to the breeding sows for a treat of sorts. The sows would see Dad coming from the house with the bucket about every two or three days, and they quickly learned that the sight of that bucket meant eats were coming their direction. It took a pretty strong stomach to empty that bucket after a couple of days in the summertime, but to a three-hundred-pound sow, it was almost like going to the candy counter at Mr. Williams's country store. It could be said that nothing was wasted back in those days. Everything was utilized, including the house waste, with nothing being thrown out as we have become accustomed to today.

Funny Drunk Pigs

Speaking of hogs and speaking of the slop being fermented, that reminds me of one of the funniest sights I ever saw as a little kid. We, in fact, laughed so hard watching the hogs that it was hard to breathe. It all happened each year about the end of summer when the corn was in the milk stage. On our farm, there was usually a half-dozen steers being fed out for market, but at Ralph Bridgford's farm, there was a feedlot that could contain seventy-five to one hundred steers getting ready for market. This took a tremendous amount of feed daily, so they produced and used what was called corn silage. They first dug a huge trench in the side of a hill that was about twenty feet across and fifteen feet deep and, many times, thirty or forty yards long. When the corn was at the right stage, they took a silage machine through the field and chopped the cornstalk and shot it into a special made wagon until it was full to the top. The wagon was backed into the trench, dumped the load to the back of the trench, and then headed back to the field for another load. At this time, one of Ralph's sons would run another tractor into the trench and push the chopped silage into the back of the trench. When the trench was completely filled to over the top, a huge tarpaulin was placed over it until it was completely covered, staked down, and was nearly airtight from top to bottom. At this point, Mother Nature took over the process, and the heat of the outside air and the heat produced inside the silage cooked the entire batch and turned it into a kind of sour but sweet-smelling composition. When completely cured, this was fed to the cattle in the feedlot. Now this is where the hogs came into the equation. As the silage was cooking from within, there were juices produced that ran to the bottom of the trench and proceeded to make a little stream that ran directly through the hog lots. It was explained to me at the time that the little stream was a lot like the liquid that the ole timers made at home called moonshine. It was pretty common knowledge that certain persons around Santa Fe was really good at this type of cooking corn and other items that ended up as corn whiskey. It was fairly easy to see why this liquid coming out of the silage could be a pretty powerful type of moonshine. At a certain stage of production, the hogs found that it resembled a little like the slop that they dearly loved but was slop with a kick. They spent most of their day either drinking the runoff or laying in it. It was when they decided to get up and walk out of the pool of moonshine that the real fun began. The bigger the hog, the funnier it became as they would stagger around, fall flat on their faces, roll over on their backs with their mouth open and tongue hanging out. It appeared that they were grinning and laughing about a joke that only they could feel or hear. This would go on for hours. When we got so sore from laughing, we had to leave so we could catch our breath. It took several days for the silage to complete the cycle of fermentation, so it took several days for the hogs to sober up. One can only imagine the amount of hangover those three-hundred-pound sows had developed after being drunk for that many days. Occasionally, a cow or steer would happen upon the stream, and ever so often, a dog would take a drink of the brew and would be staggering around. Nothing would ever be nearly as funny as watching a drunken hog try to get four feet going in the same direction when only two would work correctly.

Log Cabin and Groundhog Burn Out

Meanwhile, back on the farm. Let's go to the back east side of the place and look around at where we would spend a lot of our days as kids roaming through the hollows and back fields. Behind the Big Pond and over the slight hill was the dirt road that took you down the back side to the flat farmland, which contained the really great tillable soil. This field lay almost perfectly flat and was by all means the best dirt on the farm. It was here that as a kid we found enough places and critters to entertain us for years. One thing that always caught our interest was the old log cabin that was sitting in the woods on the southeast corner of the farm. The roof had caved in several decades ago, and all that was left was three walls and some of the floor made out of handmade rough-hewed oak. With a little imagination, the entire house could be put back together and could almost tell a story of the families that had lived here long, long ago. The cabin was not without local residents as there were holes and tunnels everywhere you could find a piece of dirt two feet square or more. Many times, we would sit totally quiet, and after a few minutes, either a red fox or several groundhogs would appear to see why things had gotten so quiet. All around the ole cabin was grown up in brush and tall grasses. Hidden in this cover, a covey or two of quail could be found within fifty yards of the place. The real problem that Dad encountered with the groundhogs, formally called woodchucks, was in the spring when the soybeans were coming through the ground. The groundhogs had been eating tree bark and dry grass for so long new little plants were like fresh salad to them. They ate nearly every soybean plant in sight. This gave reason that it was time to either kill

59

or run off as many of the critters as possible before the planting took place. Early spring after the last frost, we would go with Dad to the ole log cabin with a two-gallon can of gasoline and a five-gallon can of water. He would locate a new entrance to a tunnel and started his ritual of moving them out or killing them off. First, he would pour about a gallon of water into the hole, let it set about two minutes, then pour a coffee can of gasoline into the hole. Next, he took a little can of lighter fluid from his pocket and squirted a small but steady stream on the ground while walking backward about sixty feet. The kids were instructed to get on the hillside about two hundred yards from the tunnel entrance. When we were a safe distance away, Dad would drop a match on the ground beside the stream of lighter fluid, and within ten seconds, the fire would follow up the little stream and go into the tunnel. When the fire entered the hole, there was a huge boom, and fire would shoot backward out of the tunnel. In the same instant, there would be fireballs erupt from the ground appearing from at least five various positions, covering at least an acre or more. No less than twenty groundhogs would either be blown from the hole or come running out with their fur singed or smoking. There was little wonder that the varmints could eat two or three acres of soybeans in a single day as there were probably dozens of them within the very small wooded area that we were standing on. We usually did another blow in a couple of weeks, but usually, the mass number removed the first time pretty took care of the majority of soybean eaters. With little doubt, they would be back next year in the same place. They would come from all directions next spring to have their young and set up housekeeping under the floor of the ole log cabin. It was pretty much a fact that Dad would be back next spring with his water and gasoline to try and save as many bushels of beans as he could to help feed his family.

Close by this area was where we also planted a large plot of sweet corn, and along with this, we put in at least two rows of popcorn for use as a treat during the cold months of winter. The family had a huge bag of popcorn at least twice a week as the snow was flying. Popcorn balls were a welcome treat when candy was hard to come by. Just before you got to the place of the old log cabin was a fencerow that was grown up in a very peculiar type of bush that was not to be found anywhere but at this one location. It was told to me that this was a really large bush of hazel nut that had probably been planted there by a family passing through many decades earlier. This was not a nut that was found anywhere else on any of the surrounding farms. Each fall, we would go down the hill and gather the clumps of nuts after they had matured, ate as many as we could at one time without getting ill, then husk them out, and put them out to dry on the back porch. Not far from the hazel nut bushes were several pawpaw trees. When they ripened in the fall, we would eat as many as we wanted but never was a fruit that we kept for use other than what we ate under the tree. It was a really sweet fruit that was about the size of a small cucumber and shaped about the same but was full of black seeds that filled each piece of fruit. When they were ripe, you could find pile after pile of raccoon poop in the area that was full of paw-paw seeds. That fruit, along with the ripe persimmon fruit, seemed to be the main target in the fall for nearly every critter in the area that was seeking food to fill up on so as to gain weight that would take them into hibernation. We also looked for buckeyes in the same area, but they were supposed to be poisonous if you ate them.

Jim 4 months, KW 5 years
Summer kitchen and cistern
well in background 1947

Mary 9 years, KW 5 years,
Jim 6 months
Standing in front of house
outside Santa Fe 1947

Jim 5 years, KW 9 years 1953
New ride Summer kitchen
and ice house in background

Jim 5 years, KW 9 years 1953
Blondie quail dog Kids in
normal summer attire

We just carried the buckeye in our pockets during the winter months as they were said to bring good luck if you had one in your pocket. I always had a couple of them in my school desk just in case they did bring good luck and just in case I needed good luck at any one time.

Behind the icehouse was what we referred to as "the chicken yard." It covered about half an acre that was fenced in, kind of anyhow, to keep the dogs out and the chickens in. The fence did keep some chickens in, but those that could not figure how to get out had to be pretty stupid as there were holes big enough for a small turkey to go through. If they could not get through the hole, then it was pretty simple to fly over if they had a set of wings, which all did have available. Inside this area were two buildings, the first being directly behind the icehouse and was the brooder house or starting house depending on who was talking about it. It was small, maybe ten feet by ten feet with a sole purpose to house the newly hatched chicks until they were about three weeks old. When they arrived, they were placed in the brooder house, and most were no older than three days, so they were fragile to say the least. In the center of the room was a metal canopy that hung from the ceiling with a chain, and beside it was a really small kerosene heater that ran for twenty-four hours for days on end. The area must be kept at a constant ninety plus degree for at least two weeks until they begin putting on their pin feathers, which offered some protection from the chill of the air. Just outside the canopy was several water jugs and feeders all being close enough that the chicks did not have to venture far away from the heated area to eat or drink. There would be anywhere from one hundred fifty to two hundred new chicks all huddled together under the hood, basking in the warmth and protection of the brooder stove. Most of this flock was destined to become lunch or dinner in the very near future, and several were to be replacement stock for the laying hens. For the present time, eating, drinking, and sleeping was the order of the day and several days to come. The entire family was in charge of watching this brooder house every minute of the day as several things could and did go wrong. With every complication that occurred the first three weeks, the date of the first fried chicken dinner would be postponed until a later date. One problem that occurred was when the chicks were about two weeks old. When we returned from getting groceries in Santa Fe one afternoon, we noticed smoke coming from the brooder house. Dad grabbed a bucket and ran to the pond and then rushed into the brooder house and found the floor and litter under the heater had caught fire. When anything happens that is a little out of the ordinary, chickens and even full-grown hens run into a corner and pile up about four deep, which causes them to suffocate in short order. This had occurred as well as many were overcome from the smoke, so this entire disaster had very serious consequences with a future food source for the family. Having lost nearly half of the flock, this meant that we would be making another trip into Mexico to replace the lost chicks. This was a major setback as now we had to wait for the ones that lived to mature enough to be moved out of the brooder. Starting over with day-old chicks meant that it would be weeks before they would be old enough to move outside, not to mention the expense of paying for the second set. In about three weeks, there was another batch of day-old chicks to watch over, which meant that we were just about where we started that early spring day. Another time, we found that a possum had dug under the floor and chewed through the wood to gain admission to his own private buffet. Next morning, Dad found about fifteen of the chicks with their heads bitten off and eaten and the carcasses left strung over the floor. Needless to say, the opossum had enjoyed his last meal on earth when he was quickly sent to possum heaven or wherever possums go when Dad finished teaching it a lesson that can only be taught one time to any one individual. It did make a very nice possum hide though after it was skinned and stretched on a board to cure out for about a month. The price of that hide at Blacks Feed Store really helped lower the cost of replacement chicks, so everything kind of evened out in the end. Another time, we came home and found the bird dog pups that Dad had been training to search for quail had found that searching for chickens in the wire pen was a lot easier. Not much damage was done as they only killed a half dozen or so, but that still meant that there would be six less chickens to fry for the dinner table. Dad caught each pup and tied a dead chicken around each dog's neck and made them drag it around for a couple of days. Pretty much ended the chicken killing desire for all the pups from that day on. Another problem that seemed to make chickens disappear was when a chicken hawk zeroed in on the holding pen. When the chicks were about half grown and loafing around in the finishing pen, every so often a hawk would come diving from the sky. They made a fast plunge in among the fowl and came flying out with one in their claws. As the chicken was very alive at that point, you would hear a steady squawk that warned the entire family that a chicken was about to disappear. Dad kept the loaded double-barrel shotgun just inside the kitchen door and would come running like crazy around the icehouse with the hope that the hawk with his heavy load of future lunch was slowed down enough to still be in range. Usually, the hawk was just out of range, but occasionally, the buckshot would burn his rear end, and it would release the stolen chicken, but that really did not happen all that often. Usually, the hawk was flying west over the trees by the road, and the squawk of the chicken would grow faint in the distance. If the hawk had outrun the buckshot, then he had a really tender dinner of grain-fed chicken to either fill his craw or feed to the next generation of chicken thieves that had hatched out. In later years, the hawk population was protected from killing, but to Dad, the only good chicken hawk was a dead chicken hawk. That pretty much held true until he got too old to hunt. We explained to him that being protected meant that they were not to be shot at or shot to death and that if anyone caught him or turned him in for shooting a chicken hawk that he may be given a heavy fine. He never did say much about having shot a chicken hawk after that, but several times in the neighborhood, a hawk would have the bad luck of running into a fence with their feet tangled in binder twine.

The much larger building in the chicken yard was the chicken house that stood just east of the brooder about twenty-five yards. This had a split roof with windows up high almost to the top and was screened in on the south side with chicken wire. This was placed on the south side of the building, which let in fresh air but at the same time let in sunshine in the winter so some of the heat would stay inside the feeding parlor. To the back of the building was the roosting area that had long skinny logs placed about two feet off the floor and was staggered toward the roof. This provided an area for the entire flock to roost at night as with all fowl, the need to be located off the ground or floor is in their genetics when it becomes dark. Under the roost was an open area that gathered the droppings that the birds deposited during the night. After several weeks, the droppings heaped up on the floor, which needed to be removed by a smaller person taking a scoop shovel and pushing it all to the wall. It was then loaded into the wagon to be deposited on the fields or garden for fertilizer. This unpleasant job was for the person who was small enough to stand up beneath the roost and push the materials toward the end of the building. The longer a person put it off, the deeper it piled up and the more difficult the job became. As Jim was too small and Mary was usually busy in the house, this chore fell upon the shoulders of the middle son, which usually put it off until a better day of which really never occurred. Every time I did get around to the chore, I swore that I would not let it get this deep next time and would keep it clean at all times. It was very easy to forget this oath until the piles were deep and needed cleaning, which made it just as difficult as it was the time before.

In the back of the henhouse was located the egg-laying room. This place was totally void of light and dark at all time. Located here were about fifteen laying boxes on the back wall. It was two boxes high, and each box had a handful of hay in them so the hens could sit in the boxes during the day and lay an egg in comfort. As soon as one would lay an egg, they would cackle and squawk, which signaled the other hens that were waiting their turn that a box was vacant. Another would take the place of the one that had just finished. In a laying season, each hen would lay one egg a day for about six weeks. At this time, an inborn signal would occur in the hen's brain that would change her demeanor from a laying hen to become a sitting hen. Whenever the nest contained seven or eight eggs, this change in the hen's daily ritual went from producing an egg to just sitting on the nest to incubate the eggs for the next twenty-eight days. It was during this transition period that the easygoing down-to-earth ole hen would become a holy terror and turn mean as a junkyard dog. Reach your hand into a dark nest when one was setting and you can bet you will draw back a finger with a chunk missing. Occasionally, one would come out of the box with claws extended and beat the tar out the unlucky person that happened to be standing within striking distance. Strange how her mood would change the minute the chicks cracked out of the shell as she would return back to the same attitude she possessed before the sitting fever hit. Another situation that arose several times was when the kid responsible for gathering the eggs at the end of the day entered the dark room. Occasionally, when you reached into the laying box, you got a handful of black snakes, instead of finding several round little eggs. Snakes found that usually an easy meal in the boxes were available. You cannot imagine how rapidly one can remove their hand from within the laying box. For sure, it would linger in your mind what may be there every time you reach for an egg in the future. It would take several trips to gather eggs with a flashlight in hand before the fear of the unknown would diminish.

Memorable Moments Flashback
Searching for Guinea Nest

Each spring early in May, all chickens, turkeys, and guineas began the age-old call of the wild to reproduce. It was not all that difficult to come across a nest of eggs from the chickens and the turkeys as they could not get through the fence that surrounded the chicken yard. Not so for the guineas as they could fly as high as the house roof and higher, so they came and went as they pretty well pleased. This gave them the opportunity to travel afar when the hatching season began, and travel they did. When the chicks hatched out, they were usually in the far pasture or the edge of the woods, which gave their life expectancy fairly short-term what with the snakes, raccoons, foxes, and every other critter that was roaming around looking for an easy meal. If they did not break up the nest and eat the eggs, they would nearly always hunt down the young chicks and devour them. For this reason, the kids searching party was established. We were promised money and treats to go out and find the nest, gather the eggs, and bring them in to be placed beneath a bantam hen so that she could incubate them in a controlled atmosphere. The method we perfected was to get up really early in the morning and let the birds out of the henhouse where they were confined for the night. We would put some distance between us and the fowls and watch which direction the guineas would take. Like the chickens, they too laid one egg a day until the nest was full so they would proceed toward the nest site in an erratic nonhurrying procession to make their deposit. If anything was out of the ordinary, such as them seeing two kids hanging around behind them, then they would act as if nothing was different. They would not head to the nesting area but would amble around as if they were searching for bugs and seeds but never end up at the nest. Many times, we must stay hidden for hours until they felt that no danger was around and then would casually stroll off in different direction from the flock and disappear. If and when we did find a nest, we would place a ribbon of cloth on a branch close by as a sign that this is where we wanted to be tomorrow later in the day. We always left one egg in the nest because if the guinea hen came back tomorrow and the nest was empty, she would abandon this place and start all over again. This all sounds really simple or so you would think. It totally was not that simple as the guinea hen was extremely cautious and really, really smart, so if anything was even slightly different or if we were seen sneaking around, then she would not go to her nest. If the situation occurred often, she would leave the area and prepare another nest elsewhere. Fact: most of the time, we did not find the nest, and if we did, it was by luck and chance along with very hard work. We do not have any records to support our findings but would put the number of found nest in and around one out of six and many years equaled zero.

Journey to the Fishing Hole

As you stepped through the wire gate at the edge of the yard and preceded down the driveway, you would find yourself at a wooden gate that, when opened, led directly to the county gravel road. If you took the curve to the right, you would end up in Santa Fe about one and a half miles down the road. On the other side of the gravel road was a wooded area of about ten acres that contained the remains of a very old barn. Trees had grown over and around it so that you could not see it unless you entered the woods and followed the path that was overgrown with grass and weeds. This was the area that we spent every winter Sunday afternoon cutting wood for heat for the following week. The path led back into the woods and ended at the edge of the bluff overlooking Salt River. To get to the river, you had to walk to the spot where the rainwater of the past centuries had cascaded over the hill and had cut out a solitary strip of earth that led between two walls of rock. The path was pretty steep but easy to go down as you would slide most of the way, but coming back up was a different story. When fishing at the bottom of the draw and if we were lucky enough to snag several nice-sized catfish, it became evident that neither Jim nor I would be capable of getting anything to the top of the bluff by ourselves. We started up first with Dad bringing up the rear with what fishing tackle we had along and carrying a stringer of fish that we most generally caught. When we got approximately halfway up the hill, there was a small level spot that Dad always stopped and rested until he stopped huffing and puffing. Jim and I always wondered why we had to stop as we were very seldom breathing hard. It was not until about fifty years later it dawned on me that the reason Dad was out of breath was because adults do not breath like a kid, and the older one gets, the more prevalent this is. Once we made it to the top of the hill, we were mostly home free as the dirt path was almost level until we hit the driveway. Knowing full well that we had to skin the fish almost immediately and also knowing full well that the menu for supper would almost definitely be fried catfish and corn bread made the hard work of the morning all worthwhile.

Fishing before the Bus Arrives

One can only imagine how many times I made the trip from the house to the river during the twelve years we lived there. From the time I turned seven, I was allowed to make the trip down the hillside by myself and made that trip almost daily. When the warm days of spring arrived, the fishing fever took hold of me, and there were very few days of the week that I was either sitting on the riverbank or thinking about sitting on the riverbank. With school going on until the middle of May, there were many hours out of each day while sitting in the classroom when my mind was about one and a half miles down the road. I was thinking about that big catfish just waiting for me to throw in a ball of worms and bring his slick hide out on the bank and up the draw. When I was old enough to ride the bus to Paris for my high school years, we always met Roy Sharp at the end of the lane right at seven o'clock in each morning. We rode with him to Santa Fe where the younger kids walked to the elementary school and the older kids waited in Bill Phipps general store until the orange bus pulled up in front of the door. It was before the time to meet Roy Sharp at the end of the lane was when I was at my busiest. All the chores were done by Dad in the morning, and nearly all the chores were done by me in the late afternoon, so as soon as daylight broke enough to see where your feet would land, my steps were being made directly to the river. In my bucket was several pieces of chicken liver, beef suet, or chicken guts. And if that was not available, then the trusty can of worms was always there. Having installed six bank poles the week before, my task was to check each pole and either remove a catfish and rebait or, if the hook was empty, rebait the hook and make ready for the next fish that may be traveling down the river. Usually, there were more empty hooks than not with the line hanging slack, but just ever so often, there would be the line pulled tight as a Banjo String. When the pole was bouncing up and down, it meant that there was something on the other end. If all went well, then there would be a big catfish to haul up the draw. By the time I walked to the house, put the fish in the horse trough, grabbed a piece of toast for breakfast, changed clothes, and washed the fish and liver smell off my hands, it usually was just mere minutes before our ride was pulling up to the end of the driveway. After loading onto the bus at Santa Fe, the ride to Paris was about twenty minutes, and by the time we arrived at the unloading ramp, I had caught my breath and was ready to head to the agriculture department classroom and begin my first period of higher education. Midafternoon, we loaded back on the bus for the forty-five-minute trip back to Santa Fe and rode back to our driveway with Roy or waited for Dad to finish at the hammer mill and drive me home. My task at hand was to change clothes and head toward the Big Barn and feed the sheep, go to the granary and shell a bucket of corn, throw out grain and laying mash to the hen flock, gather what eggs were left when laid late in the day, and close the henhouse door. By this time, supper was usually ready, and the entire family was seated around the table, ready to pass the food around.

By the time I had dressed fish caught that morning, it was pretty late in the evening, so I took a shower on the back steps and lay my head down for a few hours of sleep. Arose at daybreak and started the procedure all over again. This schedule was followed until the end of the school year, and then it was all free time and do what you wanted to do for the entire summer. Problem about to arise in the near future was the fact that I was almost thirteen years old by this time, which meant old enough to do something other than fish and roam the woods and back pastures. That fateful day arrived when Dad and I were building a pen for my sow, which was my FFA project. A pickup truck turned into our driveway and proceeded to pull up in front of our barn. A guy got out, and Dad said something to the effect of "How you been, Ottie?" Unbeknownst to me, this moment was about to change my carefree and "fish when you wanted to" life. This is a completely whole new story and will be dealt with in another chapter of these stories.

Biggest fish I've ever caught. Seven years old with my first real rod and reel. Can remember almost as if it were yesterday.

Fishing with Bro. Jim sitting on the pond bank at same spot you could find us day in and day out. Caught Bull Heads by the hundreds.

Dad with Missouri Barbara Angus Heifer day before we went to show and sale in Monroe City. I cried for days after she was sold.

Four fishermen. KW, JC Kessler, Bob Moore and Bro. Jim. Must have been when I was about 12 years old because there is a light pole in the background. First got electricity when I was 11.

End of Winter and Last Wood Cutting

An even small child gets tired of cold wet days and nights and, like everyone else, begins to think of what life could be without freezing rain and snow. When I was a kid, there were many things that led us to believe change was coming and coming soon. One sign was that the wood pile that once stood ten feet tall and covered the floor of the storage shed was now down to just a few large chunks of wood too large for a fifty-pound kid to carry. This also was the time that every Sunday afternoon was spent in the woods cutting enough trees down and sawing it up into stove length to last until the next weekend. As the kids were too small to handle the dangerous saws and axes, it was assigned to us the task of taking the limbs that had been trimmed from the main trunk and pile them in a stack away from where the cutting was being done. This pile was set ablaze next weekend so that there would be ample heat to keep cold fingers and toes at a comfortable level while working in the woods. Once again, Jim and I were assigned the task of stacking limbs, but as you can imagine, Jim would be a great help for about two minutes, and then all of a sudden, he was gone poking around in hollow trees, tracking rabbits in the snow, searching for hidden treasure, or doing just about anything other than helping stack tree limbs. Made one often wonder how great it would be to be the youngest kid in the family and not be expected to work for more than a few minutes at a time. After a couple of hours, Dad would have enough wood cut down and blocked ready to load on the wagon. This was always a time of the week that made you feel good about yourself knowing that for the immediate future the cold of winter would not get hold of the house on the Willingham farm, at least not for the next week or so.

Another sign of the coming of the end of winter was the slight but ever so present few minutes of daylight that seemed to linger at the end of each day. During the month of January, no matter how you hurried to get home from school and race to the big barn to feed the sheep, you were always finishing your chores in the dark and feeling the temperature dropping before being able to get back into the kitchen next to the warm and welcome woodstove. Being in the month of February, there was still that uncomfortable feeling of numb toes and fingers, but at least now, there was enough light to see inside the barn and light enough to see where you had been after you got back. Along with this extra light, there was that little bit of comfort in the back of your mind that said spring was coming, so just hold on a little longer and the warm breezes of April would arrive.

It was not so very long until the sounds and sights of the wild geese flying north for the summer would begin. How could you forget the many times you heard way off in the distance a really faint familiar sound, a sound that can be heard to this day. Just barely visible in the far-off sky is a very pronounced large V, or maybe two or three Vs will appear and grow closer and closer. As the huge flock of geese flies directly overhead, many thoughts run through your young mind. Where do you think all those geese have been the past several weeks? How many do you imagine are in that huge far-off V? Can you imagine where they will end up in the next few days and how far will they have gone before they stop? To a child who has only been to the Missouri border and back, one can hardly imagine how much world is out there. I always wondered if we will ever get to see anything close to what that flock of geese had seen while traveling the past few days in such a gigantic flock so high in the sky. As the sounds of the geese get fainter and fainter in the distance, it leaves a nearly ghostly feeling as well as a feeling of well-being knowing that things are revolving around to start a new season and a new awakening of Mother Nature. This is also a new beginning for man and beast after suffering through and winning another bout with ole man winter and the bone-chilling winds and snow that came with the months of

December, January, and February. Things really haven't changed all that much over the years. The only thing that has changed is our age and attitudes. All else around us have remained basically the same for centuries. It's only knowing that we only walk here such a short time that we really cannot compare to see what overall differences have occurred. To me, that is one of the greatest advantages of being born and raised on a farm. You can be a part of tomorrow without getting away from all of today. It all gathers together making a reason for being little and growing bigger each day in mind and body, not to mention soul. There is just so much more meaning to being a part of the big picture and knowing that, each day that goes by, you are smarter and richer than you could ever imagine when you were a nine-year-old kid.

Elementary School Formal Education

With the subject of being smarter, this brings us to consider the subject of formal education when introduced to kids in a country school. You, for sure, can see a drastic change of what school was in the midforties and what we call education today. First and foremost, you do not have to have a multimillion-dollar facility to make education take place. If education depended upon buildings and materials, I doubt if anyone that graduated from the eighth grade at Santa Fe Elementary School would have been able to go any further than farmhand or factory worker as an occupation. Our school building consisted of two rooms; one room, the larger of the two, was approximately thirty feet by fifty feet. This was arranged with single desks situated in four rows the length of the room. The other room was about twenty feet by thirty feet and totally vacant besides a table, a sink, and cabinets on the wall that held dozens of chili bowls and glasses. In the main room was a huge woodburning furnace that heated the entire building very comfortably. It was replaced with a coal furnace and, at a later date, a coal oil furnace so as the time went on a more efficient heat was provided. When the coal oil stove came into being, it was great as the kids could bring food wrapped in tin foil to be placed on top of the stove an hour before lunch. With a little imagination, this was the start of the first hot meal program the school ever had. Entrance was made into the building on the east end of the classroom, but we were not to use that door, except during warm weather as there was no enclosed doorway. So when this door was opened during the cold times, it dropped the inside temperature about thirty degrees in a matter of seconds. Those that were sitting at their desk close to the door would almost suffer frostbite before the heater could catch up. We were to use the door on the south room as that room did not lead directly into the classroom and also had the coatracks and boot bins away from the classroom proper. By coming into the side room and not opening the classroom door, the temperature stayed a nice balmy fifty-five to sixty degrees. At the back of the room was the library. This did not take up much room as our library consisted of two bookcases of five shelves each. As all eight grades were in the same room, likewise all eight-grade-level books were in the same library. As well as could be imagined, there was not a great deal of material available for outside reading. In fact, there was actually no books available for outside reading. The only saving grace I found in the library was the presence of the *World Book Encyclopedia* and another set of encyclopedias that had nothing in them but words and writing with not a single picture to explain what the article was all about. On the other hand, the *World Book* was a wealth of information containing everything from A to Z about anything you ever wondered about. With big print and several pictures per page, this part of the library was truly a lifesaver for the kid that had little or no problem with assignments and had lots of free time to explore the *World Book* for fun and excitement. Truthfully, I lived with one of the red cover books on my desk and, at the time, could almost recite articles and information word for word of what was written.

Some of the most interesting sections are still vivid in my memory. My favorite was the section on kites and kite building, especially the part of the kite flying that was the pastime of China with the two- and three-tiered box kites that they developed. The unique models that they designed and flew were what many of my dreams were made of, and I was dead set on making one like those pictured and would fly it myself someday. I did try to make a regular kite after reading all about it, but not having a clue what materials to use kind of did a make do with what I could find around the house. Took a couple of pieces of wood out of Mom's bedroom shades as that was about as close as I could come to having a cross brace made with light wood. Wound fishing line around the outside and cut newspaper the correct size and used some wallpaper glue that I found in the store-room to fasten it together. After many hours of cutting and pasting and then removing it and starting all over, I found myself almost no closer to getting it to fly than when I started. Finally decided to just read about the kite flying and give up the idea of having my own to fly above the farm. All this was just about the biggest disappointment of my life, not getting a kite that would get off the ground.

SANTA FE SCHOOL
DISTRICT NO. 4

Faye Evans
Barbara Key
Jimmy Willingham
Jimmy Beatty
Paul Wayne Scobee
Billy Phipps
Aubrey Nolan
Carolyn Sharp

Jerry Evans
Sharon Poage
Margaret Bridgford
Janet Poage
Mary Ellen Bishop
Warren Martin
Patty Wilson
Jolene Perrigo

Kenneth Willingham
Bobby Majors
Allen Heckart
Ernie Hanna
Shirley Kesler
Lowell Ray Perrigo

J.C. Kesler
Linda Snyder
Joyce Beatty

Santa Fe Elementary School Picture
KW Sixth Grade taken March
1954 four students in my grade
total 25 students grades 1 - 8

Another section of great interest was the people of the round table and knights and such. I studied those passages for hours dreaming of what it must have been like back in the day to be on horseback and be the bravest and strongest knight in the kingdom. With a little imagination, of which I had plenty, being a part of that time in history was almost like being there. I couldn't pronounce all the words in the stories, but with what I could understand, it was fairly easy to dream away a half day of school and not once get bored with just sitting.

The *World Book* was full of animals, in fact almost every kind of weird-looking creature you could possibly imagine. It was hard to believe that there were really live animals that looked like those in the pictures especially when all we ever saw was a horse, a pig, sheep, and cows. I decided that no matter how strange those animals were, if they were in the *World Book*, then they must be for real. I actually dreamed about some of them; they looked so weird and made a really big impression on my mind and memory.

Back to the library and what it did or did not have available. I cannot actually remember for sure but can almost say that I read every book in the bookcases some time during my eight years in school. I do know that my favorite book was titled *The Biography of a Grizzly*. This book I read no less than three times from cover to cover and many other times read various chapters one chapter at a time. I truly believe that I became a part of the soul of that grizzly and lived it over and over again from the moment he was born to the day that his life was ended. Such a great book I wonder why it didn't become famous like those literature books they made us read in high school and college.

I will never forget the day that a whole new world opened up to our school in Santa Fe. That happened the day that the regional bookmobile came to our school. It was dispatched from the city of Paris, Missouri, and was scheduled to be at our school every other Friday during the entire school year. First time I entered the bus, it almost took my breath. It appeared that they must have gotten a copy of every book in the state to have that many books available at one time. As we had never been inside a real library, it was a total surprise how many books were located on the many shelves inside this mobile van. We were allowed to sign out five books and had fifteen minutes for each individual to pick out what they wanted to read the next two weeks. From that moment on, I very seldom went back to the *World Books* for entertainment. The world of outside reading books was a dream come true and would make school much more than a place to be between recesses. It actually started to be a place that a person could learn and remember about things that were outside the life of a young kid in the country.

Better back up, I got to remembering and missed out on a lot of relevant information about what it takes to be successful in an educational setting that resembles nothing one would ever think as being an educational setting. This brings us back to the second room in the building, a room that was totally bare other than a sink, a range, and a few cabinets that housed a bunch of bowls and glasses that was used for an occasional chili supper or potluck dinner that brought the city and county together about once a month. We, in turn, used the open area to spend recesses when the weather outside was way too bad to venture outside. This was not really very often, however, as we very seldom felt that bad weather was really a factor that kept us from going outside. Only the most severe weather kept us inside, and even in the coldest and most miserable times, we were outside doing whatever young kids did to have fun. For sure, the fifteen-minute recess morning and afternoon and the hour free time during lunch was fully utilized at all times. The favorite game was softball and, if at all possible, was played almost year-round if the valley was dry enough to keep the clay from sticking to your feet. The reason we called it "playing in the valley" was because years before I started attending school in Santa Fe, there was not a level place to play ball or, for that matter, to play anything as there was a deep ravine running beside the school building. Someone in the area had a dozer and, with a lot of pushing and pulling tons of dirt filled in the ravine, made a flat area that was named "the Valley." On both sides of the filled-in area was a really steep bank that ran nearly sixty feet to the top with the level part being about one hundred yards long and fifty yards wide. This made a really nice place to put a softball diamond, not to mention the really neat banks on both sides to be used as a sled run when the snow fell. The banks were also good for mud ball fights when the valley was too wet to use but had no snow on it. Everybody cut a willow switch about four feet long and about the size of your thumb on one end and narrowed down to a whip on the other end. By packing a ball of wet clay about the size of a golf ball and sticking it on the switch end, you could throw the ball like a bullet across the valley with the hope of hitting a person or persons on the other side. You could feel it when you got hit but was not a really bad hurt that would cause pain. Leave it to Jerry Evans to figure out that if you put little rocks in the mud ball, it went faster, went farther, and hurt a whole lot more when it connected with the enemy on the other hillside. Well, a couple of sissies got hit between the eyes and went tattling to the teacher, and sure enough, there went a really fun activity down the drain. The only thing left to do was go back into the empty room and shoot marbles. Most of the time, there were two rings going with a ring on each end of the room. Those that were advanced in the art of marble shooting were at the big ring, and the younger less accurate shooters were at the little ring on the side. As it was well understood that when you shot in the big ring, it was playing for keeps, and that meant you paired up against certain persons of advanced ages and ability. I was really at a disadvantage being too good for the little ring and not good enough for the big ring. To prove my worth, I usually played with the older more mature shooter and, as you would guess, usually came out of the recess with my tail pretty well beaten. Sure hated to let those guys have my best marbles but darn well was not going to let them know I was about to tear up. Times were tough on the average marble-shooting kid. The day did come, however, after the certain big boys graduated that the loser of the past had his revenge on the younger set. This gave more understanding to the old saying, "What goes around comes around." I do remember, however, giving back a lot of marbles to some of the littler kids that I'm sure felt a lot like I did back when I was their age. Guess I was a little more charitable with my marble game than some that wreaked havoc on my collection of prized glass balls. Guess my folks taught me to be slightly more charitable than the older kids that took my marbles.

Recess was such a short period of time when you're having fun, but always to get to the next recess, you had to put in your time with classroom learning. For those of you that went to a city school, you probably do not have any idea what grade school really stands for. It stands for each of eight grades to be present in the same room day after day and week after week, all studying the same subject but on different levels. For instance, Monday began with using workbooks for math, each grade level having their own workbook to follow and fill out the practice pages. All grade levels were working with math as each grade would approach the teacher's desk one grade at a time with workbook in hand, and as the instructor introduced the new material, all students in that grade stood there and filled out the example. If they did not have a question about this section, they would then go back to their desk to work on the unit, and now the next grade would move to the desk and await instruction. After all grades had received their appointed time at the teacher's desk, all students returned to their desk and sat quietly while the teacher traveled up and down the rows just in case someone did not understand a part of the assignment. What this really amounted to was that all the students were taught from the workbooks, and the teacher was available to answer questions if there was one. When it seemed all had completed the assignment, the teacher then went back to her desk and announce what workbook to bring up next, which then began another lesson on another subject. This allowed the students to usually cover three or four subjects daily with time out for the advanced classes to complete what should have been homework but of which there seldom if ever was needed. Problem that arose with my education following this procedure was that it would take some students twenty minutes to complete the assignment, and at the same time, about half of the room was finished in five to ten minutes.

This often led to massive amounts of boring self-taught time on hand, so this was daydream time on most occasions. As all students were expected to be busy even when they were in la-la land dreaming of horses, kites, fishing, or whatever. It was best to appear busy even if you were not. During one of these boring periods, I heard the older class talking about the number one million. It got me to wondering just how much is a million as it must be a really large bunch from the direction the discussion was going. I was familiar with a dozen, with one hundred, with five hundred, and even with up to one thousand. But one million had never been mentioned, so I wondered, "Just how many would it take to make one million?" This was when I made up my mind to write my numbers to one million and see just how many that really is. Taking out my Big Chief tablet and a sharp pencil and ruler, I began marking off a page in one-inch columns. After doing about fifty pages, I began with the number one, two, three, and so on until the page was full. As well as I can remember, it took about one hundred ten numbers per page so filled out the first page and continued on until the first fifty pages were completed. Marked off another fifty pages and continued right along well on my way to one million. If you have ever seen a Big Chief tablet, you know that on the front is a picture of an Indian chief, and at the time, the cost was ten cents per tablet. When the first tablet was filled, I told Mom that I needed another tablet, so next time we were in Williams General Store in Santa Fe, I got a brand-new one. About a week later, I told Mom that I needed another Big Chief tablet, so with little or no thought about it, I got a new one. The third time I asked for another tablet, Mom did ask me what in the world was I doing that was using up so many pages of tablet. I explained to her that my goal of writing to one million was well underway and that I had already gotten to almost twenty thousand and hoped to finish in the very near future. This was when Mom tried to explain how much a number of one million actually was and that it would take me at least a hundred or more tablets to get anywhere near to that figure. Now the number of one hundred tablets had some real meaning to this little kid as I had already used up three tablets and ninety-seven more would really make a huge stack for sure. Good thing she explained how big that number is, and I decided to stop at that point. Would probably still be writing numbers today. So can you imagine how much a Big Chief tablet would cost at today's prices?

Another part of education that has great meaning is that of learning from the older boys the true meaning of life as explained around the outhouse at recess. It was a time-honored sequence that the older boys told the younger boys what the not-to-be-mentioned words really meant. Today's school rely upon the health and home economics classes to explain to maturing children what the birds and bees are all about. At Santa Fe Elementary, the oldest and wisest were to explain in graphic detail what things meant, such as jokes, that were told and everyone laughed at. I did not understand just what they were talking about, but it was well understood that, to be accepted by the older crowd, one was to laugh and pretend to think the humor was very funny.

In the wintertime however, the outhouse was way too cold to stand around and visit. In fact, one waited to almost the bursting point before asking permission to make that cold long hard trip over the hill to the lone building standing at the end of the path. One trip I remember well was during the month of January on a particularly cold freezing rain dreary day. Midway through the afternoon, it was fairly evident that my bladder would not hold out for another two hours, so I wrote my name on the blackboard, which was required if you left the room for any reason. I headed out the back door to make that long trek down the hill where relief could be found. It happened that it had started sprinkling a really fine misty drizzle that freezes the moment it touched the ground or anything else it happened upon. Under foot, I could hear a distinct crunching sound that should have been interpreted as a reason to use the girl's restroom, which was located at the top of the hill and not have to go all the way to the bottom. One knew that using the girl's privy was totally against the rules as that little building was totally off limits and was never to be entered by any member of the opposite sex.

Did not really know why, but it was understood that you just didn't and, even worse, did not ask why. It was part of the culture that the women's outhouse was thought as being private, and no self-respecting male would even be seen looking in that direction, let alone use no matter what the weather condition. Getting down to the boys' outhouse was not any part of a problem, but it did not take long for a kid with an empty bladder to figure out that getting back to the top of the hill may prove to be a tad more difficult. By getting a run at it from the ever so small level area, one could get to almost about fifteen feet from the top before the leather-soled boots would lose traction, and back the kid would slide clear to the bottom of the hill. It was at this point that the little kid at the bottom of the hill began to notice that he had not taken the time to pull on the heavy winter coat that hung on the rack just inside the door of the playroom. The air was seemingly much colder than it was five minutes ago, and the trip that should have taken three minutes had become eight minutes and had every chance in the world of getting longer. The only hope the kid had was to get down on all fours and dig his fingernails into the crust and crawl up the hill and just hope with all his heart that nobody was able to see him in such a demeaning position. He did not want to be classified as that little kid that had to crawl up the hill and was not able to walk like a big kid. After what seemed an eternity, which actually was not more than one or two minutes, there was complete relief to find himself standing on the porch, standing with hands half frozen and pant legs wet, but at least no one was laughing and snickering behind his back. Much wiser was the kid that left the room ten minutes earlier that had left the room without a coat and one who had not even considered what major problems could be encountered when water turns to ice. This lesson was heeded over the next fifty years and was never mistaken as being a trivial matter that can be very dangerous when the months of winter can make your life difficult and sometimes even life-threatening.

Another event that was deemed a very important segment of youth was that of the pie and box supper that was the highlight of the school year. Cannot remember if it was in the spring or fall, but it was by all means as important an event as the annual Christmas play, which by all accounts was *the big* event. The Christmas pageant was an event that has been given an entire chapter due to its importance. As for the pie and box supper, even though it was not at the same level as the Christmas program, was within itself placed at the top of the ladder when it came to being a sought-after occurrence. This event began with all the students being given a handful of kitchen matches and a sheet of paper with which two columns of numbers were printed. One number was cut from the paper sheet and taped to a match. When all numbers had received a match, the next step was to print the matching numbers on a plain sheet of paper. The match with the number and the sheet with the number were then distributed to a child who was instructed to sell each match for a dime or three for twenty-five cents and write down that person's name on the corresponding sheet until the complete sheet had been filled. As the sheets were received, each name had a number, so when the entire set was cut up and placed in a glass jar, it was then ready for a person to draw the names out one at a time during the supper and the winner could win one of several prizes that had been donated to the school. It was explained that the reason for selling the match with a number on it was so that the school was not running a gambling scheme but was actually selling a match even if it did have a number attached to it. Often, the number was taped to a hairpin, which served the same purpose. Must have worked pretty well because it never was declared illegal, and no one ever went to jail for buying a match. The night of the big event was always on a Friday night as that was the time of week when most people were looking for a reason to come to town, so it was very well attended. Ladies of the community would each bake a pie or two, so during the night, people could eat pie and drink a Coke or sip a cup of coffee. At the end of the evening entertainment, what pies that were left over were auctioned off, so all pies were moneymaking situation. On the other hand, the box portion of the meeting was provided by single girls and women who prepared a basket of which some were filled with home-baked desserts and cookies while others were filled with fruits and candies. Each was covered with brightly colored paper and ribbons, and each was supposed to be a secret as to who it belonged to. When the auction began, there were usually several men bidding on the basket, and as a rule, most knew who had provided the one being auctioned, and the boyfriend was actually expected to win the highest bid. However, this was not the case as many men would bid against that one certain person so that, instead of getting it for a fairly cheap and reasonable fee, it was bid up so the boyfriend had to pay a really high price to win the bid. I always wanted to buy Charlotte Davis's basket as she was one of the prettiest and most popular girls in school, but it was always way too expensive as she always had a boyfriend that had better make the high bid. I did, on a few occasions, luck out and get to share with

Linda Snyder when we were younger, but the older we got, the more expensive her baskets became. A highlight of sharing with Linda was not only was she very pretty but the fact that her dad owned the general store and put some really super items in the basket that most girls did not have access to. At the end of the evening, Lyle Ramsey and his country band played country music way into the night or at least until nine o'clock in the evening. Thus ended another successful money-raising activity for Santa Fe Elementary School, and all that enjoyed it would be looking forward to it happening again next year.

Memorable Moments Flashback
The Day I Learned to Read

One moment that has played over and over in my mind took place during first grade at Santa Fe Elementary School. During the first half of the school year, my first-grade teacher was Mrs. Menifee, and as we did not have kindergarten, I launched directly into my formal education years with little or no prior experience with book learning. About the month of October, Mrs. Menifee became very ill and was not able to attend the daily school routine for several weeks. In came Mrs. Tawney as substitute teacher until her return. I took an instant like for our new teacher and thought she was the greatest person in the world to step through the front door of the school building and begin teaching all eight grades from first to eighth. At the time, I really did not think much of school and thought very little of the daily routine and in fact kind of enjoyed the classes even if there were only about three subjects taught per day. A problem did arise, however, when the reading class rolled around and all the kids in the first grade gathered around the desk to recite and read aloud the workbooks we were provided. Everyone in the class of four read their page without so much as a stammer, but when my turn came, I could not see nor recognize very few words that meant anything to my way of thinking. This went on for a couple of weeks, and the faster the other kids read, the slower I became in recognizing the words into a story form. It actually was very embarrassing and frustrating when I could not follow the story and noticed that the other three kids were watching me make a fool out of myself. Just as recess was about to begin, Mrs. Tawney stopped by my desk and said that maybe we should have a visit when all the other kids were out to play. The first thing she did was set me down facing her and handed me a beginner's reading book and said to please read the first page. As usual, I could not make any sense out of the words, so after a few minutes, she said, "Kennie, do you not know how to read?" My answer was I cannot get any words out of the story like the other kids. She proceeded to put on the blackboard in large letters: A, E, I, O, and U and said to repeat after me. We went through the letters with what she called short and long sounds and then gave me a dozen words and had me sound them out according to the letters on the board. Would you believe it that, in less than ten minutes, I could read words, read sentences, and read pages by sounds of the letters? It was as if a flashlight was turned on inside my brain, and from that instance on, I could read any and every word in any and every book. From that day on, I gave thanks to the moment Mrs. Tawney taught me how to read.

Mark Twain Park Last Day of School
May 1952
Jim First row 3rd person
KW Third row 2nd person from right
Mom in head scarf

Going to Sunday School
South side of house Santa Fe
Mary 15, Jim 5, KW 9

Sitting in front porch
Jim 5 years KW 9 years
Pups Champ and Clabber

Memorable Moments Flashback
Children Then Compared to Today

When a baby is born into this world today, it is a very scary moment due to the fact that no one can predict what the changes will bring about by the time they turn into a mature self-reliant adult. It also presented changes in the family living in the country of rural America just after the Great Depression. The changes were minimal to say the least in the early forties as all was expected to be the exact same for the next thirty years or so, and this was pretty much a fact of life. Children started working on the farm at a very early age and were expected to work for a living for the rest of their life. Today a new set of parents will immediately begin a college fund for the child by taking out millions of dollars worth of life insurance. They must start making decisions as to which daycare they will leave the child in when the parents are out of maternity leave, who will keep the child until they arrive home from a day of work and on and on. It seems that the load new parents are required to carry is almost enough to cause a severe nervous breakdown. Now let's compare this situation to my mom and dad when my birth occurred. First off, there was no disposable diapers. There was no formula. There was no new baby crib, and most of all, there was not a single thought of what will this child be doing twenty years from now. At about three years of age, the kid was out of the house for playtime early in the morning and was within one hundred feet of cows, horses, chickens, hogs, and dogs and were pretty much in charge of their own entertainment from after sunup to dusk. There was a short time at noon Mom would call us in to get a bite of lunch and would most of the time make us go lay down on a pallet of quilts for a short nap and then back to the outside theater. Things did get a little more organized at about age six as this was when morning and evening was set aside to help with or do the chores required to keep the farm alive. I can remember being required to gather the eggs late afternoon, scattering ground corn and laying mash to the chickens, and then going to the granary to stuff ears of corn into the sheller as Dad turned the crank.

As soon as the sun began to set, the hens and chickens would traditionally all return to the henhouse and select their position on the roosting poles. As soon as the last one was inside, I shut the door and put the peg in the latch. Now all were safe from the night critters that prowled around in the dark hoping to find an entrance to access the chicken dinner they so desired. Until about age eight, this schedule pretty well held year after year. At that time, the schedule shifted to being responsible for actual chores performed daily. Dad pretty well did all the morning chores, but in the evening, I and brother Jim were expected to have completed all the chores when Dad got home. Jim took over my "egg gathering and shut the door" obligation, and I moved on to putting out the hay to the cattle and sheep, feeding the weanling pigs, bringing in the split wood and coal, replacing the water bucket in the kitchen from empty to full, and any other chore that Dad told me the same morning before he left for work. This was the schedule during the school term, but when summer vacation began, it seemed that free time was not anything like it was a few years back. Now we were expected to spend many hours tending the garden, gathering produce for canning, and helping Mom snap the beans and hull the peas or anything else that pertained to getting food ready for when the cold wind was blowing. There was no telling how many hundred quarts of vegetables were canned and placed on the shelves in the root cellar. At today's standards, it would almost seem that the children were being abused, expecting them to work so many hours a day. Looking back on it all, our parents were the greatest providers and teachers in the world to show us what was expected in the possible sixty or so years to come. We kids were certainly a great cog in the wheel that made the farm and our future lives go around.

Memorable Moments Flashback
Lessons Learned the Hard Way

Education starts at a very early age, and actions taken often have consequences that are seldom forgotten. Often, things occur during your years of youth that convince you that the previous decisions you made were not in your best interest especially when it comes to comfort and/or pain. One such lesson was heaped upon me during an afternoon of loading alfalfa square bales at Ralph Bridgford's hayfield. Being somewhere around age twelve or thirteen and working with a crew of bale loaders at least two or three years older, we pulled into the hayfield about one in the afternoon when the sun was at its peak. The first thing the older crowd did was peel off their shirts and showed off their golden tan that they were all so proud of. Not knowing any better, I removed the long-sleeved shirt that offered protection from the sunrays and ever-thickening cloud of dust and began soaking up the ultraviolet rays of the killer sun. Wind was whipping up the ground cover and dust along with the invisible pieces of plant life that had edges like a knife and stuck to a worker's sweaty skin like glue on paper. When the wind was at my back, it was almost bearable but, when changing directions at the end of the field, could hardly wait until we made the trip to the other end and turned. By the time we had taken the first load to the barn and placed the bales in the loft, the itching and chafing of the hay dust around my neck and under my arms were almost unbearable. It took seven loads to empty the field, so when Dad picked me up and drove me home, I could not stand to let my arms touch my body without a searing pain and burning going the entire length of my upper torso. Leaped from the car and made a dash through the chicken yard, ran directly to the Big Pond, and did not even take time to get out of my jeans. Ran into the wonderfully wet and warm water up to my neck and found instant relief.

As I was floating on my back with arms outstretched and looking straight up into the clear blue sky, the thought came to me, *I bet this is what heaven feels like.* Lesson learned: When in the hayfield, wear a long-sleeved shirt buttoned up to your neck, and no matter what the older boys do, think twice before trying to be a part of the crowd. Too often, following the crowd may lead to pain and misery. So be original, think ahead, and make your own decisions as to what is best for your safety and comfort. Going shirtless in an alfalfa field on a hot summer day is not a wise move.

First Bike Ride to Santa Fe

A highlight of a young kid's life was when his parents considered him old enough to make a bike voyage into the city from his home in the country. At about age ten, I was allowed to get on my bike and make the one-and-a-half-mile trip into the city of Santa Fe. The first couple of times going that far, Dad traveled behind me in the car until I got up the really steep and long hill that was just across Salt River Bridge at the edge of town. There was no way that any person could ride a single-speed bike up the hill, so the alternative method of travel was to push the thing up every long drawn-out foot of a hill that seemed to go on forever. The first time up almost was the last time up because by the time I had pushed the bike, which was much taller at the handle bars than my shoulders, I was just about dead from the effort. With Dad behind me going real slow, it seemed that there was nothing to do but get up that hill if I was to ever be allowed to go the second time. About two-third up the hill, there was a driveway that went off to the left. This led to a garage behind Mr. Williams's house that was on the very edge of the hill. The garage was more of a barn than a garage as it had been where they kept their horses many years before this period of time and was now converted into a place to park their car now that horses were not anywhere to be found in the city limits. It was at this little driveway that my goal was set when first starting up the hill and was also the steepest part of the hill. It was a lifesaving spot so that I could find a half-level spot to lay the bike on its side and stop long enough for the lights to stop flashing in front of my eyes. From this point, it was only about one hundred fifty feet to the summit of the hill, so after catching my breath for a few minutes, it was a fairly simple task to push the bike up and over the edge of the hill. Once over the hill, it was level so that the bike could be mounted and the wheels could really get going for the approximately two blocks to the store on the corner and the really welcome blacktop road. Actually, the blacktop road was one of the main reasons for wanting to go to town on the bike because pedaling on the gravel roads was not only very difficult; it was downright dangerous as the wheels would slide out from under you at a second's notice. One minute, you were going like blue blazes, and the next second, you would be scooting across the gravel on your nose. When I reached the blacktop, Dad turned around and headed back home, so now the entire town was my very own bike-riding territory. The feeling of being free to do what you wanted and to go where you wanted was a real thrill even if the only place you could go was five blocks in each direction. Other than the blacktop road through the middle of town, all the other roads going in all direction were gravel like at the end of our home driveway. Basically, it was predetermined that my trip would be to ride back and forth through town for about half of the afternoon. No matter where you went, you would see people of really great interest because there were lots of businesses and lots of old retired people that came into town in the morning and sat around in front of the stores for the biggest part of the day. They then went home for supper and came back tomorrow to start all over again. Most were very interesting in their own way, but all had one thing in common: they were usually really old, probably fifty or more, and all wore bid overalls and a blue denim shirt. You could bet that they were all sitting and chewing a mouth full of Picnic Twist and spitting across the sidewalk into the dust on the street. You could tell by the dark stains on the sidewalk that most of the time they did not spit far enough to clear the side-walk but only got halfway across. It was pretty much a fact that you watched where you walked when going in front of the half dozen or so men sitting and spitting as the sidewalk was closer to the chewer than the dust in the street, so you received the better half of the tobacco juice. Another reason was that if you walked between them and the street, you may end up with a wad of tobacco juice about knee-high. You could depend on seeing Henry Heckert sitting there daily as well as Russ Scobee and two old bachelor brothers that were named John and Cecil Peak. Usually, there were another dozen or so men and women dropping by the store who would park their car and go into the store for a few items of groceries. Some of them would sit down and drink a soda pop and visit a little while then get back in their car and drive away. Oftentimes, I would sit next to Henry Heckert, and invariably, he would ask me, "Have you ever seen a hundred-dollar bill?" Of which I would say, "No, I have not. Do you have one?" At this point, he would take a folded bill out of the chest pocket of his bib overalls and proceed to show me what one looked like. No matter how many times I had seen it, I always said that I had not so that he could get a moment of pleasure out of showing his riches. About one o'clock every afternoon, a truck with a cover over the back would pull up in front of the post office. The driver would take out a couple of mailbags and deliver them into the post office building. Within thirty minutes, there would be about twenty people from all directions of town appear and go into the post office to pick up their mail. The postmasters were Phyllis and Irene Wilson who were also sisters that had worked in the post office for decades. They had never married and could be called "ole maids," but we were told that this was something we did not mention anywhere around the two ladies. They were really tall women, and when you talked to them, all I could see was the inside of their noses as they looked down at me. I talked to them a lot because Mom was in the post office a lot it seemed. At the time, we three kids were there to buy stamps for our savings books. Every time we got an extra ten cents, we would purchase a stamp, lick the back, and put it in a paper book that was called a savings bond. When you filled it, you could turn it in at the post office, and they would give you seven dollars and fifty cents in cash. If you kept them for several years, then they would give you a lot more money, but I cannot remember ever keeping them for more than a couple of days when the last stamp was stuck to the last page. I do remember that Mom would send me in to get several penny post cards and a few three-cent stamps for use in sending letters. That was around 1950, would be my guess, and that building is still there and is still the local post office, sitting on the same corner and is the same building with people coming in each afternoon to pick up their mail.

Another place I spent my time when not peddling around town was Otis Snyder's welding shop. It was way interesting to sit and watch him take pieces of metal and, using a really hot and bright flame, glues them together to make a piece of equipment. He gave me a helmet to put on while he was welding because the fire was so bright it would nearly blind you if you looked at it with the naked eye. I could watch him work for hours, of which I actually did whenever he was welding. The real heavy work was done out the back door of the shop where the Wilkerson brothers put together a rock-crusher and rock-sizing machine. They were what I call really smart guys what with the huge machines they built from scratch and without any plans or pictures.

They ended up with a really great big machine on huge tires that they took to the river and crushed and ground rocks to make different sizes that were then hauled to the various roads and spread out over all the gravel roads in the county.

State of the art grinding machine picture taken about 1950 approximately. Crew manned five of the machines with team of two taking them around a three country district.

All of the grinders lined up at the end of the day. Thomas and Tommie Hendricks sitting on the fender of the one in the middle.

Sometime during my day in town, I would sit and watch a couple of horseshoe-throwing contest. Between the building of Otis Snyder's welding shop and the old bank building was an alley that was level and about fifteen feet wide and ran the length of the buildings. This was where the horseshoe-throwing pits were built. Usually, there were two contestants, but sometimes there was a team of two men, one on each end that threw two horseshoes each time to see who could get a ringer that went over the peg or get the shoe to stop within the length of the shoe for another point. It was several years before I was able to pick up one of the shoes and throw it far enough to get to the opposite peg. Those were some really huge shoes and must have weighed fifty pounds each. As you walked down the alley to the north end, you would come out into a clearing space that led to a big shed with a door on the front. This was used to store old worn-out tires that Otis had thrown away. When other kids were around, we would spend lots of time crawling around on the stacks of tires and making tunnels to crawl through. Just to the right of the shed door was the public outhouse. It was a two-holler and must have been there for hundreds of years as it had a pit dug under it that must have been ten feet deep. It was so full they had to put powdered lime on the mount to reduce it down enough to keep using the seats. Just to the right of the outhouse was a path that led beside Thomas and Tommie's house and then turned to the right and went along the side of their hammer mill shed. This was where Dad and several other men stored the trucks that they took out each day to visit farms that needed corn or grain and hay ground up into cattle and sheep feed. When they came in at the end of the day, I would go in and watch them clean out the molasses bin and fill it up with liquid molasses so that it would be ready to go out early next morning. It was a really big building that had five doors on the front that slide to the side so that the driver could back their mill into the shed and close the door and lock it for the night. I always thought that Thomas and Tommie must have been the richest people in Santa Fe because they had a really nice new house and lots of men working for them. Tommie even had a black lady work in her house during the day, so she must have been pretty well-off.

Across the street and down about twenty-five yards was a blacksmith shop owned and operated by Tom Mowens. At one time, there would have been several draft horses tied out front to have their shoes set or repaired, but now his main work was making plow shears and other farm tools that farmers brought in for repair. My job was to stay out of the way while he was working, but it really never did bother him no matter where I stood to watch him work. When he was heating metal, it was my job to crank the blower that made the coal in the firebox glow red and roar. While I turned the crank, Tom would put a piece of metal in a long set of pliers and stick the metal into the middle of the glowing fire. When he took it out, it was red-hot and really soft so he could take a hammer and make it into a circle or any other design he desired.

Tom was about as old as he could get, wore a leather apron, and had a hand-rolled cigarette hanging out of one side of his mouth at all times of the day. It would be my guess that he was about five feet six inches tall and probably did not weigh more than one hundred ten pounds. Kind of looked half dead but seemed to be at the shop every day for all those years, and I do not remember him ever dying. His daughter was the one that really stuck in the back of my mind all these years. She was really a looker, wore jeans that were about two sizes too small, had on cowboy boots with the legs tucked in, and always wore a man's cowboy shirt. The tail was always hanging out and really did not fit correctly as it was about two sizes too small. Really doubt if she could bend over because it was formfitting, but she sure did make the old men stop talking and start staring when she walked by. Her name was Townsy Mowens but do not know how to spell it correctly. When she talked, nearly everybody listened because some of the words she spoke and the way she spoke them demanded attention. I have no doubt that if I were to use any of those words out loud, I for sure would have had my mouth washed out with soap. I really did like Townsy because she was such a fun-loving person. Whenever she appeared at the shop, she would get me in a headlock and rub my head. She usually had gum and candy in her handbag and was willing to share anything that she had with me. She did always smell of strong perfume and cigarettes but was a kind of smell that most girls did not have back when I was a kid.

Santa Fe People and Places

As you walked out the side door of the blacksmith shop, there was a very narrow driveway that led to a little square-shaped house. Out of the side of the house were many, many wires that led to a really high pole with a crosspiece on the top. The wires took off in all directions until they were out of sight. When you knocked on the door of the little house, a voice was heard on the inside, "Come in." As we entered, we found ourselves in one room that took up nearly the entire space with the kitchen on the right side and a console on the left side that filled nearly half of the room. This was what they called "the telephone office" and was owned and operated by two sisters named Effie and Bessie Scobee. They lived and worked here every day of the year with one sitting at the console all hours during the day. In front of one of the ladies was a mass of wires coming out of the desk of the console, and in front of her was row after row of little round metal holes. When a light came on, she would pick up a socket and plug it into the hole below the light, flip a switch, and announce that she was the operator. She then picked up another socket and put it into another hole and then flipped a switch back and forth until someone on the other end answered. I do remember that we had a wall phone at our house and that our call tone was two short rings and one long. It seemed that one of the ladies was sitting at the console day in and day out seven days a week, twelve months out of the year. I was in their front room several times off and on over the years, and never was the panel without an operator sitting and looking for a light to come on. My sister Mary said that she and Charlotte stood beside the lady at the console and was allowed to poke the jack into the socket and then listen to whoever was talking. I pretty much just stood in the rear and watched the calls come in and go out. I do remember that they both were not very thin ladies, and when they sat on the stool or the chair, there were several inches of lady hanging over each side. You can bet that there were not a better-informed couple of ladies in Santa Fe when it came to the latest gossip going around especially if it was spoken on the telephone. Most women around Santa Fe listened in on the party line several times during the day through their home phones, but Effie and Bessie got to listen in on all of them and even got paid for it.

Santa Fe Christian Church. This was the church we three kids attended every Sunday for years to go to Sunday school. We never missed a day of Bible School that was held for a week each summer. Christmas programs were a holiday tradition. The inside of the sanctuary is almost the same as it was during the 1940's and 50's.

This is the Baptist Church located in Molina Missouri and sits just one block west of where the general store was sitting. This was where Aunt Naomi and I would attend the revival each year during the hottest part of the summer and would sit in a varnished pew until your pants soaked through with sweat and stuck to the seat. This was where I went forth at about nine years of age and was baptized in Cline's pond one really chilly day in April. This was also where Mary and Laverne got married just a short time later.

Stepping out the front door of the telephone office and heading west down the little driveway and going right on the gravel road would take you directly in front of Grandma and Grandpa Burl's house. If the weather was even close to being warm, you could find Grandpa Burl sitting on a folding chair under the tree in the front yard with a flyswatter in his right hand and a chew of Picnic Twist in his left. Very few cars drove by their house during the day that Grandpa did not see and always waved at them. When he was not sitting in the front lawn, you could be assured that he had walked down to the Santa Fe Bridge and was sitting on the riverbank with two poles baited and sitting on Y twigs stuck in the mudbank. Not many days went by that Grandpa did not make the trip down the road, go up through town, took a left at the post office, and down the hill to the bridge. Usually, he made a detour to the right that went past Gene Williams's barn and garage and followed a well-beaten path to the riverbank just below the place called the "Big Rock." Big Rock was a huge boulder about the size of a small house that sat at the edge of the water about half in and half out of the river. It was a rock that was different than other rocks; this one was a lot softer, so over the years, many had carved their names in the side of the rock, and many of the dates were forty or fifty years old. Rumor had it that this was not really a rock but was a meteorite that had fallen from the heavens many years before. As a kid, I did really doubt that theory as we all knew that rocks that fell from the sky burned up before reaching the earth; at least, that was what was written in the *World Book Encyclopedia*. There was also another huge rock just behind the Mica Hill on the way down toward the bridge and was located back in the woods. This too had many cravings in it as well. Mica Hill was about halfway down the hill toward the bridge and was the only place in the area that you could find crystal formations sticking out of the dirt bank. Whenever it rained hard enough to move some dirt off the top of the ditch, one could find several pieces of Mica, of which some were fairly large. It was not unusual to fill a tin can almost full. About the only purpose it served was to write on sidewalks and mark off hopscotch play areas.

Customer counter inside the front waiting room of the Santa Fe Post Office. It is exactly how it looked the first time I saw it in 1946 but minus the stick on decals.

Santa Fe Post Office as it looks today. Is also how it looked back
around 1948 except there was no deposit box back then.

Returning to Grandpa, he constantly fished the strip of water just
west of the bridge and was well-known to bring home a big catfish quite
often. If he did catch one of bragging size, the townspeople saw him
walking down the middle of the highway the entire length of town. If,
on the other hand, he did not fare as well, he was known to take the
indirect route home through the back alley. The people that knew him
well called his catch either a "Main Street fish" or, if not so successful,
called it a "back alley fish." He was known for bringing home the big
ones, but even the really good Willingham fishermen can have a down
day and for sure did not need those looking on to make snide remarks.

Many times, I stayed overnight or over weekend with Grandma
and Grandpa Burl. I was about the only one that made it a practice
of staying at their house but did stay many times during the summer.
Strange thing about staying with Grandpa, especially in the summertime, when the weather was known to make a turn for the worst
during many afternoons in the summertime and clouds rolled in real
quick, no storm ever snuck up on Grandpa Burl. He was like the cows
and horses; he knew when a storm was coming long before the black
clouds and thunder rolled around. At the first sign of a change in the

weather, Grandpa Burl grabbed his flashlight and grabbed me by the hand, and within seconds, we're in the cellar waiting for it to go over. No matter how minor the weather showed up, we did not come out of the cellar until it was way gone down the road and into another county. Bad weather really never did seem much of a danger to me; in fact, not nearly as scary as being in that dark, wet, moldy, full-of-mice-and-snakes cellar. If Grandpa was not around the house when a storm was brewing, Grandma did not head for the cellar, but if there was a lot of lightning and boomers in the area, she would make me lie down on the bed with my head on a feather pillow. This was supposed to prevent the lightning from striking if your head was on a feather pillow. Must have worked pretty well because no matter how much lightning was flashing around, we never did get hit with a bolt.

Just across the street from Grandma's house was a tall two-story home that belonged to Mable and Shennie Davis. Now this house was really, really nice, everything new in each room, carpet on the floors, or shiny hardwood floors going into the kitchen and down the hallway. Every room had real fancy curtains and blinds with just the latest wallpaper on the walls and ceilings. It was top-of-the-line living and was even more so when you walked out of my grandparents' plain little farm décor home and stepped into the big-city decorated house of the Davises. His job was that of a livestock hauler and each day drove his big stock truck to St. Louis with a load of hogs or cattle. I guess he made a pile of money because I would classify his house as being about as fancy as any dwelling in the city of Mexico, and there were many rich people living in Mexico.

Just to the north of Shennie was the home of James and Alice Davis. They must have been brothers because they both had the same last name, and both of the houses were way above the average home in Santa Fe. James was the owner of the general store down town or at least was half owner as Mac Snyder owned the other half. It was not really all that close to being as nice as Sheenie's house but was a house that was much above the average dwelling in the area. When comparing to the house that we lived in out in the country, this house would be classified as being really close to a castle. This was where Charlotte Davis lived, and as mentioned before, this kid thought her to be one of the prettiest girls in the area. Kind of strange how she was the only child in the family and was lucky enough to have the best of everything, including a new bicycle and lots of new clothes or about anything a kid would ask for. When she was about ten years old however, she unexpectantly became a big sister when baby Randy suddenly appeared. My sister Mary and Charlotte were best friends, so from this point on, we got to see a lot of little brother Randy. It just so happened that they were riding home with us one midafternoon, and just as we were getting out of the car in front of the house, we were met by Dad's dog, Champ. Randy was the first to depart the car and made a beeline to pet Champ. As the dog was taken by surprise by seeing a really small person approaching with arms outstretched, he snapped at the kid and jumped back. In about an instant, Randy had a chunk taken out of his ear and let out a scream that woke up the entire countryside. As it turned out, the damage done was minor, but my parents had to call Alice and tell her that her little son had been dog bit, so the remainder of the evening was pretty sober to say the least. Randy did come out a few times after this episode, but never was the dog allowed to be in the area when they arrived.

Dad and Blondie, best female dog in the country. Sante Fe house in the background June 1954

Charlotte Davis age 15 and sister Mary Kay age 16 dressed like twins July 1953

Champ, son of Blondie
proven to be one of the best
dogs in the State of Missouri.
June 1960, already retired.

K.W. Warren Martin, Sharon
Poage and Patty Wilson.
K.W., Warren & Sharon
all 8 grades classmates.

Behind Charlotte's house was the only sawmill in the area. I had forgotten all about the many hours we spent rolling down the huge pile of sawdust until Mary reminded me of it being there. It was great fun, but when the fun ended and we headed in another direction, it was then that the presence of sawdust down the neck and inside your trousers, socks, and shoes became a reminder how bad a person can itch from inside out, which became nearly unbearable before we could find a water pump to wash most of it off.

Main Street taken from the South side of the main business square. Building to the left is James and Mac's General Store, center building is Otis Snyder's welding and machine shop and on the right is the Santa Fe Bank that was by then being used as a feed storage building. Picture below is the same bank building when it was being used as a bank.

Same buildings taken from a different angle and about 10 years later.
Pretty busy day with cars lined up parked next to the city sidewalk.

This is at the bottom of the hill looking North just at the edge of the bridge that went over Salt River. This hill was the final challenge for a little kid that road his bike from home to Santa Fe. It looked a lot steeper back then and truly was about all I could do to push the bike up and over the top to see the main block of Santa Fe about fifty yards ahead.

Looking West over the bridge rail you can see the "Big Rock" just before the river makes a bend to the South. This rock was very soft for being a rock so at the time had dozens of dates and names carved upon and around the surface. It was said that it was not really a rock but was possibly a meteor because of being different from all other rocks. After nearly 60 years of floods and rushing water flowing over and around the rock it now is about half the size it was during the late 40's. This was also the exact location where the story took place of me falling through the ice and making it to Grandma's house just before my feet and legs froze.

Down the road were several houses and families, but the one most worthy of mention was the little farmhouse of Carrie and Cash Scroogins. This couple was really special as they had moved from a big city somewhere called Chicago. Cash was a little wisp of a man and had so little to say that one would almost forget that he was around. On the other hand was his wife Carrie who was never to be overlooked. She was a very happy person that was always talking and laughing, so you were always being aware of her presence. She was not a very large person; in fact, she was almost a miniature but moved around at almost a run. She really reminded me of Minnie Bell Bridgford as they both covered a lot of ground in a very short period of time when they were working in the kitchen. It was in this house that I saw my very first television. Sitting on a table in the living room was a wooden console much like all the radios you found in nearly every home. The difference was that on the front of this box was a very small screen about six inches square. It was lighted, and when you stood in front of it at just the right angle, you could see pictures of people moving around. They were much too small to really be recognized, but it was readily evident that this was a marvelous instrument and way different than anything we had ever seen before. We were not even close to ever imagining what this little screen would turn into for those of the next several generations. We spent a great deal of time at the Scroogins's farm that summer because her grandson and two granddaughters from the big city came to live with them the entire summer. They were three of the neatest kids I had ever seen. The boy and girl were older than me, and the youngest girl was about my age. They had kind of a golden skin that looked like a beautiful summer sun tan. They had coal-black really thick hair that was mostly curly. They were a lot of fun to be around as they were not at all like their grandfather Cash but mostly like their grandmother Carrie by their actions and quick moves. It was kind of interesting to listen to them talk because they had real funny ways of saying things, things that we knew what they were talking about but nothing like we had been hearing all our lives. Really did enjoy seeing them that summer, but when school started and they returned to the city, they were certainly missed. Suddenly, one day, the bad news came to us that the boy had been killed in a street fight, and he was only sixteen years old. The next year, the news reached us that the oldest girl had died suddenly, which only left the youngest little sister. Mary did stay in contact with her, but I never saw her again the rest of my life. I also never stopped feeling sorry for Mr. and Mr. Scroogins as they lost nearly all their grandchildren in such a short time.

Memorable Moments Flashback
Charlotte Davis's Winter Weekend Visit

Sister Mary and Charlotte Davis were best buddies, so very often, they hung out at each other's homes during the weekends and quite often during the winter months. Seldom did they come to our house on a Saturday afternoon that we did not make saltwater hard taffy. Charlotte was the world's best when it came to knowing exactly how to bring the gooey concoction to a boil and exactly when to remove it from the heat. We made it many times without her being there, and it hardly ever came out to be a sweet chewy chunk of candy. It was usually either rock hard and not chewable or was one big glob of hot sticky goop. On the other hand, Charlotte would make a huge ball of warm taffy and pulled and stretched it and rolled it around to make a large ropelike string out of it. She pulled it and stretched it until it had a light coating on the surface. She then rushed it outside and placed it in a snowdrift and in a matter of minutes was what she termed "setup." By using a large wooden-handled knife, she would whack the end of the long rope of candy, and it would shatter into a dozen or more small pieces. We wrapped each piece in a square of waxed paper and twisted the ends, and there it was, a bowl of fresh wonderfully chewy taffy pieces ready to enjoy for many minutes in the future. I can remember her making a batch about every time she came over, and not once did it turn out to be anything but perfect.

Fun at Scott Holland's

Leaving the Scroogins's farm and heading back into town, taking the first street right, and going one block, you will find yourself in front of the house owned and lived in by Scott and Virgie Holland. This house was an eye-catcher of the entire town. Sitting on a corner lot with a really large front lawn covered with a blanket of deep thick grass was a two-story house that had a porch that went from one corner of the house around the front to the other corner on the east end. A lot of houses had porches but nothing like this one because on this porch were white pillars that had rolled scallops of carved wood across the entire top and rails that were made of beveled solid wood post, and everything was painted white. It looked as if it was redone almost every week so that there was not a single spot of peeling or chipped paint to be found on the entire house. You could see in the really big plate glass window that there was layer upon layer of thick curtains that almost screamed of expensive. Scott Holland owned the local garage and Ford Motor automobile dealership, and word had it that people came from all over Missouri and the neighboring states to buy their cars and trucks from the business in Santa Fe. Another rarely seen item that was with the greatest house in Santa Fe was that of a sidewalk constructed of concrete that started at the top of the hill on the west side of the lot and continued to the corner of the lot where it circled to the left and ended at the east corner of the lot in front of their detached car garage and workshop. Nearly at all times, you could find no less than a half-dozen kids standing on roller skates either slowly making their way up the hill or rapidly flying down the hill, trying to keep on their feet and on the sidewalk when they approached the round corner at the bottom. To make matters more difficult, there was a huge maple tree just outside the curve in the sidewalk that had roots going under the concrete and over time had raised the slab of concrete about six inches above the rest of the walkway. It was here that a large number of kids would lose contact with the walk and end up flat on their face in the ditch that ran alongside the road. The skates of that time were held on to the feet with a strap around the ankle and clamps on the side of the front part of the skate that hooked over the edge of the sole of the shoe. It was tightened with a small piece of metal that was called, of all things, "a skate key." Stability was not a part of the skates, so about half of the time you were skating was spent opening up the clamps and putting them back on the shoes and screwing the clamp back tight again. Cannot ever remember having a Band-Aid available but for sure do remember falling face forward onto the sand paper concrete and leaving several layers of skin from either my hands, my elbows, my knees, and sometimes my nose or all these parts at one time. It was pretty important to try to go off the sidewalk to the left each time because it was a whole lot less painful to go sliding on the thick grass than down the sidewalk or go off the right side of the sidewalk as that puts you face-to-face with the gravel of the street that began about one foot from the edge. Must have hit the wrong place a dozen times or more over the years but really do not remember being all that painful. Must have been a lot of fun to keep coming back to the place of pain and not remember it being all that much a danger. Another time that we were used to seeing Scott and Virgie was during the Saturday nights throughout the summer. As we kids got a little older, of which I was eight or nine years old, we were allowed to branch out and try to find our own entertainment on Saturday nights while Mom and Dad were sitting either outside the store or inside the store visiting with the same ole crowd that showed up every Saturday night year in and year out. Before we were all sitting inside watching TV for the first time and before the TV had made its way into the country store at Santa Fe, the old folks would sit and visit every Saturday night. We the kids were pretty much left on our own to find something to pass the time with as little danger as possible. Many times, the entire crowd of kids, which may be only three or four or at other times may amount to ten or twelve ages varying from eight years to fourteen and fifteen, would all gather on the front lawn of Scott and Virgie's for the evening. Usually, just laid around on the grass and talked and joked about who was whose girl– or boyfriend or who was seen doing whatever last week but for the most part was pretty calm most of the time. Red Rover was a favorite game that was played many evenings, and sometimes this would be the starting point of the cross-country venture of follow-the-leader. Red Rover was played by choosing up two sides, each team getting on each side of the yard facing each other and each member holding hands or locking arms. The group would then decide who they would choose first to dare over, and when all agreed, they all would chant, "Red Rover, Red Rover, we dare Kennie Willingham over." This meant that I was to pick out a pair across the lawn that looked the weakest of the line and run like my butt was afire toward that couple and plow chest first into their arms. If they held together, then I was deemed out of the game until the start of the next session. If I did break through the hold, then I could choose which one that had to sit out. The strategy was to dare over the weakest and smallest first, and then when the little ones were out, the big guys and girls would be trying their hardest to knock down the next strongest. It got right down dangerous toward the end when all that was left were the big kids that were going all out to wreak havoc on the line at the other side. We smaller kids were glad to be watching from the sidelines and not have to be some of those that were getting hammered by the heavyweights.

Another game we often found interesting was follow-the-leader. Everyone was to bring a red bandana or other type of scarf from home when heading for Santa Fe. The oldest boy or girl was usually chosen to be the leader, which was usually the biggest guy in the group. His job was to take command of where and when we were to go. Everyone but the leader and the person at the rear was blindfolded. None of the followers were able to see where we were going or where we had been. We all took hold of a hand in front and a hand in back so that there was a long snakelike line with a leader at the front and a leader at the back. If you got caught with your blind off or peeking out to see where you were going, you had to go to the back of the line and follow along like a little lost sheep. It was not unusual for the leader to take you through town, through the fields outside of town, across the riffle on the river, through the graveyard and snaking between the tombstones, through buildings and barns, or just about anywhere a person could go as long as the line could hold on to the other person. After about half an hour of meandering through the unknown, the leader would stop and announce that we were to take off our blindfolds and try to figure out about where we had ended the train and how did we think we would go to get back to Scott Holland's front yard. Today a person could look around and see lights on top of towers or tall buildings that were lit up or see or hear sounds or sights that would give you a clue. Back in the late forties, there was seldom if any pole lights available and very few roads that were carrying enough traffic to make a noise or show any lights. This made the group at the mercy of the leader to get us back to civilization. Do not think we were completely lost at any one time, but there was several moments when the leader proceeded to get us back to town after many minutes of wandering and found that he also did not know exactly which way was town. We always did make it back to town but not always by going in a straight line.

Another fun thing we did was acrobatics on the lawn. Larry Talley was about the strongest guy, so he would lie on his back with his feet on the ground and his knees bent. Two other guys would stand about ten feet from the top of Larry's head to act as spotters. We kids would make a run toward Larry and put our hands on his knees and flip over him. His hands would catch us in the middle of the back and pushed us up and over. We would do a flip or, in the case of the really brave or ones that wanted to show off, would do a double flip and hopefully would land on our feet and move toward the catcher. The more we did the flip, the faster we tried to run and the more flips we tried to do so that those who were watching would be in awe of how brave we were at the moment. It was usually the smaller kid, girls as well as boys, that did the flip, but you can rest assured it was not good for a girl to do it better or go farther than the boys, so this would many times lead to desperately try flying through the air about fifteen feet and not land on the top of your head.

Was a good thing that Scott Holland had that really thick layer of grass because not always did the catcher do their job of catching. All the time, this wild circus of kids was tearing up the very well-attended yard Scott and Virgie would be sitting on the porch in the porch swing watching what was going on under the single light bulb that shined over the yard. Not to say we were in their yard every single Saturday night, but we could be expected to show up more than just occasionally, and no matter when we arrived, they would turn on the light, and unless it was really a chilly evening, they would sit and watch for hours from the porch swing.

After an evening of tearing up the lawn and soon as we heard one or more car horns honking, we knew it was the signal that the parents were ready to head home. We all slowly but surely made our way across the gravel street and up the hill to the parking lot beside the store. One particular evening when I got out of the car at home, it suddenly dawned on me that I had left my ball cap hanging on the side of the steps at Scott and Virgie's. We attended church the next morning, so as soon as it was over, I made a dash for the corner play lot. Looked all around the area, but nowhere was my red ball cap to be seen. As I was standing beside the step, the door opened, and there stood Scott Holland, and sitting on the top of his head was a red baseball cap. He did look kind of strange at the time as the hat was way too little for him and him being totally bald, except for a little ring around his ears. I guess I was a little taken aside. He took advantage of the situation by talking about the weather and other things that really did not have any interest to me but to get my hat back and be gone. After several minutes, he said something like "Did you lose something?" I said something like "I think that may be my hat that you're wearing." He let out a laugh and reached down and put it on my head, and without any further ado, I made a very hasty exit toward town.

Four days later, we were sitting on the steps of the post office when we saw Scott Holland and several guys come from behind his business building, and they were carrying a tire in each hand. They disappeared around the old skating rink building and entered a door under the steps of the building. This was where they stored all the used tires that they had traded for and would occasionally come here to get a used tire and sell it to a farmer for his wagon or cart. Suddenly, there was a really loud yelling and shouting. We could hear all the men talking really loud. One of them came running up the little hill and disappeared into the garage that they had come from. Just as sudden as he ran into the building, there were five other people running out the door and rushed to the lower building and disappeared. In about two minutes, four guys came out the door carrying Scott Holland who was lying limp in their arms and looked like he was sound asleep. They put him in a car and went flying down the road toward Perry that was about twelve miles to the east. That was the last time we ever saw Scott Holland, and for whatever reason, we never went back to our favorite play yard ever again. Story was that he had reached up to move a tire about shoulder-high, had a heart attack, and was said to be dead before he hit the ground. Such a sad time and such a change of having so much fun in their front yard, and suddenly he was gone forever. A few days later after the funeral, I started thinking just what was a heart attack and how do you get a heart attack. All I could think about was the way he looked just a few days before in my cap, and then it dawned on me, could you catch a heart attack like you can catch measles and mumps from other people? It really played on my mind about how maybe I could catch the same thing that Scott Holland had and could have caught it from him wearing my hat just a few days before he passed away. Mom realized that there was something really bothering me, and when she asked what was the matter, I spoke out the entire worry. She said there was nothing to worry about since a heart attack was not catching. Talk about a load off my shoulders, I felt that all was once again perfect in my world. I would really miss seeing Scott Holland, but at least I was past the danger of getting what he had that caused him to die so suddenly.

Memorable Moments Flashback
Jim and His First Chew

Back in the day, tobacco was utilized by nearly every adult and many times by those who wished to appear as an adult. It was not sold to kids, but seldom did anyone have a second thought when a kid was caught taking a pinch of snuff out of a snuff can or take a chaw off a picnic twist or plug of Red Top. When a group of more than two got together behind the general store, usually one or more of the kids had a piece of tobacco in their pocket. Often, the older kids would go into Mr. Davis's store with a dime in their hand and tell him that their dad needed a plug of tobacco and was seldom refused. One such time, we were behind the old bank building and had passed around a plug with everyone taking a bite off the corner and passing it on. Little brother Jim was among the group, and he said that he wanted some. When he was told he was too little, he started throwing a fit, which got him the plug without hesitation. He took a bite, chewed a few seconds, and swallowed the chunk as he would have swallowed a piece of gum. Within seconds, he was gagging and screaming bloody murder. Did not take long for him to throw up the chew, throw up the candy he had previously eaten, and—without much doubt—threw up what he had ingested for breakfast earlier that day. He quickly cranked the handle on the old well pump that was located at the corner of the old bank building and tried to wash out his mouth, but this did little to improve the situation. After it was over, we started to think that maybe getting water from that old discarded well was not all that good an idea, but he never got any sicker from the stagnant water than he did from his first chew of tobacco. Along the same story happened when we were behind the skating rink and tried smoking grapevine sticks.

Jim did not try those when he saw how red in the face those that tried it quickly became. I did try them one time, but when you took a puff of the lit grapevine, there was a very vile hot and pungent smoke that came from the stick and entered your mouth, nose, and eyes. Usually, it only took one puff to convince the smoker that this was not a good idea and was in fact really stupid to have done in the first place.

Memorable Moments Flashback
Gee Dunlap and His First Smoke

Another instance happened one Saturday night behind the pool hall located to the rear of the post office. Several younger kids were gathered in the grassy area beside the post office and were sitting around talking and killing time. I was about nine years old with a couple of my buddies the same age and several others a year or two younger. I had by chance several days earlier noticed my dad's pack of cigarettes on the kitchen table. Quickly removed one from the pack and hid it in my coat pocket. I mentioned the fact that I had a cigarette in my pocket while we sat around beside the pool hall and asked if anyone wanted to take a puff. Very few said that they did not with the majority jumping at the chance to do something less boring than what we were doing. Tinker Dunlap, couple of years younger than me, said that his dad had matches in the truck, so into the darkness, he disappeared. Several minutes later, he arrived with the book of matches in hand. The entire group disappeared behind the pool hall out of sight of any adults that may be in the area. We lit the end of the cigarette and passed it around. Everybody took a puff and blew the smoke into the air. Tinker's little brother Gary was standing beside him and kept jerking on Tinker's shirt, saying that he wanted a puff too. No one paid any attention to the kid seeing as how he was about five years old and much smaller than most. He became angry and began yelling at the top of his lungs. It was loud enough that the adults could hear him inside the pool hall. I told Tinker to give him a puff so that he would shut up and not get us all in trouble. Gary, whose nickname was Gee, took a puff and, instead of blowing it out, inhaled instead. The kid went into instant choking and coughing, was down on his knees, and turned red in the face. Scared the bejesus out of us standing around. I told Gee's other brother, Dallas, to go get his dad and get him quick. When his father came around the corner, he asked what happened. Tinker said right out that Gee took a puff from a cigarette and choked. His father picked him up and patted him on the back a couple of whacks, and Gee started breathing normal almost instantly. Bob never said a word. Took Gee into the pool hall and got him a drink of soda pop, and all was well. Must admit though none of our group wanted to puff on that cigarette anymore.

Memorable Moments Flashback
Gee Dunlap Remembers His First Smoke

The theory of the story of brother Jim and the chew of tobacco actually pretty much followed the scenario of the events that occurred behind the pool hall. Here, the older boys were puffing on a cigarette, and the little kid known as Gary Lee "Gee" Dunlap demanded to smoke also. It was explained how sick the little kid got from getting a lungful of smoke and nicotine for the first time. Fast forward sixty plus or minus years later, I was attending a century-old celebration of the first Christian church in Santa Fe when in walked an individual carrying a toddler. This person seemed to resemble the little kid that had turned green behind the pool hall. Only difference was that this man was about five feet eleven and dressed in bib overalls. I immediately made my way through the crowd and asked if he was the same kid we knew so many years ago by the name of Gee, and he said that he was. Told him my name, and he said something to the effect of "Kennie Willingham, I remember you." My first question to him was do you smoke or had he ever smoked? He said he does not but did try it several years ago and got so very sick that he never touched another cigarette. I explained the story of how it happened, but he had no recollection of the event. He did say that all his brothers and cousins always smoked, but he remained smoke-free for all these years. My last words to Gee was that just maybe I had saved his life by keeping him from smoking and for sure saved him mega bucks but did apologize for making him such a sick little kid back in the good ole days.

Lela Williams and the Rug Loom

O n the other side of town was the home of Gene and Lela Williams, and in their basement was another place where I was found killing time very often. Their place was sitting right on the edge of the hill that led to the bridge over Salt River. They had a really beautiful view of the Salt River valley when looking out their screened back porch. You could see for miles of just where the river ran west and then circled back to almost going due east. The view, however, was not why I stepped into the screened-in porch on the back of the house. It was instead to enter a set of steps that led into the basement or cellar under the house. Here you would find a really neat, really old piece of equipment they called a "loom." It filled the entire room and barely missed the floor joist overhead. Hard to explain what you were looking at as you almost had to be looking at it to understand what you were seeing. The huge console had a bunch of rollers facing each other and must have had a million spools of string on the back near the floor that went up and over all the rollers until it came to a level platform on the front. This looked like a table made up of strings lying side by side so that it appeared to be a solid piece of material. Lela sat on a bench with her feet touching a separate pedal, and the platform of strings was just above her knees. When she stepped down on one pedal and relaxed, the other pedal half of the strings would raise about two inches, and the other half of the strings would lower about two inches. In her hand was a little piece of wood that looked like a little toy boat and had strips of material wrapped round and round the piece of wood. She placed the piece of wood with the ball of material between the two layers of string and pulled it out on the other side. With her other hand, she held on to the wood and pulled the material tight. She then reached about halfway up the layer of strings that was coming straight down and pulled another board that was attached onto a hinge and hit the material that was between the strings a couple of pretty hefty whacks. This struck the strip of cloth, which packed the strip really tight against the strings. She then reversed her feet raising one and lowering the other so that the strings would change places and be holding the packed material in between the strings. Then came the little wooden boat back through the strings, pulled it tight, grabbed the hinged board, and slammed it against the material that was now tight against the strings. Back and forth, she sent the little boat and was working so rapidly that you could hardly see her hands move. When the little boat ran out of strips of cloth, she would reach into a brown paper sack at her feet and take out another ball of strips and wind it round and round the little boat until it was full. When she started pushing the little boat between the strings, she was moving so fast that you could not make out which strings were up and which ones were down. After about fifteen or so minutes, she would have her lap filled with what was called a "rag rug." Sometimes the rug was about three feet long, and there were times it would be five or six feet long. Depending on how many strings she began with, the width would vary from two feet wide up to four feet wide. It was a fact that when I was a kid nothing was thrown away, and this rug making was a great example. Today when anything is slightly worn or deemed out of style, it is thrown in the garbage can and taken to the landfill. Back then, this same material would be cut into small two-inch strips and rolled into a round ball that would end up in a rug or throw piece. Our house never had carpet in them, but there were rag rugs by the dozens scattered around the floor to prevent cold air from entering the house. It was a safe bet that all these rugs had at one time been a ball of cloth in a sack beside Lela and her rug loom. Just maybe some of these rugs had been one that I had practiced on for many times Lela would set up the loom and leave while I sat and threaded the little boat of cloth through the strings. Would give it a whack and then raise and lower the strings, making ready for the next strip. I never in all those years got even a fraction as fast as Lela, but many hours were spent in her basement over the years, and there is no telling how many rag rugs that were placed in hundreds of homes that had a couple of inches of my loom work done on them.

Nighttime Entertainment
and Consequences

Normally, my life as a well-behaved, well-adjusted child running around Santa Fe during the daylight hours or hanging around the city life after dark was as expected a quiet and uneventful occurrence. Approximately 85 percent of the time that I was hanging out around the local retired or nonworking element of society that could be found in front of the general store would find me without the benefit of others in my age group anywhere to be found. This actually was pretty much entertaining in itself by quietly listening to and learning from the extremely diverse group of people that daily gathered in front of James and Mac's grocery store. When a group of five or so arrived and with the average age being about seventy to seventy-five years old, this would put a kid that had been in this world less than ten years in and among three hundred years of stories and experiences. Without any female participants sitting among this group, it did have a tendency to bring forth some pretty vivid jokes and stories, but at the time, most of what was said pretty much flew over my head as not being all that easy to understand. Many, many hours went by over the years with me sitting and listening to often the same story repeated time and again, but it really did not seem to matter what was said, but just the way it was said made it an entirely new and interesting adventure.

As mentioned before, 85 percent of the time, there was none of my peers or older individuals around to assist me in seeking entertainment. However, the 15 percent of the other times was what tended to bring forth experiences that I probably would not have thought of without the help of older kids that came to town looking for a change of pace in their lives.

One occasion that comes to mind is the Saturday night that the crowd of about a half-dozen guys were sitting around the parking lot when one mentioned that he just happened to have a package of balloons that he had found in his little brother's toy box. Another said why not blow some of them up and put them next to the fan blade on cars parked along the street. Back in those days, the car hoods did not have a release inside the car but could be opened from the front just over the grill. After installing half-dozen balloons in various automobiles, the only thing to do was wait for someone to come out of the store. They would start the engine, so the loud bang would complete the task of making the driver wonder what had just blown up and would provide the group a laugh or two. After standing around for many minutes and no one leaving the store, someone then mentioned why we don't sneak down the alley and get some turnips out of Mr. Snyder's garden to snack on. Quickly and quietly, the group melted away into the darkness. We traveled down the alley between the mill and the blacksmith shop and arrived at the turnip patch in a matter of minutes. Of course, being quiet was really not that easy to do, and what with the house windows open and many years before TV or radio playing to cover up any outside noise, the sound of the screen door opening on the other side of the yard along with the sound of a hammer clicking on a shotgun rang out loud and clear. Those sounds were very noticeable, but when the shotgun trigger was pulled and the black powder discharged into the very heavy night air, there was very little thought of needing a turnip to snack on. The only thought we had as the buckshot came sprinkling down on the dry plants of the garden was to make haste in any direction away from Mr. Snyder's turnip patch. The group ran like our butts were in line to be in front of the next shotgun blast. I was in the very center of the group, and as we crossed the gravel parking lot in front of the mill going at a full run, my foot ran directly into the foot of Kenny Moss that was half a step in front of me. Instantly losing my balance and falling face forward, I fell into the gravel with the right side of my face grinding into the gravel like a scoop shovel. As the lights flashed and went dim, it was of little doubt that my night of turnip snatching was about to come to an end. I remember to this day every moment that led up to this dozing of gravel with my nose and not another memory until I woke up in the emergency room in Mexico. It was told to me that I walked to the store, sat on the bench outside, and was talking without making any sense, and when my parents took me home, I told all about putting the balloons under the hood, taking Mr. Snyder's turnips, and other gibberish that made very little if any sense. They decided to take me to the hospital in Mexico to be checked out, and when we arrived there, we went directly into the emergency room. When the attendant began cleaning the gravel out of my face with the antiseptic or whatever, the burning pain brought me around. A few days with a concussion were in order, and all was well. This also ended any further adventures of turnip snacks, and to this day, I would have to be really hungry to ever eat a turnip—raw, cooked, or in any other form.

Saturday Night Entertainment and Visiting the Ballpark

When television came on the farm scene life as we knew, it took a dramatic change. It went from making our own entertainment to sitting and letting the silver screen predict what we would be doing and thinking from dark to bedtime. When all the neighbors bought their own TV, the many nights of going into Santa Fe and sitting around the general store or going to the neighbor's house and passing the time of day disappeared totally. Each family stayed home and seldom if ever spent a night or evening without the television going full blast. With this change, it did not take long to forget how we filled our time to keep from becoming bored. We now had many hours totally wasted.

Before TV, Saturday night at James and Mac's general store was for many years a way of life. Massive amounts of information were passed down from farm to farm and family to family by conversations while sitting and listening and giving opinions. This was done in addition to enjoying a cold Coke and whiling the time away swapping stories and reciting family traditions. With the addition of the TV, all forms of listening and talking disappeared. Thinking back to pretelevision, one of the highlights on Saturday night was the arrival of Ulmer Wilkerson in the town of Santa Fe. Ulmer came into town with his completely restored model T Roadster and gave anyone a ride through the country and around town that wanted one. It was really great when he would go through town with a load of kids and open up the horn through Main Street. It made a loud "aaaauuugggaa" that ricocheted off the buildings and eliminated the quiet night whenever it sounded. When the crowd had been given a thrilling ride and the horn was silenced, Ulmer would bring out his guitar and settle down on a bench in the feed store located in the old bank building. He would play and sing many familiar tunes, and all the while, the crowd stood around or sat on soda cases and sang along with him. I remember two songs he sang every session, one being "I'm Dreaming of My Blue Eyes" and the other was "The Little Old Lady under the Bed." Ulmer was very original as he had a speech impediment and could not pronounce certain letters, so when he sang "I'm Dreaming of My Blue Eyes," he called it "I'm Dweeming of My Boo Eyes." This one particular song has remained with me for the past several decades and became a totally original part of Ulmer Wilkerson who will remain alive in my memory until my last breath.

Another activity was the summer softball games scheduled on most every Tuesday and Friday nights during the warm weather. The park was built on the farm of Russ Bishop just across the road from Henry and Rosie Heckert's house. This was about a half mile from our farm, so about six o'clock in the evening on the selected evenings, we drove to the park and parked on the west side of the road on Henry's grassy field. There was a fee to get in which was a dime for adults and free for kids.

This was to pay for the lights and to buy new balls a couple of times per season. There were two sets of bleachers on the west side and two sets on the south side, and just behind home plate and back-stop, Russ Bishop had a concession stand that he operated during the ball games. There was a soda box filled with ice and water with several flavors to choose from. The most popular was Coca-Cola, but you could have Grapette, Orangette, root beer, or cream soda. On the table in the center were three kinds of candy bars. There was Babe Ruth, Hershey's, and PayDay. On the corner of the table was a single hot plate with the cord hanging from a single bulb in the center that heated a one-burner hot plate. On the plate was a metal pan that boiled half-dozen hot dogs at one time. Occasionally, I worked in the stand for Russ, digging out hot dogs, putting them on a bun, wrapping them in a napkin, and handing it to a customer.

Russ would collect the money and make change. At the end of the night, Russ would give me a nickel for helping, and if he felt real generous, he would give me a dime. If things were slow inside the stand, several kids would take an empty soda case around the bleachers and pick up empty bottles that people had thrown under the seats. If all had been picked up, then we stood around the end of the bleacher and watched individuals while they were drinking. Soon as they were empty, we asked for the bottle. There were usually two or three kids with cases early in the evening, so competition was severe early on. After about an hour, most got tired of standing around, and as the big number of bottles was gone, most lost interest and moved off to play elsewhere. I usually hung around and hawk eyed the crowd for that one more empty bottle so I could finish a case, turn it in to Russ, and receive a shiny nickel for my work. We were always on the lookout for a foul ball going over the backstop fence. This was worth a nickel when you turned it in to Russ so that it could be used again in the future. When one went out, there was a maddening rush of nearly a dozen kids pushing and climbing the fence to get to it first. On a good night, there may be as many as five or six foul balls hit backward. If you were in the right place at the right time and was tough enough to hold on to the ball, it was a rather easy five cents. Many times, we drove our bikes to the park the next morning to search beneath the bleachers to see if anyone dropped a coin the previous evening. In a really rare instance, a foul ball may not be found in the dark, so whoever got there first could keep it and take it home. A new softball was an item held in high esteem when it was free.

Many teams made the road trip to Santa Fe to play softball. I can remember well some of the pitchers that performed on the mound for several of the teams. Our pitcher was Jackie Crigler who was known for his curve ball and his fastball. Man could he smoke that thing over the plate. When I was several years older, like twelve or thirteen, I had the privilege to warm him up before games. I can remember the first time I knelt down behind the plate early one evening to catch his warm-up. Having never caught anything but a kid's windup and release and never been in front of a professional fastball pitcher, I had no idea what a softball looked like coming about sixty miles per hour. The first catch I made about tore my hand off, and the sting went up my arm. The second throw hurt almost as much, but all after that, I had no feeling as my hand was totally numb. Another pitcher was Jackie Davis, but I never did catch him or any other team's pitcher. Roger McCreery pitched for Stoutsville, and A. V. Grimmes pitched for Perry. All of them were good beyond anything we had seen before. The first game of the season was a special occasion, and when the season ended, it was much missed by the entire neighborhood.

Mrs. Blaker and Brother Jim's Warts

After sitting in front of the loom in Gene and Lela's basement and working at making a rag rug for an hour or more and having produced not more than two or three inches of rug, we usually figured that it was not as simple as it seemed when Lela was throwing and hammering the material among the strings. It was a very interesting way to kill an hour or more but not a job that we would like to do day in and day out and still not make more than seventy-five cents an hour. After becoming bored with the loom, we would leave the basement and look toward town to find something to fill our time before Dad was done at the hammer mill and ready to pick us up.

When you walked up the street from Gene's house, you had to pass in front of a little house on the right side that had a screened-in porch on the front with a small wire pen on the side facing south. This was the home of Jerry Evans's grandmother, Mrs. Blaker. Whenever Jerry was running around with us, we would go say hi to Mrs. Blaker knowing full well that there would usually be a cookie or two available in her kitchen. I always thought of Mrs. Blaker as being a really tall woman, or at least to a scrawny kid looking up to her, she seemed to be extra tall. I would say that she was much taller than most of the women in Santa Fe. She usually did not say very much but spent most of her time smiling and watching us eat cookies, which was kind of strange as most of the women in Santa Fe seemed to never stop talking when they all got together. The worst thing in her house was three little long-haired dogs that looked like tiny rag mops with a sharp nose and beady little eyes looking at you from inside all that hair. When you opened the door to go into the house, they started barking and, with all three of them yipping at the same time, almost hurt your ears. Once they started with that shrill loud little bark, they would not let up until you walked out of the house and made it halfway down the street. Mrs. Blaker did not even seem to hear them, but to an outsider, they were all that you could hear.

The reason I mentioned Mrs. Blaker and her dogs is, because of brother Jim, I would make a visit to her house at a later date. It seemed that many in town felt that Mrs. Blaker possessed powers beyond what a normal person would possess. At the time, Jim must have been six or seven years old and had a real problem with warts on the back of his hands. When I say warts, I do not mean a spot or two on either hand, but I mean covered with warts on the back of both hands. Having seen several doctors and each giving him a different medicine or potion and having followed their directions very close for a number of days, nothing seemed to get rid of the warts. They would almost disappear and then suddenly would be back just as bad as before. The worst problem with the warts was that Jim was constantly hitting or scraping them when playing, and they would bleed and become sore, which would take days to heal. Someone mentioned to Mom that Mrs. Blaker was known to rid adults of warts so that it might be wise to take a child to her and see what she could do. One afternoon in the middle of the summer when we were all in Santa Fe, Mom said to me that she wanted me to take Jimmy down to see Mrs. Blaker and have her look at the warts on his hands. First thing that came to my mind was "No way will I go there by myself, and no way would I take Jim into a strange place to have his warts looked at." After a great deal of discussion and with the promise of candy and soda pop, I finally agreed to do what I so dreaded and did not want to do. Walking with Jim toward the house and not being able to go slow enough to keep from getting there, we were standing in front of the screen door. The moment I knocked, all heck broke loose with the noisy little dogs barking and jumping up on the door. If they had not been the size of a rat, a person would think that they were going to jump up and rip your throat out. Mrs. Blaker appeared and asked what did we need, and I tried to tell her in a polite way that someone down town said that she could perform witchcraft, and maybe she could cure brother Jim of his warts. She just smiled and said to come in, so we followed her onto the back porch. She told Jim that she needed to see where the warts were, and Jim with eyes about the size of half dollars raised his hand toward her. She raised the hand toward her glasses and looked at one hand and then looked at the other. She said for us to come on out on the back porch, and she sat down on the top step and pointed for Jim to sit beside her. I was told to just sit down in the chair by the door, so sit down I did and did it quickly. I can still see her sitting beside Jim with the sun shining directly down on them and her holding one of his hands. She sat holding his hand for what seemed a terribly long period of time. She then reached her other hand up and, with her fingers, touched each and every wart and all the while mumbled something under her breath but just loud enough so that we could hear the sounds. After about two hours, which was actually about two minutes, she put down his hand and picked up the other one and began the same procedure, touching and mumbling until she had touched every last wart on Jim's tiny little hand. She then looked up at me and said that she was done and that if there were any warts left after five days to come back, and she would take care of them at the time. Do not remember who made it to the front door first, me or Jim, but it did not take long to be half a block away and far enough to not be able to hear those noisy yapping dogs. When we got back to the store, sure enough, Mom did buy us a soda pop and a candy bar apiece. So in a few minutes, all was forgotten about Jim and his case of warts. We watched the back of his hands for the first couple of days, and nothing different had occurred, but on the fourth day when Mom checked his hands, she let out a surprised yelp and said that they were actually gone. We all looked for ourselves, and sure enough, the back of Jim's hands was as smooth as silk with not one wart visible. I know what you are thinking as you read this, but to my dying day, I will stand by this story as being the absolute truth and the total truth and did happen just as you read it. Mrs. Blaker got rid of every single wart, and from that day, he never had a wart return.

Change of Season

It seemed that the best part of life was when the robins appeared on the front lawn, and what seemed like millions could be seen hopping around the pasture looking for the first earthworm to appear. We could hear great numbers of geese flying so high that you could hardly make out any individuals but looked like a huge V in the sky and knowing full well that the V was heading north to places totally unknown to a kid born and raised on a farm in the middle of Missouri. We did know that the snow and cold that made our lives so much harder was going to be but a memory in the days and weeks ahead. When spring was about to arrive, God gave us many signs of what was to come. The Jonquils that were located by the path that led alongside the garden that ended at the privy were always the first to show their little green pointed tips above ground. At this same time, the leaf buds on the lilac bushes began to swell and, in a few days, opened into tiny leaves that gave the entire bush a light ting of green. This announced to all that saw it that the sun was becoming warmer by the minute, and the danger of frost was rapidly going away not to return for many months in the future. As the leaves began to take form on the lilac bush, there appeared small clusters of flower buds that would be a bud one day and develop into a clump of flower buds the next. It sent out an aroma that drifted with the spring breeze and seemed to have a smell that only a lilac bush could produce. Many decades of springs later when the lilac blooms open, the distinct smell will halt you in your tracks, and once again, the great memories of being a kid on the farm will come rushing back. As a kid, I saw baby lambs had arrived earlier and could now be found lying together in large groups that looked at a distance to be a huge puddle of white soaking up the warm sunrays. Newly arrived calves were running around the pasture pushing one another with their heads trying to show just which one is the strongest and which one may be the leader of the herd in seasons to come. Fruit trees became covered with blossoms; fields and pastures went from a drab dead brown to a solid sheet of green, and the woods across the road from the house began filling into a cover of green that blocked your view when entering the woods with a mantle of leaves. Everywhere you looked, you had to marvel on what a new awakening was taking place before your very eyes. Everything seemed so much in sync, and when you met up with neighbors and friends, there seemed to be a change in attitude that must have come from the promise of new hope and greater prosperity than the year before.

Best of Springtime in the Country

Every time the robins appeared and the frost and ice were in the past, all the new world around you led one to think about when would be the first time that we can get to the river and catch that catfish. It was for sure a fact that whatever size it was this time last year, it would be a great deal larger now. It was now time to get out the fishing tackle and give it a thorough check over. A quick inventory was accomplished by laying everything out piece by piece on the bedroom throw rug. There was to be extra hooks, several sizes of lead weights, a heavy-duty fish stringer, a pocket knife, and a container to carry a gob of live worms, which was usually a Prince Albert tobacco can. Last but not least was to inspect the rod and reel making certain that the line was in good shape and the reel was taken apart and oiled. Pretty hard to imagine how looking at and checking out this small amount of equipment would take the largest part of a day, but as I looked at each piece, my mind would wander back in time to the first fish I ever caught. It then went back further to what Grandpa Burl said and then to what Aunt Naomi had taught me, and time and time again, what Dad had said was really important to remember about catching the elusive huge catfish. When reliving the many experiences we encountered during childhood, invariably the folklore of the snapping turtle would reappear and reinforce a kid's fear.

It was told many times about how dangerous these seldom-seen reptiles of the water could become. Many tales were told about how people had been scarred for life when a big snapper was caught in a river seine and pulled out on the bank with other fish. There were stories of men having their fingers snapped clean off when a turtle was snagged or how chunks of meat was missing on a person's arm when bitten underwater. There were many other stories that made me believe that the mythical snapping turtle was a horror to behold. Mom said that if a turtle clamped down on your hand, it would not let go until the thunder sounded. Do not know if that is true or not, but I have seen a big snapper that was caught going from the river to a pond, and some of them were as big as a washtub. Some of the braver kids would touch its nose with a broomstick, and when that turtle snapped down on the piece of wood, there was no way in the world to pry it out of its beak no matter how hard you pulled. Now that would give you an idea of what it would be like if it had gotten hold of a piece of your flesh. I so much remember how many times we lost hens and chickens to the snapper in the pond next to the granary. The snapper would come up to the edge of the pond and be totally submerged, except for his nose and eyes. The chickens would go to the edge to get a drink, and that would be the last drink many of them got because the snapper got them and pulled them into the pond. Chickens were always pretty stupid that way.

Usually, the first fishing of the season was when Mom took us down to the Big Pond with our cane poles and a can of fishing worms that we had dug fresh from the huge manure pile behind the cattle barn. Was a real nasty place to get fishing worms, but just to fish in the Big Pond made it all worthwhile to turn over the chunks of rotting manure and get the really huge slick to the touch worms. We were not allowed to go on the pond dam side as it was really deep, so we fished on the shallow side with cane poles and bobbers set about a foot deep. Action was almost guaranteed with the huge number of blue gill fish that was in the pond. With the four of us fishing, it was expected that someone would have a cork bobbing or at times all four going under and reappearing. Mom was the world's worst at letting the cork jump up and down without pulling it in. She spent more time laughing at the bobbing cork than trying to get the fish out of the water. I did not agree with that train of thought as the major objective was to catch more fish than any of the others standing on the bank. Jim usually caught the most, but that was with his count, and his count could easily be off a half dozen or more. Mary, on the other hand, wanted to fish but did not want to put the worm on the hook, so she would bring along a piece of cloth to hold the worm so as not to touch it.

Some of my earliest recollections of catching fish were when I was five or six years old. As with the Big Pond, we had to have an adult along, but with the littler pond next to the granary, it was open season on any fish that happened to be found in that smaller puddle of water. It was full of bullhead catfish about five inches long but was too small to bite on a hook, so Jim and I used a big minnow trap to capture them. By leaving it overnight in the middle of the pond, we usually procured six to twelve small bullheads. On real rare occasions, it would hold a huge fish about twelve inches in length, so when this occurred, we would be set to run the trap for another two weeks thinking that it would maybe happen again. Problem with this pond was the fact that the water was about two feet deep, but the mud on the bottom was another foot deep. If you were a little dirty when you entered the water, for sure you would not be any cleaner when you got out. We did fish with a cane pole and a gob of worms on a hook often in the little pond, but too often, a snapper turtle would take the bait, and that was a critter that you did not want to tangle with. We didn't know there was nor had any idea that there was big fish in the Big Pond until one winter when the surface froze over and as we were skating and riding on sleds, we came upon a channel catfish that had died of natural causes and was embedded in the ice. He was really huge or at least looked huge compared to the five-inch bullheads we were used to seeing. From that time on, my goal was to hook one of the big ones, but that just never did happen.

I learned a lifetime of fishing knowledge from my parents and several of my close kin, but the art of fishing was best described and taught by my very special aunt who we referred to as Aunt Naomi. She was my dad's younger sister and was a person that was a totally unique individual. She stood about five feet two and was a bundle of action with a great love of life and knowledge of the great outdoors that every person wishes they could possess. When school let out for the summer, my suitcase was packed with nearly everything I owned and headed for Aunt Naomi and Uncle Jody's cabin in the woods. It was located way back in the woods at the end of a wooded lane that could be reached by going across two dry creek beds and through about a half mile of cattle pasture that led to a little cabin in the woods. She said that they lived so far back in the woods that the chicken hawks were all the time beating up on the hoot owls. Just as soon as I arrived at their place, the first task was to get our fishing gear in top condition so that we could hit the river the first available minute. Now fishing with Aunt Naomi was a far cry from fishing with my mother in the Big Pond. We did use worms, but on the riverbank, the rule was to throw in at least two lines and sit until something took the bait and ran down the river with it. If nothing took the bait, then the rule was to sit and wait until a hungry fish came along. Now that could take five minutes, or it could take six hours to happen, and all there was to do was sit and listen to the sounds of nature and be patient. Being patient for a ten-year-old kid was pretty hard to do, but a rule was a rule, so sit and listen I did. Usually, we did catch several fish, but sometimes there was little to take home for supper, but just to be there had more meaning than doing just about anything else at home. One time, she fixed us cheese sandwiches for lunch. When I say cheese sandwiches, I mean just plain cheese sandwiches. There was nothing on the bread but cheese, and to say that it was a dry lunch would be like saying the river was a little wet. After eating lunch, I noticed that there was nothing to drink—no soda, no milk, and no water, just nothing to wash the dry cheese down with. After about four more hours of no fish and no water, she finally said that it seemed nothing was going to bite, so we may as well go on home. I have never heard a bunch of words that sounded so great as that and was afraid that something would jerk on one of the lines before we could get them out of the water and make us stay another hour or so.

Aunt Naomi was also the first person to teach me how to rock fish. In fact, I think she was one of the few women back in that day that did rock fishing. We would get on an old pair of shorts and wade down the river until we came upon a big rock that was partially or completely submerged. These rocks usually had a hole under it, thus having a place for a big catfish to hide and lay their eggs in the spring.

As there were usually two entrances, it was my job to go around the big rock, find the opening, back my rear against the hole, and stop anything that was hiding under the rock from escaping. She would then cover the other hole with her hands feeling inside to see if anything was hiding there. If it thought it could go past Aunt Naomi, then it should have another thought coming because if she touched the fish, then she had hold of the fish. Usually, she came out of the water with the fish by the lower jaw and hung on with the determination of a grizzly holding on to a salmon. It was very seldom that anything ever got past her, and most of the time when she got a hold on it, the only place it would or could go was home with us for supper. Several times, I would watch her hanging on to a pretty large fish and see blood streaming down her arm from where the sharp little teeth were cutting into her flesh. I cannot ever remember her letting go or even acknowledging that there was any pain involved. I called Aunt Naomi one of the smallest tough ladies in the county.

Aunt Naomi and Uncle Jody. This picture was probably taken somewhere around 1945. So much of the early childhood was spent living with this couple. I stayed with them at least 6 weeks out of every summer from age

6 on to age 12. My dad taught me a lot about the great outdoors but Aunt Naomi taught me how to make do with what I had and used the great outdoors to provide the basic essentials to live. We spent hours playing and enjoying all that was natural and available through Mother Nature.

Actually, I owe a lot more to Aunt Naomi than my many lessons in the art of outdoor living. She saved my life one Sunday afternoon when the Willingham clan was at the river for one of the many all-day picnics that occurred very often. After lunch, all the kids—of which there were about ten or twelve—spent the afternoon swimming and swinging on the rope swing hanging over the river. I was able to stay on top of the water by dog paddling but was not a swimmer by any means. Cousin Donny was about six feet tall and was standing in chest deep water while I was in about three feet of water when he yelled for Uncle Bob to come on out. I thought I should go out also as it looked to be lots more fun than where I was playing. Took three steps, and the bottom fell out of the river, and under I went. Looking up, all I could see was water and a shimmering light, which seemed to be just out of my reach. Running out of air quickly and paddling hard to get to the top and not making any progress in that direction, it seemed as if I had been down there an awful long time. Suddenly, there was a set of hands grabbing me by the shoulders and bringing me to the top into the very welcome air. Aunt Naomi had been sitting in a chair at the water's edge fully clothed in her Sunday go-to-meeting outfit, which included her best and probably only pair of good shoes when she noticed I had disappeared. She plunged into the river and accidently bumped into me. According to others around the swimming hole, none had seen me go under, so without a doubt, I owe my many years of life to my really special aunt Naomi.

As special a woman as Aunt Naomi was, she definitely was not much in the realm of domestic engineer. Housework or cooking was not her real strong point. We really never did go hungry around her house, but if you did not care for the dish she prepared for dinner, then that was pretty much your tough luck. If she fixed a main dish and put it on the table, that was what you ate as that was the only dish on the table. If we had fried fish, then we had fried fish. There was no salad, no corn bread, or hush puppies; but there was a lot of fried fish. That was not all that bad really as my favorite food was fish, but the day we spent in the woods cutting greens was what we had for supper, a huge kettle of greens. If you have never eaten greens, then it should be explained that greens are in the spinach family. In the wild, it was a variety of plant tops that when separated from the plant became greens. Having never really acquired a taste for spinach, then you have an idea of what that particular dinner offered for me. Another meal that sticks out in my memory was the meal of sauerkraut and wieners of which we had a huge amount. So as not to hurt her feelings, I ate what she put on my plate, but believe me, if my mother had put that stuff on my plate at home, it would never have been touched, let alone eaten. After dinner, things got worse as my uncle Jody took down the milk pail and proceeded to the barn to milk the cow. I crawled up into the hay mow and sit on the edge of the upper story and was watching while the milking took place. My uncle took out a plastic pouch from his pocket and bit a huge chunk off the Picnic Twist tobacco plug that he always carried. He asked me if I wanted a chew and, not thinking any better of it, said, "Why, sure." He threw the pouch up to me, so I proceeded to take a piece off and started chewing. Having seen other men chew, I knew full well that as you chew, you spit the amber fluid in your mouth out on the ground and continue to chew and enjoy the moment of chewing and spitting. I suppose the art of spitting was a little more difficult than it looked, for as I spit, some went out into the air, and some went down my throat with the large percentage going down my throat. In about three minutes, give or take two minutes, the world started taking on a weaving and dizzy feeling that was pretty much about to push me forward over the edge of the loft. Climbing down the ladder as quick as possible and about the time my feet hit solid ground, there was a rapid expulsion of kraut and wienies along with about anything else I had eaten that day. To be real truthful, the kraut was not all that good going down, but coming back up was by far more dreadful. Thus, a clear lesson was taught: when chewing tobacco, make sure all the spit is outward. Second lesson, do not eat kraut, and if you do, do not chew tobacco. I now have no problem staying away from both such items to this day.

Three days after the chewing lesson, Uncle Jody asked me if I wanted to earn five dollars. Not being able to imagine how much candy, soda, and fireworks could be purchased with five dollars, I immediately said I sure would. I asked just what I had to do to earn that huge amount of money. He told me that he had a job of docking and cutting lambs the next day. As I had been around lambs most of my life, there did not seem to be any problem helping my uncle with a few little lambs. Next day, we got to the farm about eight o'clock in the morning and found a really pretty place with a two-story farmhouse, a nice garage, and a huge red barn out past the smokehouse. We walked into the barn where the early morning sun was streaming in, which was almost a perfect picture of what farm life was all about. The farmer had already set up a couple of bales of straw to serve as an operation table, and everything was in place and ready to go. My job was to go around the corner and bring in the lambs, catch one by the back leg, place it on the bale of straw, and hold its body up straight with the lamb's back against my chest and with its hind legs beside its small body. Uncle Jody used a lopping shear to cut off the tail, and if the subject was a male, he removed the testicles so that they would grow faster and get ready for market much sooner. My thought was "Now this is really going to be an easy five dollars, so let's get started." I was told to go around the corner and bring in a few at a time, so around the corner I went to retrieve the first few little lambs, finish the job, collect my wages, and head for the candy store. As I turned the corner, you cannot imagine the sight that greeted me. There were not a few lambs in that corral, which must have contained at least two hundred head. And where I was expecting small little fluffy critters, they must have been in the thirty- to forty-pound range and far from fluffy. To make a long story shorter, we did not get away from there until early dark that evening. I was covered from head to toe with sheep manure and blood and was so tired I could hardly stay on my feet, and the worst part was where the lamb was held up against my chest with their feet in the air. All was well until the tail was cut off, and then they exploded by slamming their head against my chest in rapid succession. You can just imagine the movement of the lamb when the males had their privates snipped. I was black and blue from below my chin to almost my waist and so tired I could have cared less how much the wages would be. It took several days to get back to not hurting when I moved, but to be truthful, the five dollars did make it all worthwhile after the pain went away. Lesson learned, ask questions when someone offers you huge sums of money and have complete understanding of what the job entails before you say yes to any offer that sounds too good to be true.

Uncle Jody and the Bobcat

This very exciting moment happened while I was staying with Uncle Jody and Aunt Naomi. It was middle of the summer about midevening with a slight breeze coming through the open windows. It had been a really long day trying to keep up with Uncle Jody, so I was totally spent and too far into sleep to even dream. Suddenly, there was a bloodcurdling scream that brought me out of a deep sleep and sitting straight up in bed. All I could think was some woman was in terrible pain. As Aunt Naomi was the only woman around for miles, it just seemed reasonable that she was in terrible pain and agony to have let out such a loud scream. Suddenly, there was another ear-shattering scream that found me out of the bed and halfway down the hall in a split second. I met both of the adults halfway down the hall, and they were about as spooked as I was, thinking that it was me that made the scream. As another scream pierced the night air, we said almost together, "It's in the front yard." We quickly went to the front window and looked out into the bright full moonlit yard where we could see almost like it was daylight. As we were staring out the front window, we saw sitting on the corner post a huge bobcat. Every couple of minutes, he would stand on his back legs and paw at the stars while letting out a scream that made the hair stand up on the back of your neck. Uncle Jody said that he was going to get his shotgun and get rid of that chicken-killing cat before he gets in the chicken house and kills off all their flock. As bright as it was outside in the moonlight, it was just as dark in the house. Just as he took two steps, he fell with a crash over a rocker that was sitting in the middle of the floor. The cat turned his head toward the sound and made a leap that took him halfway to the road and, with another leap, disappeared into the darkness, never to be seen again. Was kind of glad the big critter got away and did not end up on Uncle Jody's skinning board. To this day, I have never seen a live bobcat again but have in fact heard several at a distance. Still to this day, the hair on the back of my neck and arms stands straight up from the sound of that high-pitched scream.

Uncle Jody at Simmons's Stable

The next day, we got a call from the manager of the Simmons's Stables in Mexico, saying they needed a load of oats first chance we got. If you have ever been around show horses in the state of Missouri, then you would have seen Art Simmons thousands of times in the show ring, winning every champion class of saddlebred horses all over the United States. It took about two hours to scoop off a load of oats, so I was left to entertain myself, and my favorite place to be was sitting on the fence at the corner of the big barn next to the training arena. At any one time, there would be three or four of the most gorgeous show animals you can even imagine seeing working out and going around the arena. They each would work out for nearly an hour going at a fast and furious rack with heads held almost straight up, ears cocked forward, and front feet coming almost to their noses with every step they took. Their trainers were holding them back with double reins and were sitting in the little pancake saddle as if they were sitting in a rocking chair. The horses pounded the ground and made the earth tremble every time they came around the bend at almost a full run but in complete control of where each foot landed. From where I was sitting, you could feel the wind off them as they thundered past and could smell the sweat and wet leather as each rushed past me at what seemed to be a hundred miles an hour. I can remember as if it were yesterday how they would appear to be looking at me with huge bulging eyes that never blinked and had the appearance of a half-crazed animal snorting and blowing with each movement. I almost expected one of them to break stride and go crazy, trying to kill whoever was unlucky enough to be in

153

their way. When they came around the turn where I was sitting on the fence, they would be pounding the dirt as they made the turn picking up huge chunks of dirt and throwing it toward me. As one of the huge beast came around my turn, the right front shoe came off and flew directly toward me like a cannonball shot at close range. The shoe hit the side of the barn a mere ten feet from where I was sitting, shattered a board, and stuck there like an ornament on the wall. The rider brought the horse to a stop as quick as he could, but quick was about halfway around the arena before stopping. He handed the reins to an attendant and came over to where I was sitting and asked if I was OK. It was then that I realized that it was the owner of the stable, Art Simmons himself, who was standing before me. He asked Uncle Jody if it would be all right if he took me inside to see the horses up close. Away we went into the very center of the largest saddlebred stable in the world. To be very truthful though, it should be said that he turned me over to a stable boy that worked there, but I did see many horses that made history during their lifetime as being the best of the best all over the world. The stable is still standing to this day and has been designated as a historical site for Missouri and is being totally remodeled inside and out and has become a saddlebred museum, which will stand for all to see like I saw through the eyes of a kid.

Simmons Stable as it was when I could be found sitting on the fence rail at the north end. Grain bins are still there to this day.

Art Simmons mounted on one of the dozens of show horses he took around the world during the 40's and 50's. This is exactly what the horse I have written about in my memory of sitting on the fence looked like. You can see by the look in it's eye that this horse is wired for 220. It was a sight to behold as it came at a full rack around the corner of the track about 20 feet from where this kid was sitting.

Simmons Stable today which is about one-half the size it was in the early 1950's. This portion has been totally renovated with most of it to be used as an International Saddlebred historical museum.

Grin and oat bins at the end of the training track exactly where they were 60 plus years ago. While Uncle Jody scooped oats into a bin I was watching the show horses work out on the dirt and cinder track that ran along the entire east side of the stable.

Larry and the Dead Rooster

This episode took place at my aunt Mildred and uncle John's place just outside the city of Molina. I usually stayed several days each summer with my cousins Ginny, Larry, and Robert. I was about ten years old when this happened on a mild summer day some time about mid-July. Like all other families during this period of time, Aunt Mildred had a flock of old hens that provided eggs nearly year-around and baked hen whenever the laying flock became too old to produce. It also was not unusual to have at least one rooster that ran with the flock. In this instance, there was a huge red-and-white rooster that was the king of the chicken yard and would crow diligently each morning at sunup and walk around the yard with head in the air and strutting as if he owned the place. Who knows, maybe in the chicken kingdom, he was at the top of the pecking order. One day, Aunt Mildred said that she was going to walk to the store for some flour and that we were to continue playing in the tree house as we had been doing all morning. No sooner than she got out of sight, cousin Larry spotted the ole red rooster and made some comment that we should catch him and tie him up. Sounded like a good idea to me as little harm could come from catching a red rooster and tying him up. Having been trying to fly kites earlier, we had a long strip of material about two inches wide and six feet long that had been used for the tail of the kite. Larry proceeded to catch the ole rooster and tied his feet with the long strip. The rooster of course flopped around and eventually got one leg loose from the knot that Larry had tied and then proceeded to get away from us at a rapid pace. Before we could catch him, he made about five steps and looked over his shoulder to see where we were. Seeing out of the corner of his eye the long strip of cloth dangling behind him startled him a great deal. Every step he took made the strip of cloth jump, which we guessed made him think of a snake or something about to attack, so with a loud squawk, which was almost like a scream, he took off like a shot out of cannon. When he became tired and slowed down, looked back over his shoulder, and saw the streamer jumping at him, he let out another squawk and flew out like he was possessed. We were standing at the gate laughing so hard we could hardly breathe, and the more he squawked, the funnier it became. Suddenly, the rooster came to an abrupt halt, looked up at the sky, and flopped over without so much as a quiver. We looked at each other and slowly walked to where the pile of feathers was lying in the dust. Larry poked him with his toe, but not a move of any kind did the ole rooster make. Picking him up by one wing, Larry said almost under his breath, "I think he's dead." Wasn't any doubt in my mind he was dead, and the thought crossed my mind that there was every chance that we would be better off dead than when Aunt Mildred got home from the store and saw the end of her prized rooster. Larry was the first to get his speech back and said that we better get that rooster out of the yard before anybody saw him. Out the gate, he ran with the rooster slung over his shoulder and disappeared down the driveway. Nothing was said about the rooster until that evening when John put up the chickens for the night and just mentioned that the ole rooster was gone. He said that probably one of the chicken hawks or maybe a red fox must have made off with him. We said nothing, and to this day, the reasoning of the chicken hawk was about as good a reason as could be to explain that missing rooster. Lesson learned, never put a string around the leg of a chicken unless you have them in a really small area or make certain that there is a lot of chicken hawks in the area.

Uncle John and the Skunk

Another very exciting moment occurred when I was staying with Aunt Mildred and Uncle John. It was about the time the chicken hawk made off with the rooster but a bit later in the year. Robert, Larry, and I were sound asleep with the windows open in the middle of summer when suddenly there arose a really loud commotion from the chicken house. It was located about twenty yards just west of our bedroom, so we were easily close enough to hear the racket and become awakened instantly. There was a terrible sound of chickens squawking and flying around in the chicken house beating their wings against the window screens. Everyone in the house was up in a flash to investigate the cause of what the entire ruckus was about. Uncle John was the first outdoors with his six-cell coon-hunting flashlight and double-barrel shotgun clad only in his boxer shorts and pair of boots. Next came me and cousin Larry, and immediately behind him was cousin Robert, sister Jennie, and Aunt Mildred. Robert was not much more than five years old and had a habit of every time he set foot outside the door he carried with him a stick that was a lot taller than he was but nevertheless always present in his little hands. As we neared the chicken house, you could hear the chickens making a terrible ruckus, and above the noise, we could hear a distinct thump, thump, thump, which sounded like someone was slowly beating on a toy drum. Uncle John swung open the door, shined in his six-cell flashlight, and saw in an instant what was causing all the commotion. Standing on a washtub turned upside down was another of those black-and-white critters that looked somewhat like a cat. This one was all fluffed up with tail in the air and, with its front feet, was making a thumping sound that kind of raised the hair off the back of your neck. Being the smallest of the crowd, cousin Robert was in the rear pushing his way to the front of the group so as to see firsthand what all the noise was about. Larry pushed him out of the way so as to retain his position in the front just beside Uncle John. Robert, having nothing to do with being pushed around, made a lunge to the front. Remember the stick mentioned previously? Well, as it happened, he was holding it in front, pretending that it was a shotgun like his daddy was holding. With a lunge forward, the stick—also pointing forward—jammed Uncle John square center in the middle of his rear. He let out a yell and jerked up the shotgun, and one or both barrels of the shotgun discharged. The roar of the blast was deafening as was the yell of Uncle John. As the smoke cleared, it was evident that the varmint was blown to smithereens, the tub had a hole the size of a basketball in it, and two old hens were shot dead. As the old saying goes, "If you shoot skunks, never shoot it with its tail in the air." According to folklore, when the tail is raised, the critter's gun is also loaded, and that being the case, the air was filled with gunpowder smoke and pole cat scent, both of which made a really pungent odor. Usually, Uncle John was a person of few words, but by the time the blast had died down, Uncle John became a person of many words, most of which I cannot quote in this passage. When all was said and done, a large portion of the night was spent scalding and plucking old hens for the noonday meal in the coming days. Can't remember what became of Robert's stick but do remember that he spent the next day finding a replacement. The excitement of the night events was easy to remember as the night air was coming directly from the chicken house toward the open window, and with the night breeze came a really strong smell of deceased pole cat.

Memorable Moments Flashback
Seining Salt River

Back in the good ole days, the rivers were teaming with a large number of fish. This was when seining with a floating fishnet was legal. At least once a year, the men of the area gathered together and drug the seine up the river to procure fish for a fish fry. The seine reached across the entire width of Salt River and was dragged toward a riffle about a half mile upriver. There was a man on each end holding a pole upright that had the seine connected at the top and at the bottom with floats about three feet apart across the top rope. The string mesh then went from the top rope to the bottom of the river that was held down by lead weights. As they proceeded downriver, three or four men waded behind the net so that they could dislodge the bottom rope if it became snagged on a rock or submerged log. Brother Jim and I were wading along behind the procedure, holding an inflated inner tube under our arms so we could float when the river bottom disappeared beneath us, which often it did. You could tell when the net was starting to gather fish as every so often the floats would submerge when a huge flathead catfish or a really big carp tried to go back upriver but was stopped by the net. One time, I remember well when the pole guys came to a riffle and pulled the net out on the sandbar. Suddenly, the water exploded with big and bigger fish beating the surface of the water into froth. We all went over the top of the net and started grabbing flopping fish and stuffed them into a gunny sack for safekeeping. I looked up, and brother Jim, not bigger than minute, had a really big white perch in a bear hug holding on to it as if his life depended upon it. He had it upside down so that the tail of the perch was right in line with his face, and no matter which way he turned his chin, the fish would slap him on one side of the face and then the other with the large tail. He did not turn loose of that fish until one of the men grabbed it, so for sure, Jim came out the winner with that fish fight. I can also remember another time when I was much too young to go with the crew that they unloaded a pickup truck of fish one afternoon at Shannon

Roberts's dad's backyard. Two of the flathead cats were monster big, and they hung them from a tree limb and butchered them. Another time, they had an alligator gar that was so big that it was bent in a circle in the truck bed, and its body touched all sides. Soon as everything quieted down, the men all took out their skinning knives and sharpener and began dressing the fish one at a time. They skinned, gutted, deboned, and chopped into chunks the entire truckload. We headed to the Santa Fe Ball Park with the fish and found, when we got there, that others had preceded us and had two or three large fires going each with an iron kettle of lard heated to a boiling point over the flames. Basket after basket of fish was fried; hush puppies were cooked last, and finally the entire county of folks took turns going past the kettle and carried away as much fish as they could eat. This was known as the Santa Fe Fish Fry, which was an annual event that occurred for as long as I can remember.

Memorable Moments Flashback
Putting Up Hay at Russ Scobee's Farm

As the hay crew moved from farm to farm, it was the responsibility of the wives to prepare food and have it ready to eat at high noon. Kind of a potluck organization where the wife of the farmer where the crew was baling did most of the cooking, and the rest of the wives were expected to bring desserts or whatever and to be available to assist having the food on the table when the noon bell rang. Oftentimes, there were too many workers to fit into most kitchens, so a long table and benches were set outside so everyone had a place to be seated. This all went according to plan except when it was Russ Scobee's turn to host the crew. He was by most accounts classified as an old bachelor as he had never married as well as his two sisters, Lucy and Ruby, who all lived together in their parents' old homeplace. Russ was a rather large man that probably weighed close to three hundred pounds or slightly more and wore bib overalls and a blue denim shirt every day of the week, including Sunday at church. The two sisters made sure he was always wearing clean clothes, which were pretty much a surprise when comparing him to others in the same living conditions. Russ always had several gold foil-wrapped cigars in his chest pocket, but never did I see him smoke one. Instead, he would unwrap one like a banana and bite off a third of the cigar, rewrap it, and start chewing. Many times, I saw him sitting in church on the back pew by the door on Sunday morning during preaching and open the door and spit a mouthful of amber fluid to the outside. When the hay crews arrived at his farm, it was well-known that the two sisters did not need any assistance getting lunch ready for the hay crew. When the dinner bell rang, the crew found tables set in the huge kitchen with room enough to seat everyone and room to spare. Laid out before us was a buffet that boggled the mind. At least four meats, half-dozen bowls of fresh vegetables, enough mashed potatoes to feed an army, bowls of gravy, and plates and plates of freshly baked hot bread with fresh churned butter. After the meal, the sisters would pass around various pies and cakes so that each man could choose either one or several pieces to finish off the meal. I will never forget the roast beef and gravy that I put away during those visits to the Scobee sisters farm luncheon. You can only imagine what it was like to leave the table and walk across the front yard thinking about going back to work in the hot dry fields that were covered with bales of hay. I for one could only think about finding a shade tree and fall into a food-induced coma. For sure, it did not seem to affect Russ all that much. When we returned to the field, it was a fact that Russ would always get there first so that he could seat himself on the tractor. This kept him from having to walk along the ground and pick up bales and took the job that I usually filled. Instead of an eight-year-old boy doing the driving, it now belonged to a fifty-year-old man. When asked why he was on the tractor seat, Russ always explained that he was kicked by a mule when he was a teenager and had bothered him ever since. It was unusual, however, that the only time this old injury affected him was about hay baling time. There was one time, however, that we did see Russ move rather quickly, and that was when he got off the tractor to empty his bladder. He was standing beside the tractor, which was parked next to an electric fence. As he proceeded with his bathroom call, someone called his name. He turned to see what they wanted. When the stream of urine crossed over the electric wire, the effect was rapidly felt throughout Russ's body. Now this day, he actually had a reason not to work the rest of that afternoon.

Memorable Moments Flashback
Community Hay Baling

Each year about midsummer, you could almost mark your calendar when the hay crop on our farm and the neighbors would reach its growth peak. It was now ready to mow, bale, and store into the hay barns preparing for the winter blast that would soon arrive. In our area, there were five farms that depended upon one another to go from farm to farm with all the equipment and manpower to fill each barn to capacity with hundreds of bales. At one farm, the mower was cutting down the grass, which then two days later would be raked into windrows. When cured, a baler showed up to bale the grass into bales about two feet by three feet weighing approximately forty-five to sixty-five pounds each. When the bale hit the ground, there was a crew of eight or ten men walking beside the wagon and quickly stacked the bales onto hay wagons stacked five or six bales high. When full, the tractor pulled the wagon out of the field and took it to the barn where it was unloaded and stacked in the top story of the two-story barn. When I was eight years old, it became my job to drive the tractor in the open field and weave between the rows of hay. When the load was completed, I would crawl on top of the load and ride leisurely back to the barn. At Ralph Bridgford's place, the barn was huge, nearly twice the size of most barns, and it held enough hay to feed his herd of several dozen Angus cows and calves. My first memory was watching the men use barn hay hooks to get the bales upstairs. It consisted of a set of ropes that ran through pulleys that was connected to four huge hooks that were dangling from a pulley above the window on the second floor. When the hooks were lowered to the ground, two men would put eight bales of hay in a stack and then drive the spikes into the bottom bale. A team of draft horses would walk away pulling the rope, which raised the bales to the open window. When it hit a certain spot, it touched a rail that entered the top of the window, which tripped a lever sending the stack of hay into the loft. When the guy in the loft released the hooks from the bales, they signaled the horses to back up, and the hooks came back down to the exact spot the last bales were raised. I was not allowed to go into the loft because Dad said that it was much too dangerous to be around the bales and hooks as they were swinging loose. Years later, Ralph purchased a hay chute that was a long narrow track on wheels that contained a chain running up from the bottom so that when a bale was placed at the ground level, it pulled the bale up the chute and delivered it into the loft. It was powered by a small gas engine, so with the trailer parked at the end of the chute, I could throw off the bales to a guy standing on the ground. And up the chute the bale went and disappeared into the window above. Soon as the field was cleared and the barn was full, it was time to move on to the next farm.

Memorable Moments Flashback
Uncle Ronald's Yellow Fishing Boat

With the amount of time we spent either fishing or swimming, a dream we had was to own a rowboat that would let us get up and down Salt River with ease. When Otis Snyder gave us a homemade car hood boat, we thought this was a dream come true. It was to some degree a big help, but the dynamics of a boat with a rounded bottom caused a great deal of swim time as we were in the drink more than we were in the boat. When two people got in the boat at the same time, it was virtually impossible to keep it in an upright position. Quite often, we ended up in the river chasing our floating fishing gear downriver. One Sunday afternoon, we were at Uncle Ronald and Aunt Odell's place when he opened up the garage door and showed us a super great rowboat that he had built. It was painted yellow and was big enough to hold four people, which meant it was a really large boat.

As I was marveling about how sturdy it was and how this would be an ideal boat for our fishing purposes, Uncle Ronald asked if we would like to take it home and keep in on the river down steam on Salt River. I thought he was kidding and kind of laughed, and he said that he made it to put in the back of his pickup truck and move it around from place to place but found that, when it was finished, it took at least three strong men to get it off the ground. Putting it into a truck was way too much work for the amount of fishing time they got out of it. Dad and I drove over with the hay wagon the next day and took it home. Next day, we drove it down to the river behind Herb Moore's place and, by backing the wagon into the water until it was almost submerged, soon had the boat floating. Bob Moore and I ran lines and fished out of it on many occasions. We did realize that it was *big*; in fact, almost too big to maneuver in Salt River, and that river was plenty wide enough to turn an ordinary boat. Several weeks after we began using it, we tied it to a tree on the riverbank overnight instead of putting it back in a still water cove like we usually did. Would you believe we had a toad strangler downpour that night and the river went out of its banks? After the river receded, we made a trek down to the river to check on the boat; it was nowhere to be found. The chain was there, but the boat was missing. We walked downriver for a mile or so, but that boat was nowhere in sight. In school the next day, I got out the *World Book Encyclopedia* and read about the rivers of Missouri. I came to the realization that somewhere many miles down the Mississippi River, someone must have found a yellow boat floating along and thought, "Where in the world did this *big* yellow boat come from?"

Fishing with Grandpa Burl

Another fishing story began when Grandpa Burl picked me up, and we headed for the river. I had just turned nine years old and, for my birthday, received a new rod and reel that replaced my trusty cane pole. Not being able to cast this new piece of equipment correctly, I did the next best thing. After putting a gob of earthworms about the size of a turkey egg on the hook, I let the line dangle in the water and then stripped many feet of line off the reel and let it lay in a circle at my feet. By casting the rod tip toward open water, the line would flow through the eyelets, and the glob of worms would fall into the river and sink to the bottom. After doing this at least three times and not placing the hook in just the right spot, I decided to try it one more time. I noticed Grandpa watching me over the rim of his glasses about to go crazy wanting to say something. Finally, not being able to hold his tongue any longer, he gave me words of wisdom that to this day is one of my favorite quotes. He said, "Son, you ain't going to catch any fish if you don't have your line in the water." I use this phrase often as it pertains to so many instances when you are working with people. As I did have my line in the water and pretty sure I did not dare to try again as bad as I wanted to, I left it be and sat down behind the pole. The line was just too close to the bank, and I knew that there would not be a fish even close to this side. I also knew that I was not going to bring it in again what with Grandpa watching and waiting. This is where my education began.

Suddenly, the line began jumping; reel began screaming, and the belief that you had to throw the bait to the other side to catch fish totally went out the window. This hit came only a few feet from the bankside, but could you believe there it was, pole bent double and line making a mad dash down the middle of the river. After what seemed to be an eternity of fighting that huge unseen fish, all ended when at my feet was one of the biggest, shiniest, floppiest huge white perch I had seen anywhere but in my dreams. It was now imbedded in my brain that grass isn't always greener on the other side of the fence, and the fishing isn't always better deeper or farther out. As we were admiring the large fish swimming on the stringer, I could once again hear the wisdom of his words, "You can't catch any fish if your line ain't in the water." It is hard to ever forget the feeling of excitement the few minutes where the fish was lunging at the end of the line but do believe that at that moment I became a true Willingham fisherman that has lingered to this very day.

The story of fishing with Grandpa Burl does not end here, however, as another clear lesson was learned just as the trip was ending. This did not carry the weight of the experience of catching the trophy fish but was etched into the very innermost side of my brain. This occurred after a very long time of sitting on a flat rock on the riverbank with my back resting on a large flat rock that was imbedded in the mudbank. For the longest time, I sat there in one spot occasionally reaching behind me to grab a stick to whittle on and help pass the time. We sat at that one position for at least an hour without getting another bite. Then came the welcome sound of Grandpa closing his tackle box and getting ready to call it quits for the day. Now I could go to the house and maybe even go to Santa Fe and show everybody the really once-in-a-lifetime fish I caught. Suddenly, the words of Grandpa caused me to freeze, and my heart to skip a beat when he said in a really serious tone, "Kennie, do not move. Stay perfectly still." The tone of his voice caused me to become instantly scared, and to say the least, I did not even breathe, let alone move. He said, "Lean forward and slowly move away from the rock you're sitting on." He did not have to say to move forward but once when this little guy was many feet away in the blink of an eye. Turning around and looking at the spot where I was sitting but a moment before, Grandpa had taken a long stick and proceeded to bring out from under the rock one of the largest copperhead snakes that I had ever seen, especially at this close range. As the massive reptile slithered away, I saw that the huge poisonous snake had been coiled up under the very rock I was leaning on and had been there the entire time we were sitting and fishing. Grandpa Burl said to me, "Kennie, there is nothing about a snake to be scared 'cause he doesn't like you any better than you like him. Let them alone, and both of you will be better off."

Now Grandpa Burl has been gone for a number of years, and the young lad that he took fishing so long ago is a grandpa himself several times over. The words he gave me will hold true until I too will be gone. There is and was so much to learn from the older generations. As long as I am able, his strengths and knowledge of life will be passed on so that Grandpa Burl will live through generations to come. It can be truly said that my life has been strengthened and enriched by what my grandparents and my parents told me over the years, and I hope that I can leave a legacy to the generations below me.

Memorable Moments Flashback
Rotten Egg Battle

Often, one will refer to a bad smell as smelling like rotten eggs. I doubt if many alive today have actually run across a truly rotten egg. When we were kids, it was a common occurrence to find a nest of eggs that for one reason or the other the ole setting hen abandoned. After several warm days, the eggs will decompose internally but looks like any other egg. Usually, anything round and not too large was good for throwing, and the object to throw at was usually one another. Gathered up three eggs, and Jim had one in each hand, so with very little thought, we quickly hurled an egg at each other. My throw hit Jim just above the eyes, and his hit me dead center on the bare chest. If you have not thrown a rotten egg, then it should be explained that when they break open, they not only break open but actually explode with the liquefied center having a spattering effect. Brother Jim's face was pretty much covered with a mucus-type liquid that was dripping off his chin. Within seconds, one of the worst smells imaginable filled the air and was in fact so bad we both started gagging and choking from the terrible stench. We immediately headed for the watering trough but found that water had little effect on getting rid of the awful smell. We ran to the house and went flying into the kitchen, yelling for Mom to come quick and help us get this horrible smell off our skin and out of our noses. Her first words were that we were to get out of the house and get out immediately. She did, however, bring a wash pan full of warm water and mixed a cup of Cheer laundry detergent in it. This formula did help to rid most of the bad smell. From that point on, Jim and I did know what was meant when a person said it smelled like a rotten egg and certainly left them alone from that time on.

Farm Kids Eat the Best

When thinking back to days of our youth, it would have to include what foods we were raised with. When I was under twelve years of age, there was no electricity available to our farmhouse. Can you imagine walking into your kitchen and not have a refrigerator available? You did not have an electric oven, not have a microwave, and not have a washer and dryer. With Mom and Dad and three kids in the house, it was a fact that there was need for three meals a day for seven days a week. If you wanted to eat out with the family, that would mean that you took your meal outside and had a picnic because the nearest restaurant was many miles away. Besides that, we could not afford to give those prices when we could eat at home free. It was expected by all concerned that all meals were organic; all meals were home-raised produce, and all meals were some of the best-tasting food in the world. If you were ten years old, it was a fact that you had never in your lifetime while living on the farm ever gone to bed with anything but a full stomach. In the summer, there were fresh items from the garden, fresh chicken from the brooder house, large portions of pork and beef—either cold packed or fresh frozen and stored at the locker plant in Perry. This was a small town about six miles from where we lived. Our diet was supplemented with rabbit, ducks, geese, squirrels, and all other wild critters living in the woods that surrounded the house. From the river west of the house came catfish, white perch, carp, buffalo, and occasionally a mess of frog legs. We captured frogs by using a cane pole with a short line and hook and a small piece of red cloth that we would dangled in front of a huge bullfrog. I would handle the pole, and Jim would come along behind with the gunny sack. In the spring, we had mushrooms, greens, asparagus, blackberries, wild strawberries, rhubarb, and mulberries by the gallons.

Breakfast was the first meal of the day, and there was no excuse that would keep any family member from the first meal of the day. In the colder months, there was always a big cooker of oatmeal sitting on the woodstove calmly bubbling away. When someone sat down at the table, this was a signal to Mom that she needed to dip out a bowl of oatmeal and toast a couple of pieces of bread for either one kid or all three. Several pieces of homemade bread were stacked on the table, and available were homemade butter, homemade jelly and preserves, and—during seasons—fresh berries and honey. There was a pitcher of milk along with a smaller pitcher of pure cream that when added to oatmeal made a completely different-tasting bowl of cereal. On special occasions, Mom would make a kettle of hot chocolate that was a great place to dip our toast and provide a taste and memories that lasted kids a lifetime.

During the school year, Mom would start about five o'clock in the morning with a skillet of grease frying chicken or pork chops or hamburgers for Dad's lunch on the hammer mill and in our lunch boxes for the noon meal at the elementary school in Santa Fe. After finishing the noon meal preparation, she would make milk gravy and put on our plates pieces of meat and biscuits left over from a previous meal. The kids were usually up and eating at the same time, but early in the morning, we very seldom saw Dad as he was doing chores before the sun came up and had already eaten breakfast with Mom while we were still sound asleep. Dad would show up in the kitchen for just a few minutes in the morning, gather up his lunch pail and coffee jug, pat us each on top of the head, and go out the back door heading for the hammer mill barn ready to begin his day. Sunday morning was an entirely different time of life. Mom would have a special menu for this morning that included several eggs over easy, bacon and/or country ham, biscuits and gravy, toast, fried potatoes, and a pot of fresh brewed coffee. We kids got about three tablespoons of coffee in our glass of milk so that the taste let us pretend that we were almost adults. Dad did something that we never did figure out why. He ended every breakfast by pouring a huge cup of coffee from the percolator, added sugar and cream, stirred it, and then poured the entire contents into his cereal bowl. He drank his coffee from the bowl instead of the cup. He continued this practice until the day he passed away. We never did understand why this took place every breakfast during the ninety plus years that he lived.

Sunday noon was always spent at Grandma Clair and Grandpa Burl's house in the country outside of Molina, Missouri. Parents would pick us up after Sunday school and church at the Christian church in Santa Fe and head to Grandma's house. The entire clan would be there by eleven thirty in the morning, and by eleven forty-five, there would be a table full of bowls prepared by each lady of the families along with meat prepared by Grandma. On the counter was a least five pies and a couple of cakes along with several plates of cookies prepared by the mother of each family, which was the specialty of each particular woman. First through the line was the really young children, of which there was seemingly dozens. Then came the age six through twelve, and then came the menfolk with each filling their plate to overflowing. When the men were out of the way, the womenfolk would bring up the rear and usually find that the best platters were empty, so they got what was left over. There never was a word spoken as to why the men and kids got the best fare. I often wondered why the women accepted the leftovers and presumed the men were supposed to be treated like the head of the household. It was pretty much a fact that the women were the ones that had the most brains and usually were the ones that made things right when mistakes were made by the men. After the meal, which was consumed in a matter of minutes, it was time to quietly sit around and visit, and in some instances, the men and kids would lay on the throw rugs and sleep off the huge meal. Late afternoon, the clan gathered up their kids and picnic baskets and headed off to their respective homes to meet again next Saturday morning in Mexico and be at Grandma's house Sunday at noon. This went on for years until Grandma became unable to prepare the meals, so as it occurred, most families' kids were old enough to meet at their parents' place for Sunday lunch. Tradition faded into memories of old age, and new traditions were established within each family and are now passed down to the third and fourth generation from the days of Grandma's Sunday dinners.

The only time of the week that Mom remained free from the kitchen was Sunday evening. After the chores were done, we all gathered around the kitchen table for Sunday supper. Actually, we all gathered, but rarely was a meal placed before us. Instead, there was usually a pot of mush, which was a cornmeal-based concoction that was a whole lot like oatmeal with a different consistency. I found it pretty much distasteful when put in a bowl out of the pot; but when laced with a huge gob of butter, two teaspoons of sugar, and enough whole cream to make it float, then it became a much more tolerable dinner dish. This was the only time we were allowed to have store-bought cookies. By taking a bite of cookie and then a spoon of mush, it was a filling meal and not all that bad once you got into it. Some Sunday suppers consisted of beef chunk vegetable soup and other times a pot of chili, which was mostly hamburger and a few beans flavored with chili powder and other unknowns. Other times, there was a stew that you really didn't know what it contained but did have meat of some kind and canned carrots, canned cabbage, canned green beans, and any other vegetable that was a leftover dish from a previous meal. Usually, I had corn bread with this but really was never to my liking, so I usually crumbled up a handful of crackers to complete the feast and then retired to the living room with the one bare bulb hanging from the ceiling. That was before we got our first TV, so there was a lot of family togetherness for most evenings. Reading and drawing became kind of boring after a few minutes, so we became sleepy very early and headed for bed. We would awaken early Monday morning and start all over again.

Memorable Moments Flashback
Feeding and Breeding Rabbit Colony

One of my assigned chores was to daily pull a hefty amount of grass and feed the rabbits that Dad had in cages beside the garden fence. There were four does or females and one buck. So every four months, we had a new litter of rabbits. About the time we were finished dining on fried rabbit from the previous bunch, there would be a new litter weaned and getting close to market size. Dad had it all figured out when the next litter would be born, so we always had fresh rabbit to make our dinners more interesting. I had gotten tired of pulling grass every day, so I came up with a plan to make my life a little easier. I located a wooden crate behind James and Mac's general store that was used to deliver vegetables from store to store. I asked permission to take the crate home, and they said it was fine to carry it away. When I arrived home, I turned the crate upside down, and when I put a doe in the crate, they did my work for me by eating the lush grass beneath their feet. My job was to wait about ten minutes, put the doe back in her cage, put another one in the crate, and let her eat to her heart's content. Plan worked like a charm; each rabbit got their fill of fresh grass for the day, and my work was as simple as sitting around and watching. All went according to plan until the folks said that today is the first day of the Audrain County Fair and thought that we should attend. I was so excited I could hardly wait to load into the Chevy and get to the big city and see all the sights and lights of the county fair along with rides and eats and drinks. Suddenly, Dad's voice brought me back to reality when he asked if I had pulled grass for the rabbits, and if not, then we would not go until the chore was done. A rule around Dad was that if there was an animal penned up away from their natural surroundings, then they had the right to be provided for before any of our personal wants were to be considered.

The animals ate first, and that was the rule that always was in place. Aw, man, I had forgotten all about the rabbits, and now those lop-eared critters were going to ruin my fun and stop me from all the excitement I so much dreamed about. I knew that it took so much time for each to eat their share. So to hurry up the feeding, it just made sense that instead of letting them eat one at a time, why not put them all in at the same time and get the job done a lot quicker. All was going well when I put the four does in the crate as they were very happy to be placed where the green grass was available. Things took a turn for the worse when I put the male rabbit in the crate. Instead of eating calmly like the does, a big problem erupted. There was fighting and banging around in the crate until I had to sit on the top to keep it from turning over. Suddenly, it became calm and quiet, and the only movement was the male wrestling with one female and then the other. Totally relieved that they had calmed down and was eating quietly, I thought that the plan was working great and we would be able to head for the fair in a matter of minutes. I did notice that one of the rabbits was not eating but just figured it was not hungry, which was not my fault, so not to worry. After a few minutes, I started to take one out at a time to return to their cages when it suddenly dawned on me. They all looked alike. Which one would I put back in the buck rabbits' cage. Whatever, Dad would be able to tell me, so I went into the house and told Dad that I needed help. After putting all the rabbits in the crate, they all looked alike, so I needed help finding which one was the buck. Was really surprised how fast Dad jumped up and headed for the pens. Really was surprised when he began talking to himself and mumbling something about a breeding schedule. He did give me instructions to not ever put the buck into the crate when the does were eating but never did explain why that was a big problem. The next time it was mentioned was when I was about fifteen years old and was talking about a girl in my class at Paris High School.

Community Butchering
and Fresh Meat

There should be many pages written about the good ole days and how healthy we were by having tons of fresh fruit and fresh vegetable and how they were all organically grown. However, it is very hard to remember how good the carrots were when the thoughts of fried pork shops or fried T-bone steak or fried sausage or fried chicken with fried potatoes come to mind. I can't remember a fried carrot or a fried green bean that stands out in my memory, so there must not have been many unforgettable vegetables. We did eat vegetables daily, so it must have been because Dad said we could not get down from the table until our plates were clean. Many years later, my favorite meal is something fried with mashed potatoes and cream gravy. Another piece of information is that there is no comparison between margarine and butter. Butter will be second choice to this day with margarine taking first place. If anyone that reads this disagrees, then let me see you churn at least a half ton of butter, one-gallon churn at a time, and still come out thinking that butter is all that great. Occasionally, I give buttermilk a try just to see if I dislike it as much now as I did then. Turns out, I dislike it even more the older I get, so there is little chance that my mind will take a turn to just how good buttermilk is.

I wonder what my grandchildren would think if they were required to exist on what we had available in the midforties. I would guess that 95 percent of our food was produced within a stone's throw of our house. When the weather turned off cold and the temperature held around the freezing point, the entire neighborhood started thinking about scheduling butchering time. To get the meat processed in a timely manner, every family would have one, two, or—with the large families—three hogs finished out by the first of November as well as one or two steers ready to slaughter and get ready for the canner. I can remember the five families that brought their hogs to a central location farm each year. A trench was dug long enough to hold several hardwood logs and wide enough to set a huge tub on the edges so that a very hot fire was going under the tub. It was filled with water and brought to a boil early in the morning. When the first neighbor arrived with their hogs, the killing process began. It was first come, first served, so usually by the time the first one had been put down, the entire group was there ready to proceed with the butchering. The first hog was shot between the eyes with a .22-caliber rifle; their back legs tied to a wagon single tree and hung from a tree until the carcass was swinging off the ground. The throat was slit so that the blood could drain, and within a few minutes, the entire hog was taken down and placed in the water vat. After several minutes of scalding, it was hung back in the tree where two men with sharpened butcher knives scraped the entire body until the hair was totally removed. The next step was to gut the pig, cut off its head, and then cut it in half from top to bottom. It was removed and each half hung in a nearby tree after being marked with a tar stick as to who the two halves belonged. Every man had a certain task to do, so in a few minutes, each procedure was being done on a different carcass. Within the hour, every hog that was delivered to this farm was halved and hanging in a tree. Usually, you could count on at least eight to ten hogs processed within this first hour. As I was six to ten years old, I cannot remember all the steps carried out but can remember that it was carried out with precision and every member of the crew was a very important part of the butchering. When all the hogs had been halved, the entire crew of men stood around the wagons and separated the various cuts, pork loin off the back, pork chops below the loin, ribs removed and sawed into pieces. The hams were separated from the leg portion, which was the last cut made. Any parts that were left over was stripped of any meat pieces and placed in huge washtubs to later be ground into sausage. A large iron kettle was placed over the hot coals. All pieces cut off the carcass that was without any meat attached was thrown into the rendering kettle. When it hit the hot kettle, the pieces actually melted down into a liquid they called lard. When the kettle was full of boiling liquid fat, they drained off the top into a lidded can. This was to be used the coming year for cooking and baking. This had the consistency of Crisco but slightly less white, and the can weighed several pounds. What was left over after the rendering was pieces of cooked hide called a crackling that was like a potato chip being brown and crispy. Everyone took a handful and had a tasty snack; however, the rule of do not eat too many was important. After a certain amount was chewed up and swallowed, the stomach would give you pains that said maybe that last bite was one too many.

A new kettle was placed over the coals and a coffee can full of small skin pieces were thrown in. After a bit of stirring around with a wooden paddle, the skins would puff up almost like popcorn. This was also a treat to eat hot out of the kettle and was called pork rinds. Not nearly as greasy as the cracklings, but the same rule applied with the amount consumed.

The next procedure was grinding the sausage. All the giblets and pieces of meat removed from the bone was run through a grinder and collected in a washtub. When the tub was full, a designated person opened several five-pound cans of spices. He very carefully measured out certain amounts of each and mixed them in a bowl. As the men worked the ground-up pork with their hands, the spice man would pour a cup at a time over the meat until it was completely mixed up. It seemed that this one man was trusted by all others as being top spice man, which made the sausage not too hot and spicy, but he knew when just the right amount would make it perfect. It should be mentioned that all these pieces made a massive pile of meat and fat, so when the grinding started, it took all the men to keep the grinder going until finished. Each would turn the handle ten or fifteen minutes, and then his relief would take over. This was by far the hardest part of the butchering and took a lot of time to grind all the sausage. One year, somebody in the group had an idea of taking an automobile and jacking it up, removing the back tire and tying the handle onto the rim. This really worked as it nearly cut the grinding time in half. One guy watched the grinder, and two guys kept the meat hopper full, and everybody else stood well out of the way as occasionally the grinder clogged and the power of the car motor made things go around rapidly. The closest person may find his hand and arm being whacked with a runaway grinder. At the end of the day, all tubs and buckets of fresh pork was loaded into each family vehicle to be taken home and packaged the following day. The hams were salted and put into gunny sacks and then hung in the barn or smoke shed to cure out for future use.

The next day, Mom and the three kids came together in the kitchen to cold pack some of the meat and to wrap the rest in freezer paper. After we washed the dozens of canning jars and placed them on the table, Mom came along with a bucket of sausage and filled each jar about two-thirds full of raw pork sausage. These were capped and ringed and each jar placed in a canner of boiling water. After so many minutes, they were taken out and placed back on the table to cool. In each jar was a layer of meat and about two inches of white grease floating on top. During the next several months, Mom would take one of these jars and dump the grease and meat out into a bowl, and when mixed up once again, it was fresh sausage or almost like fresh sausage. When cooled, we kids carefully carried two jars at a time and placed them downstairs in the cellar among the green beans, peas, pickles, beets, and in some jars a whole chicken that had been dressed and stuffed into a quart jar. Occasionally, Mom would take out a chicken jar and separate the bones from the meat, and it was chicken pot pie time.

The part that I most dreaded about butchering was when Dad took the hog's head and lay it on the floor in the north storeroom. He intended to find time later on to make hogs headcheese, but in the meantime, the head that had the cold staring eyes was in a direct line where I had to walk to get to the back door to head toward my chores. At least twice daily, I had to walk past that head within inches of where it lay looking up at me with eyes wide open and mouth grinning as if to say, "I see you, look me in the eye, and you will have a spell cast upon you." I just hated having to make that trip, and it seemed almost forever before Dad got around to processing it. Everyone really thought hogs headcheese was a treat but not me. I placed it a close second to fried brains or blood pudding, which all were something that I would not touch unless starving to death.

The highlight of hog butchering was what we could expect for supper many nights in the future. Anything that was not taken to the cellar or taken to Perry to the locker freezer was fair game to be consumed locally. I always looked forward to getting home, finishing the chores (Jim was excluded because he was too little, and Mary was excluded because she was a girl), and then sitting down to supper with fresh pork chops fried crispy on the outside and tender juicy on the inside. Along with this was a huge pile of mashed potatoes in a bowl with a gob of butter pushed down inside the pile. As I watched the gravy being dumped out of the skillet into a huge bowl with big chunks of giblets floating around, I could hardly wait for Jim to say his two-liner prayer so we could begin passing around the food. Night after night, Mom would put before us a meal that we would remember for at least twenty-four hours, and then it was time to start over again with a meal so special it stayed in my memory for a lifetime.

Memorable Moments Flashback
Terrible Home Health Remedies

As you read about the wonderful meals and foods we enjoyed as small children, it must also be mentioned about the dreaded home remedies that we were forced to endure. This occurred once annually or, in some instances, two or three times a year. One can remember that, as small children, we were never allowed to have soda pop at home and never had bottled pop of any kind available. When Mom came from the general store with a bottle of orange soda, it caught our attention instantly. At this moment, we all three realized that the dreaded dose of castor oil was about to be introduced into our soul and memory bank in the very near future. Sure enough, early in the evening, our parents would take the cap off the bottle of that thick clear liquid and pour a huge tablespoon. This bad-smelling liquid filled the very huge spoon. They then pushed it toward one of the three kids' faces. If Mary was first, then she got to hold the orange soda pop bottle just below the spoon, and immediately after the nasty concoction was stripped from the spoon, she would quickly take big gulps of the orange. Hopefully, this would replace the taste with orange before the gag reflex kicked in. I actually started gagging before the spoon was placed in my mouth, and even the taste of orange soda pop had little to do with making it any better from a bad disgusting experience. Cannot ever remember Jim taking it because I was so overcome with a gagging and chocking sensation that time seemed to stand still and memory was erased. Later years, we asked Mom, "Why were we being punished with that vile stuff?" She said that it was very important to take this, so the body could fight off sickness later on. My idea was that I would rather have a bout of the croup or stomachache than be forced to put that nasty stuff in my mouth. We were also given a little blue pill once or twice a year to get rid of pin worms, but that is a completely different flashback that we will not mention maybe forever.

Memorable Moments Flashback
The Day Dad Got Sheep from Wyoming

From an early age, we farm kids were familiar with a variety of animals. On our farm, the main interest was raising cattle, hogs, sheep, chickens, and bird dogs. We always had a few sheep around but not in any great numbers. Early one spring, Dad came home and said that he was going to go into a deal with a guy on his grinder route. He wanted to go out west and bring home a semiload of sheep that was for sale, really reasonable. They took off for Wyoming early one morning with a rented eighteen-wheeler pulling a two-tier hog trailer with destination of Cheyenne, Wyoming. Late in the afternoon three days later, they pulled into the driveway and proceeded to back the trailer toward the barn south of the house. When they lowered the back-end gate, there was a huge rush of leaping sheep that erupted like a flood of wool all heading in the same direction. What I saw was fifty or sixty wooly animals that looked like a rack of bones held together by the thin layer of wool. They ran about fifty yards from the truck and then suddenly noticed that they were standing nearly knee-deep in green grass. They began eating as if their life depended on it. Afterward, we decided that the reason they were so thin was because they had spent their entire lives trying to stay alive grazing on what little vegetation that was available, but the sand had destroyed their teeth down to stubs. It was safe to say that the bunch of sheep had never seen so much green grass beneath their feet in their lifetime. They truly did not raise their heads for the first three days but continued eating the entire time. Within the next three weeks, that herd of thin sheep went from a bag of bones to a herd of healthy well-developed breeding ewes. Year after year, the entire bunch produced dozens of offspring and tons of virgin wool that made Dad many dollars above and beyond his original investment. Until his dying day, Dad would tell you that, without a doubt, he made more clear money with the truckload of sheep than any other livestock on the farm in his lifetime.

Lost Sheep and Newborn Baby Lamb

A very vivid animal memory keeps coming back to me over the years, and that memory is of my real dislike for the wooly animal named "sheep." The dislike of this animal was bad enough but took on a much more hateful meaning during a certain winter down on the farm. Being the middle of three kids and being the firstborn son, it fell upon me to have the distinct responsibility to watch for any mamma ewe (pronounced "you") that seemed to be missing or having trouble during the lambing season. The good part was that Dad seemed to nearly always be around when problems occurred, but just ever so often, things went from bad to worse when he was not available. One such time was the afternoon I got home from school and, after counting the sheep, found that one was missing. Now you have heard of the good shepherd that went out to look for the one missing sheep? Well, I was not one of the good shepherds because I did not want to go looking for any stinking sheep that was missing because about now it was starting to mist a really cold rain. It was one degree off becoming a really cold snow, and after a day of higher education and learning, mostly being hard marble shooting during recess, I was ready to do my chores and head back to the warm and toasty stove in the kitchen. What then made this young man leave the protection of the barn and head across country to find one missing sheep? Was it the desire to make sure the animals were all accounted for, or was it the need to feel pride for being so trustworthy and loyal? It may have been a fear of what Dad would say when he got home and found that one of the sheep was missing. Maybe his middle son had not gone out looking for it but decided the warm kitchen stove was a much more comfortable place to be? Probably had a lot to do with the part of what Dad would say one would imagine. Well, whatever, the farmer's son started out to follow the fence line and hope that the stupid wooly was easy to find and not hidden in some ravine between the barn and the back eighty acres. Sure enough, I found her about as far back from the barn as she could get. To make matters worse, she was having a baby and having all sorts of trouble getting it into the world. Not having a strong desire to get into the mess of things, I sat down on a dead tree trunk and thought just maybe, if I watched long enough, things would work themselves out. It did not take long to figure that this was not going to happen. Rolled up my sleeve and did what I had seen Dad do a dozen times before, ran my arm up alongside the slick little body, found its leg, and straightened it out so Mother Nature could take its course. Sure enough, there it was, on the ground squirming around like it wanted to get up and get up right now. Seemed like a good idea to me as it was starting to get dark, and the weather was taking a turn for the worse and getting more uncomfortable each minute that went by. Grabbed up the lamb and started in the direction of the barn. Took about a dozen steps and noticed the ole ewe was not following me as was to be expected. They always jumped up and came directly toward where their baby was to check it out. Going back a few steps in the dimming light, I could see what the problem was. Of all times, the one I was carrying was about to have a little brother or sister, as a twin was being born at that very moment. Great, now I have two lambs to get back to the barn, and one slick kicking animal is hard enough to hold on to, so that meant that two would be twice as hard to carry. By me not being but about nine years old and being not that large a person to begin with, it would be quite a feat to carry that much even on a good day, let alone on a cold, dreary, misty, rainy, early evening, getting dark day. What else to do but gather them up and head for the barn. Getting the old mamma ewe to follow was not a problem now as she was very interested in what had become of her new family. She figured that I was about to do harm to her newborn, so protect them she must. Just about every fifteen steps I took, she plowed me directly into my behind for the complete trip from woods to the barn. This tallied out to be one heck of a lot of butt-bruising jolts from behind. The only thing that saved me was just before I arrived at the barn, good ole Dad had come looking for me, and believe me, he was just about the finest sight a guy could behold at a time like this. I could have made it to the barn by myself, but you really cannot imagine how relieved it was that the ewe would have two people to knock around instead of one. Arriving at the barn a few minutes later, we placed the lambs in a stall, and mamma sheep took over the duties of caring for her babies. It did give me a bit of pride when Dad said, "Good job, son." It did not take away the feeling of both cheeks being totally numb from the banging I had previously received. I did, however, feel good that I had made the right decision and gone looking for the lost stinking sheep and not gone directly to the warm stove in the friendly farmhouse kitchen. It did not take me long to heed Dad's advice when he said, "Go on to the house and warm up while I finish your chores." Never have the warm glow of a fire and the friendly snapping of burning sap been such a welcome sight and sound as that one time. Speaking of memories, for almost the better part of the next week, I had no lack of memories about the previous encounter with the forehead of a sheep. I especially remembered the trip whenever I sat down on the hard seat of the desk found in the classroom of Santa Fe Elementary School.

Memorable Moments Flashback
Annie, Annie over the House

Many times during the day, brother Jim and I were looking for some type of entertainment that would not tend to get us into trouble but something that would cause time to go by a little more rapidly. One such game we played was Annie, Annie over the house. This was played with a ball being thrown over the house with one or more persons on the other side of the dwelling. Usually, it was more fun when you had a group of kids, but it could be played with only Jim and me. The ball we used was about the size of a softball but was rubber filled with air, and the idea of winning was that you would catch the ball and quietly run around the corner of the house, trying to surprise the kid on the other side. The purpose was to throw the ball at the kid, and if you hit him, you were the winner. If missed, then the thrower had to go back to the other side of the house and throw the ball from that side. The ball we used was my very favorite ball that was given to me for my seventh birthday. It was very unique because it had a smiling face molded on one side and the image of a baseball hat on the other side. Having owned that ball for three or four years, I had taken great care of it and made it a cherished possession. I had to really be careful to keep it out of the front yard when we were playing because it was also highly sought-after by Dad's bird dog pups to play with. One day, it totally disappeared, and after days and days of searching, it could not be found. It never did show up, and when we move from the farm eight years later, I was still trying to think of where it could be. I never gave up wondering what did actually happen to my prized possession.

Christmas Tree Search with Brother Jim's Help

This story is a combination of memories of anger and the smell of cedar. Everyone has at one time or the other noticed the pungent odor of a cedar tree that has been bruised or cut, not to mention the glue effect of the sap that comes from any injury to the trunk or limbs. On our farm, we never were without a Christmas tree, and we never were with anything but a live cedar tree cut and transported to the kitchen and placed in a bucket of rocks and water. It was then decorated with one or two strings of popcorn and tons of aluminum tensile and occasionally a bit of spun glass angel hair for effect. We did not have electricity, so obviously, it was not lighted. If you were raised with cedar in the house at Christmastime, then every time you smelled cedar, it should bring back a flood of pleasant memories. In my case, the smell brought back nothing but the great times of family, of thinking about baby Jesus, of dreams of what we would find under the tree Christmas in the morning, and all the other things that made that time of year so great. All memories were of good times—all memories but for one year I should add. To understand my feeling of anger toward cedar, you must have a brother—even better, a younger brother. In my instance, it became very easy to possess an instant dislike for the little brother, but I could not get even because he was younger, and younger was held in a higher regard because they are little and supposedly protected from all harm. A younger brother was one that you would die for if anyone other than yourself started to cause danger toward but one you often wished you could beat the holy tar out of but knew that he would go straight to Dad to tell all kinds of fibs about you. Even worse, they always seemed to believe him and not me even if his fib was bigger than my own. Him, being my younger brother, was also the younger of three and him never having to do any of the dirty part of the chores, always getting the best of everything or as it did seem. Well, you know what I mean by "favorite child" as it would seem he always got the best part of everything given. It was the first week in December of my tenth year and Jim was four years younger. I decided there was really no need for Dad to take time to go cut a Christmas tree. Jim and I would do just fine by ourselves, so I volunteered to get the tree and set it up in the kitchen for the holiday season. Having been to the back of the farm at least a thousand times, I knew just where we would start looking. So midafternoon, we gathered up our trusty crosscut saw and headed to the back forty. Temperature was about thirty-five degrees, little wind and sunny, just a beautiful day to go searching for just the right Christmas tree. I knew full well that by being trusted to do this by myself, I would have to really make good so as to show how grown-up I had become and how I could be trusted to do things that had previously been done by adults. Little did I know that the future was to hold a lot of instances that would make me wish that I was still a child and had not put myself through the self-imposed anguish of trying to be an adult.

With just a good dusting of snow on the ground, it was a picture-perfect afternoon to be out on our own, communicating with Mother Nature. This would prove to the world that we were men and could do what men did best, bring back a great Christmas tree. After walking for about an hour and locating no less than fifty trees that were all just not good enough to be called "our tree," we finally spotted one that really did seem to be a best tree. It really was the dream tree, tall, shaped just right, could be imagined to be the most beautiful tree we had ever decorated, and could be deemed the most perfect tree ever to sit in our kitchen during the Christmas season. One problem that surfaced almost instantly was the fact that it was about twelve feet tall and had grown in a fencerow among several other smaller uglier trees and was surrounded by briars and thistles.

Surveying the situation, I figured that we would have to make two cuts, one to fell the tree and the other to cut off the part that would be transported to the house. So with great gusto, I began making the first cut. With a trunk that was about four inches thick and green and full of sap, this first cut undertaking quickly turned into more of a chore than originally planned. I called upon Jim to come and help, but he was crawling through the tall grass investigating mouse runs, and his answer to my call for help was "You're not my boss," and with this statement, the first words spoken by the older brother did nothing to help shape the outcome of the task ahead. Finally, after many threats, pleading, and making promises I did not plan keeping, Jim finally came over and pushed on the tree trunk while I was sawing. This really did help as the tree was not binding the saw nearly as bad, and much progress was being made. Progress that stopped the instant Jim said he was tired of holding the tree and was not going to help anymore and that I couldn't make him do it if he didn't want to. In the meantime, a little breeze had kicked up, and unnoticed by me, the sun was getting to a spot that pretty much meant daylight was not long for the asking. With a drop in temperature, good ole younger brother Jim said, "I'm cold, and I'm going to the house, and I'm going right now." I pleaded and threatened as much as I could, but there went Jim over the hill, and to the warm fire he did go, leaving me to do all the work, work of which there was still plenty to do. Kneeling under the tree and using my shoulder to push it over a little bit, sawing with one arm, cedar falling down my neck, sap sticking my hands together, getting colder by the minute, and lo and behold, the tree fell with a thump. It fell, but it fell on the fence and rolled over on the side of the fence away from the house. Minor setback, not to worry, just cut off the part that would be used as a Christmas tree, take it to the house, and everything would be just peachy. Now it's getting dark, breeze is colder, saw won't cut, tree is binding, Jim is warm and toasty beside the kitchen stove. Anger beginning to build, going to get this tree to the house if it kills me, and the way it's going, that just may happen in the near future. As you well know, the madder one gets, the more determined one is to finish the task even if it gets to the point of life-threatening; it will get done with no compromise. Now it's done, cut into two pieces, one piece to leave for rabbit cover and the other to be deemed the best tree we have ever decorated. Assessing the situation, it seemed that there were three steps that must be completed to get this tree to the house. One, I had to get it over the fence. Two, I had to drag or carry it a quarter mile to the house. Three, I had to grab brother Jim and wring his stupid little neck. At this point, these steps wouldn't necessarily have to be carried out in that order. Heaving, pushing, rolling, sweating, cursing, all seemed to be going according to plan, all but the fact that the tree was still on the wrong side of the fence and getting heavier by the minute. With great effort and all the strength that a worn-out ten-year-old could muster, it rolled sideways and ended up on the house side of the fence. Now we were ready for step number two. Grabbed a branch at the end of the trunk, and over the hill and ditches we did go, moving at a fast pace and making lots of headway toward home. Was now almost able to imagine how great the warm kitchen fire and supper was going to be when the tree and I arrived. After pulling for an eternity and stopping for a breather, I made the mistake of looking back from where I started. In the quickly slipping light of day, I saw that we, meaning me and the tree, had gone a mere fifty yards and had an unimaginable amount of distance ahead of us to even see the light of home, let alone getting to supper. Surveying the situation, the mind of a ten-year-old had to come up with a plan that would give me an advantage. Leaving the tree and going on without it was not one of the alternatives. It dawned on me that what I needed was a horse and harness to hook onto the tree and drag it quickly and effortlessly to the back door. Back to reality, we did not have horses anymore as Dad sold them and bought a used International tractor, one that I was not allowed too much more than sit on in the shed, let alone go get and drag a tree home. It suddenly dawned on me that, even if there was no horse, a harness would make it easier. Pulled off my belt, put the buckle end around the trunk, and—holding the strap end over my shoulder—found that this raised the trunk end off the ground and let the tree branches act as runners instead of digging into the earth. This was a huge improvement, made the moving much easier. But with all things better, there is often something going on that makes you keep thinking, "Why did I ever volunteer to do this stupid tree-getting job?" The problem that was occurring had to do with the tiny cedar needles that had died off during the summer but had not fallen to the ground. Now they were breaking off, and nearly every single one of them were going down the back of my shirt to end up directly against sweaty skin that held them in place so that sharp little points were eating into tender areas and getting rawer and rawer. Finally, there in the distance, lights, so bright and beautiful, lights that were shining from the coal oil lamp that Mom had put in the window to guide me home. The light ahead in the dark at long last said that my journey was about over. At long last, this self-inflicted pain was about to end. I really cannot remember much more of that long-fought battle other than Dad was coming after me with a flashlight with two strong arms that would take place of a much-needed horse with harness. The next thing that I really remember was sitting by the stove drying out and being slightly proud of myself for having a plan and some parts of it working. Such pride in being a part of putting the most beautiful tree ever standing in the kitchen window made things that happened almost worthwhile. Almost maybe, but in the back of my mind, a little voice kept whispering, "Don't you ever volunteer to get a tree ever again." What about brother Jim? Well, I'm a much bigger person this day because I've finally forgiven him for abandoning me that cold December day. Well, maybe forgive him really isn't the total truth. I guess you could say that I have somewhat forgiven him but have not forgotten the sight of seeing my helper's hind end going over the hill toward home. I do still remember the major dislike of anything that looks like or smells like the totally disgusting cedar tree. To this day, artificial Christmas trees are forever present in my house during the joyous season.

Christmas Pageant Night before Christmas

As little kids, we sat in church Sunday afternoon, and being just the week before Christmas, it was very difficult to keep focused on what was happening with the musical cantata we were practicing. If you were raised around Santa Fe, it seemed that each and every season followed the exact itinerary as the year before. When the church door opened the night of the presentation, you could expect the entire town and most of the surrounding farm families to be present. We knew every person by name, and the adults knew the entire history of each person in each family. Because the group was so tightly knit for so many years and most were third or fourth generation, it just stood to reason that there were few if any secrets kept from public discussion. There was always a Christmas presentation each year at the Christian church, and it was held the following Sunday after the grade school pageant. When preparing to present the play, Minnie Bell Bridgford was in charge with Mrs. Godby accompanying on the piano. Several parents were present to help corral the fast-moving and difficult little ones that were aged three to five. All of the participating kids were to sit on the front two rows of pews with the older ones toward the back and wait for their turn to practice their particular skit. On the night of the presentation, the place would be standing room only. The little ones came first so that they could be turned over to their parents, so the kids would be their problem to keep corralled. The old favorite Christmas hymns were always sung by the individual groups, and when they had all finished their parts and the little kids had done their thing, it was time for the older group to go behind curtains in the rear of the church. We put on bathrobes and wrapped towels around our heads and took off our shoes so that they would look the part of shepherds and wise men coming to look for baby Jesus. The floor around the latter part of December was anything but toasty, so by the time the congregation sang no less than four songs, the feet began to become slightly frostbit. During the songs, the actors came forward with crooked staffs and stood around the girl and boy that represented Mary and Joseph. I always wanted to be Joseph as that was a character that seemed to be held to a higher degree than the lowly shepherds that left their flock of sheep and stood around with cold feet but never was chosen for that honor. Then entered the wise men carrying great gifts for baby Jesus. They also got to kneel down at the bottom of the steps to the stage and did not have their bare feet in contact with boards that were a few degrees warmer than ice. To make matters worse, Minnie Bell had done a tremendous amount of work by taking a coat hanger apart and made a loop on each end. To this, she attached huge wads of sheep wool that had been dyed black and wound it around the wire. This was the beard for the shepherds and wise men used year after year just for this presentation. It would have been much better had she used wads of cotton from her kids' stuffed bear than the use of raw wool because, after wearing the wool for a few minutes and breathing through the wool, the aroma of a wet sheep would drift from each beard. This smell entered each wearer's nose, and the longer we wore them, the stronger it became. The songs seemed to go on forever, and all we could think about was getting that wad of wool far away from our nose and faces. No one would dare say a thing about how terrible it was to wear the foul-smelling things because everyone dearly loved Minnie Bell, and hurting her feelings was the last thing that any kid would want to be a part of. Needless to say, when the last song was sung by the audience, the first thing to go was the beards, and the second thing to do was get your socks and shoes back on so that your toes could thaw out. As the applause began to die down, there suddenly was heard a loud ringing of sleigh bells in the back of the church. Santa Claus would come waddling down the aisle, picking his way between all the parents that had filled the church. What a thrill to get the beard off and, to make it even better, see the red-and-white-suited bearded man coming toward us with a huge sack over his shoulders. We were instructed to all sit down on the floor, and when it began to quiet down, little packages were taken from a box, and when our names were called, we got up and took the wrapped gift from Santa Claus. After opening the gifts and placing the torn paper in a box, Santa would reach into his bag and bring out a mesh bag that had some of the greatest candy canes and ripple candy along with an apple and an orange that you could ever imagine. Now you must realize that when we were kids, oranges and apples in the middle of the winter were looked upon as a great treasure. These two items were seldom if ever available, and if they were, someone had paid a premium for them. Along that same line of thought, every year at Grandma Burl's Christmas dinner, there was a huge bowl of tangerines, which we thought was a rare treat but only was available at Christmastime. Back to church and after Santa departed with several *ho ho ho*s and disappeared out the back door, the adults were served hot chocolate and homemade fudge and cookies, and the kids started in on their bags of candy. Thus ended another Christmas program that we all knew would be right back here one year from tonight. We then realized that now came the long, long night ahead waiting for Santa to visit each of our homes. After the candy and sugar intake and with the excitement of Christmas morning in our heads, sleep was really hard to come by. After getting home from all the activities at the church, it was usually pretty late at night and way past our bedtimes. Well, actually, it was about nine o'clock in the evening, but for us, that was pretty much after bedtime during the winter months. After we were tucked in bed, we were told not to get up and amble into the kitchen so as not to spoil any surprise Santa left. We slowly drifted off to slumberland with the faint rattle of metal, or a series of tap, tap, taps could be heard late into the night. It was many years later when we had become parents did it really dawn on us why Mom and Dad stayed up several hours into the night. What with instructions that made no sense to anyone other than the manufacturer and parts that did not fit, we knew completely what all that sound was about. As a little kid however, the excitement went on for years, and to this day, I can pretty much remember what gift we received each year. There was always one really special present that we had asked for along with several smaller but greatly appreciated toys that would greet us on Christmas morning. At our house, Christmas was always celebrated Christmas morning and remained such until our kids left home. I truly hope that we have given our children some memories about the Christmas season that they can enjoy the rest of their lives just like Mom and Dad did for us. This was some of the greatest moment of my life and remains totally alive seventy plus years later. Thanks, Mom and Dad.

Dad's Fly Rod and the Kids with the Hornets' Nest

With the hot days of summer hanging heavy each day we were not in school, kids had to find something interesting to do for entertainment. This must not be something that would be harmful nor be something that would cause their parents to be forced to teach a lesson by the rule of the hickory switch. That usually meant going to the river to catch bullfrogs or going to the woods on the north side of the farm to throw rocks at squirrels, but this usually got old pretty fast, so we were forced to look elsewhere. As we were not allowed to go to the Big Pond by ourselves, then the rules laid upon us really narrowed down the field of entertainment choices. Usually, the most exciting things were happening at the big barn or in the grain shed beside the house or the old icehouse, which was way too close to the house to really be any fun. Parents could hear sounds made by Jim or myself that usually meant we were doing something that should be looked into. Therefore, the big barn was the most exciting place to hang out and a place where we could most generally not get into trouble looking for something to do. The ropes hanging from the roof beams could be utilized with a small amount of imagination to become pretend grapevines of which Tarzan would have used if he had been in Missouri. Before the hay was harvested each year, the storage section of the barn was almost empty and had about three feet of loose hay scattered over the floor. With a little moving and stacking of what bales were left over, it made a very open swinging area. By standing on one side of the stacked bales and making three or four steps sideways, a kid could propel himself in a huge arch and either end up on the other side of the room or find himself landing with a thud on the loose hay on the floor. Bad part was when one let loose of the rope and landed on the floor where the loose hay was not very thick, then one would find himself looking up at the roof with various lights blinking before your eyes.

After swinging for an hour or so, Jim mentioned that he needed to find a bathroom as he disappeared around the corner of the barn. A few seconds later, he came running back into the center of the barn going about as fast as a little kid's legs could be made to go. He said that there was a really huge hornets' nest just around the corner and up under the roof of the barn. When he looked up, they made a dive for him. Nothing in the world hurts any more than a hornet sting unless it is two or three hornet stings, so a kid would be wise to leave them alone and look for excitement elsewhere. Well, you can bet that was not going to happen as this was a new challenge to be accepted. Very carefully, we peeked around the corner, and sure enough, there it was, about the size of a basketball and covered black with little insects that at a distance did not look like anything that could be dangerous. By throwing clods at the nest from behind the corner of the barn, it was pretty evident that we were not going to be able to put much harm upon the nest. We began thinking of ways to teach that bunch of hornets a lesson without getting ourselves stung a half-dozen times. There was not a stick available that was anywhere near long enough to reach around the corner to whack them. Suddenly, little Brother Jim said, "What about the fly fishing pole that Dad has in the box under his bed?" That was about as brilliant an idea as Jim had ever come up with. It was really light, about twelve feet long, and would reach the nest with length to spare. About the fly rod, when cousin Donnie was stationed overseas in Japan with the navy, he purchased for each of his uncles and his dad a handmade bamboo fly rod. It came apart in pieces and stored in a long thin wooden case that was built with a really soft velvet lining that held each separate section completely safe from becoming scratched or broken. Dad made it very clear the rule was not to ever take the rod from the box and use it as a fishing pole at the river or Big Pond. Jim and I both knew better than to ever take it fishing, but nothing was said about taking it and very carefully beat the tar out of the hateful and nasty hornets' nest. Jim went into the house through the back door and, finding Mom out in the garden, took the four pieces of the fly rod and quickly headed to the big barn by way of the chicken house then around the pasture and ended up on the south side of the big barn. This pole would make us the perfect tool to wreak havoc upon the totally unsuspecting hornets. Putting the pieces together was a piece of cake, and in a few seconds, there was a trusty twelve-foot-long hornet stick ready for step two of our planned assault. Jim said that it was his place to poke the nest the first time as he was the one that thought of the idea and he was the one that got it out of the house. Being the senior of the two, I quickly convinced him that this was very dangerous and only the oldest should tackle such a dangerous task. With no further discussion, I reached around the corner and whipped the tip of the rod directly into the center of the nest and— after a couple of hardy pokes—dropped the pole and made due haste in the opposite direction of the dull roar that was coming from the disturbed wasp nest. After a few minutes, Jim and I carefully snuck up to the corner, looked around, and found that the hornets were still very disturbed but were all back on the nest, trying to put things back in order. I picked up the end of the pole, peeked around the corner, gave it a couple of profound whacks, dropped the pole, and made a leap that put me in front of Jim and ran to the safety point that we had used previously and watched the black swarm working around the pole. We laughed ourselves silly from all the excitement and relived the past several minutes over and over. As the swarm disappeared around the corner, we could hardly wait to make another attack on the nest. Jim got there first, grabbed the end of the fly rod before I could tell him how dangerous it was to do such action. Raising the rod even with his head, he swung it with all the strength a kid could muster, hit the nest direct in the center, and knocked it to the ground. Before either of us could make a move to run the hornets tuned in on our location and were coming at us with a vengeance, Jim let out a war whoop when a hornet nailed him, forgot to drop the fly rod, turned to get away from the angry hornets, and ran head-on into the barn with the rod tip. Instantly, there was a loud snap, and where originally there were four pieces of rod, there was now transformed into twice as many pieces and much shorter. The hornets, not having a nest to return too, saw two shirtless nest killers making a cloud of dust trying to put distance between themselves and a very angry cloud of insects. We did make it away from most of the flying insects, but several did catch up with us and taught two kids what real pain consists of. Had it not been for the stock water tank we dove into, there is no telling how many stings we would have received as part of our lesson learned about leaving hornets alone and not making a plaything out of them.

Now you are probably going back to the part about the special fly rod that Dad was so proud of. It is all pretty much a blur from the part of waiting for Dad to come home from the mill to the part where he used a torch to destroy the nest and then came back with the several extra pieces of fly rod in hand. To be concise, one of the pieces was about the length of a hickory switch, and as well as I can recollect, the oldest received the first part of the lesson taught. I do remember that the hornet stings did not seem to hurt nearly as much as after Dad spoke to us without saying any words.

Memorable Moments Flashback
Ice Cream by the Tons

Very seldom did we have the pleasure of eating ice cream other than the few times we were on the way home from Saturday in Mexico. There was a dairy on the north side of town that was called Herrers Dairy and Ice Cream Parlor. Three brothers operated the dairy, and just outside the door of the ice cream parlor was at least forty dairy cows that provided the vast majority of the milk for the entire city. When not milking, they all three were inside the parlor, making several different flavors of ice cream and freezing it into two-gallon buckets. These could be seen under a glass counter so that we could pick out which flavor we wanted. My favorite brother of the three was the one that wore a baseball cap tilted on the side of his head and did not have a tooth in his mouth. When you asked him for a single dip cone, he would dig into the bucket and continue digging until there was a ball of ice cream about the size of a softball. One dip was five cents, and two dips were ten cents, but never in all the times we visited did we ever order the two dips. It was doubtful that anyone could get around two dips the way it was piled on top of the cone. This was also the place that Uncle Jody and I stopped when heading out of town to Molino after delivering grain to the bins of Simmons's Stable.

On the other hand, we did have homemade ice cream occasionally but had to buy an extra block of ice. We put it in a gunny sack and broke the huge chunks into small pieces that would fit beside the metal bucket that was inside the wooden freezer bucket. Mom would cook a custard type stuff on the stove that was boiled milk, sugar, and pure cream cooked until it was thick and became an ice cream mixture. Everybody took a turn with turning the handle until the mixture became so thick that the handle would not turn anymore. It was always vanilla, but Mom had chocolate syrup or caramel topping and in-season chopped peaches or strawberries. The pure cow cream was what made the ice cream rich and smooth. This made the ice cream to stick to the roof of your mouth for many minutes after the bowl was finished.

Another treat was when we had the first really big snow of winter. When the drifts were about a foot or more high, we would go outside and get a huge pan and pack it with snow until it held a large ball of frozen water. Inside, we would put a huge dipper of the snow in a big bowl, pour a spoonful of sugar on top of the snow, and then cover it with pure cow cream. Added a small drop of vanilla on top and beat it until it became a yellow white sludge of which we called snow ice cream. As there was not a shortage of snow nor was there a shortage of cream, one could eat as much as he wanted or any time he wanted. They say that you can make the same stuff today but that the environment is so full of pollutants one cannot be sure what the snow contains, so they suggest that you not make snow ice cream anymore.

Smells of the Farm and Trapping the Skunk

I f you were born and raised on a farm, there are certain things that you take for granted. Some things would include seeing and being directly involved with a huge menagerie of animals and fowl. With these, one would expect: one, there will be a variety of smells involved; two, there will be a potential for moments of danger and fear for your well-being. The first expectation, that of smell, can come from a various degree of slight odors to pungent, instantly overwhelming, gut-wrenching, life-consuming stench. It is also expected that the person that receives this may react to the smell with a slight indifference or, as in my case, an instant engagement of the gag reflex. The most prevalent smell around farm animals is that of the distinct odor of manure. This smell was one I found easy to tolerate. That is easy unless it was deposited in large amounts and placed on the body up close and personal. In this case, the reflex kicked in automatically. Many times, we found it necessary in the spring to put cattle in a small enclosure to either treat them for a variety of wounds and/or sores or vaccinate and worm each individual cow. It was a fact and one that should be considered that for the entire winter the herd had been feeding on dry and boring grass hay. It is now spring, and for the past several days, they had been gorging themselves with the tender and abundant fresh grass that was available everywhere. Pretty sure you all have heard of a cow patty or a manure pile or a cow dump. It's a fact that each and every cow kept eating until their stomachs and sides where extended from overfeeding day and night. When jammed together in a small area, each animal is subject to pressure from all sides. Usually, someone is the designated driver, so to make the group go forward, the person must walk behind and occasionally tap the ones in the rear on the top of their tails. Thus, when the driver is about as tall as the back of the subject cows and having to be rather close to make your presence known, one can readily surmise what action takes place. To explain, when the very full cows are confronted with pressure on the stomach from the outside, it will expel a green, very hot, and very wet substance toward the person driving the herd. Being just tall enough to see over the cow's back would put the driver's chest and face directly in line with the fluid ejected. No matter how fast you think you can move when this happens, most will find that by the time you see the matter appear and the time it makes contact is usually a matter of microseconds. With a little imagination, you that are reading this but have never been in this predicament will usually say that this is really not a big deal. For those that have participated in this bringing in the cattle would not be at all surprised as to the ending of this chapter. You of all people should have realized the warmth of the moment and that the degree of coverage usually totals at least 90 percent. No matter how much hot water you use or how much soap you rub on, there will be a smell that is totally unique to country living.

Another odor that was overpowering to me was the day Dad decided today was the day that we would clean out the barn section where the cattle and hogs had been standing all winter. In most instances, we would clean out where they had been standing for more than one winter. The straw and animal droppings were approximately a foot deep the entire length of the barn. Dad started on one end and sank a pitchfork into the thick layer, leaned back on the handle until it broke loose from below. Took a couple of steps toward the barn window and threw the aged poop out and into the manure spreader. Before Dad had disturbed the layer of debris on the floor, there was really not much of a smell inside the barn. That quickly changed when the first forkful went through the window. My fork was not really a pitchfork but was one of the tater-digging forks that was kept in the barn for just such purposes. I swear to this day, any person who was in that barn during the dig and pitch had a set of eyes that literally burned and tears ran down his face. This was the material that Dad threw into the spreader and spread over the vegetable garden each spring before planting took place. If you were chosen to remove this stuff from the barn and then watch it spread over the garden and then get down on your hands and knees to plant the little seeds, you would have to consider this addition to the soil when you gathered the produce and took it into the house to eat. A person needed to sit at the dinner table and only concentrate how good the food looks and smells and dispel from your mind those hours of digging and removing barn manure. A great benefit from the pile of rotten poop outside the barn was the huge earthworms produced around the edges of this pile. When you were looking forward to sitting on the riverbank, seeking the huge catfish, you knew that the big juicy worms grown here would give you a great advantage over the fish, so now the smell did not seem all that bad.

Another odor that brings back memories of those days long ago on the farm is that of a visiting black-and-white animal that resembled a cat but had a really fluffy tail. The tail was used as a signal that, when it was raised straight up from the back of the cat-looking animal, meant that there was shortly to be a really pungent and sickening odor coming your way. The worst I ever encountered was the winter Dad was running a trapline. He would check them morning and evening to make sure they were set for the night. The most sought-after hide was that of the very rare mink as it was sought-after but seldom caught in the trap. The lesser-value coon or possum and occasionally a red fox made it worthwhile as to bring in extra cash. I hopped in the pickup early one morning to ride along and break the monotony of sitting around the house with Jim who became a real pain after about ten minutes. With the traps, who could tell maybe this would be the day that lots of excitement may happen. First couple of traps was untouched, rebaited, and hoped to be more productive on the next run. The third trap was set under a little wooden bridge that spanned a small stream and stood about four feet above the water level. The moment we got out of the truck, it was a definite fact that the trap was not empty. There was also a definite smell that gave us an idea of what type animal was caught in the trap under the little wooden bridge. Dad leaned over the edge and, with a long two-by-four board, tried to open the trap by pressing down on the trigger. Not being able to open the trap from this position, he handed me the board and showed me where to hold it. The moment I reached over the edge of the bridge, I found myself staring face-to-face with a beady-eyed little critter that looked nothing like a cat. To make matters worse, it just happened that there was a slight breeze that was going under the bridge and came up over the edge where I was standing and went directly up my nose. The stench was terrible, and no matter how long I tried to hold my breath, it eventually had to be let out and another breath taken. Dropping the board and getting away from that terrible smell was my next move. That move faded when I saw Dad right beside the trap and did away with any idea of letting the board drop. I knew full well that my well-being would be in question when Dad got back to the truck from under that bridge. In just a few minutes, it was over; the trap was open, and the critter was making a dash to the other side of the county. In the meantime, a smell remained that would be in my clothes and in my nose for the rest of my life. To this day, whenever a skunk is within smelling distance, my throat tightens, and my gag reflex kicks in automatically. I get slightly nauseated every time that smell is close by. You can bet I will never set a trap knowing full well that one of those black-and-white varmints may become really close and personal.

Another smell that is totally synonymous with the farm, especially in the summertime, was that of an animal that had met their demise either by lightning, illness, or accidental. Today we are required to hire a backhoe and bury them at the earliest opportunity. Back then, you called the dead animal wagon. This wagon usually came through the community once a week, and if the call was received just before the scheduled time to be in the area, then everything was usually of very little notice. However, if the animal was deceased just after the wagon made the local circuit and if it was during the hot months of summer, a week was a really long time to have a three-hundred-pound hog or a one-thousand-pound cow or steer lying around. The natural decay process of Mother Nature usually took its normal process, and all those within a half mile or closer from the carcass was reminded of the need for the return of the wagon. Having watched the dead animal wagon and the man operating the winch several times, I have little doubt that this guy has absolutely the worst job in the universe. For a young man with a delicate gag reflex, there would be no amount of money received to make this an occupation.

With the past points in mind, now would be a perfect time to mention that there was and is today a massive number of smells on the farm that are a real delight to the senses. One sweet smell is that of newly mown alfalfa lying like a thick carpet on the ground. Then came the smell of that same hay baled and stacked in the barn to finish curing and making ready for the time when the snow blows and the animals are standing ready to receive the high-protein bundles. Another is the lilacs in the spring, fruit trees in full bloom, Mom's flower garden with dozens of different colors and aromas, the smell of freshly washed clothes hung out to dry, fresh air just after a rain cloud dumped its life-giving water, the smells of the forest and river when you're sitting on the bank at sunup. There also are scads of smells that arrive on the gentle breezes from across the cornstalks or milo field. It must also be said that the aroma of Grandma Burl's frying country cured ham in the morning and making red-eye gravy with biscuits was right up there with the smell of the first mess of fried chicken in the spring coming from the big iron skillet sitting on the stove.

Fresh air is something we have on the farm that we take for granted. If you were not born and raised here, it would amaze the city visitors. We take it for granted that everywhere in the world has a deep blue sky with snow white puffy clouds and star-studded nights that shine extremely bright and seems to go on forever. What little kid never lay on their back in the deep moist grass and looked up at the heavens, wondering just how far is the universe.

Saturday Morning in Mexico

For the first ten years of my life, the Willingham clan met very early Saturday morning on the north side of the courthouse square for the entire summer. If we pulled up to the parking spaces after eight o'clock in the morning, we would be considered late and knew full well that all the other brothers and sisters would be there, wondering where their older brother and his family was. It was as if yesterday that we kids would pile out of the back seat and stand on the sidewalk looking directly at Dad ready to receive the fifty cents, which was our allowance for the coming week. It rather boggled the mind of the many decisions I was facing as to where all this money would take me in the very near future. First decision to be made was where I would eat my noonday meal. Would it be at the Rexall Drug soda fountain and grill or Uncle Johnnie's Night Hawk Café or just spends it all on candy at the Woolworth's five-and-dime store. Most generally, noon would find me at Uncle Johnnie's Night Hawk Café. My order always consisted of a hamburger hot off the grill, chips, Coca-Cola, and a piece of pie. Being kinfolks, he always gave me a discount or threw in the piece of pie, so the bill was thirty-five cents, which left me fifteen cents to jingle around in my pocket. Within the hour, my footsteps would lead me directly to either Mattingly's or Woolworth's five-and-dime store and found myself standing on tiptoes to see over the counter watching the little trays of roasted peanuts going round and round while putting out the greatest smell imaginable. The purchase here was five cents' worth of hot roasted peanuts, which the lady behind the counter would reach in with a metal scoop and put two scoops into a colored wax bag, twist the top, and hand it to me. Without a doubt, there was enough peanuts in that bag for three people my size, but without fail, the bag would be empty by the time I had walked around the courthouse block three or four times.

The next place to visit was usually Montgomery Ward basement located across the street from the courthouse on the south side of the block. When entering the store, you had to walk between aisles of shirts, overalls hanging on hangers, boxes and boxes of shoes that really smelled of leather and glue and then past the dresses and, just before the steps down, the stacks and stacks of women's undies and unmentionables. At the bottom of the stairs began the greatest section of the store, that of hunting, fishing, trapping gear, and softball gloves and bats. And toward the back were gardening tools of any equipment a farmer would need. My favorite area was the fishing counters. It was nothing to stand between the aisles and pick up every box of hooks, try out the many reels that were sitting on their boxes, check out the poles. For about an hour, I would dream of what it would be like to be able to come into this place and buy anything you needed to become a great fisherman. Very seldom could I buy anything because I only had ten cents left in my pocket. If there was anything that cost a dime or less, I already had it in my tackle box sitting in my room at home.

From here, my journey would take me to the toy and candy store on the west side of the square. The place was stocked with rows and rows of bright and shiny toys, but my sight was usually set on the candy counter on the right wall. The task here was to figure out what the next nickel would be spent on. Usually, it narrowed down to either the chocolate-covered peanuts, the red-hot covered apple, the caramel-covered apple on a stick, or just the plain bag of red-hots. No matter which one was purchased, it would be my favorite for this period of this certain Saturday afternoon.

With a grand total of five cents left in my pocket, the urge for something cold and wet would lead me to think about a bottle of root beer sitting in the cooler with ice chunks floating on the water bath. This did present a problem of sorts as the nearest place that this could be found was the pool hall just a half block off Main Street.

The problem was that my parents told me that I was not to go there because of the crowd of rowdy, heavy-smoking, bad-language crowd you always found there. After thinking about the consequences of being caught in this place or thinking about that cold great root beer just inside that door, the idea of the root beer usually won out. After going back and forth past the door several times, it seemed safe to quickly open the door and disappear inside. Immediately upon entering, I made a quick right turn and found myself standing next to two tubs with pop bottles sticking out of the ice-cold water. It was not difficult to find the root beer as it was the only bottle that had a cork in the neck and had a wire over the top to keep the cork in place. Putting a nickel on the counter, I grabbed a bottle, looked around for any signs of danger, and then made a beeline to the back of the hall. I located a seat in the back of the building that would give me a place to quietly enjoy the forbidden drink. All around was thick, heavy smoke and lots of men shooting pool and talking and laughing loudly. Really did not understand what they were talking about but did figure that what they were saying was probably why I was not to be in there in the first place. By the time the bottle was empty, it was pretty much time to get back to the north side of the square and get ready to head for home. By this time, I was flat broke, not the least bit hungry, and had just enough energy left to get home, do my chores, and go with Mom and Dad to Santa Fe and visit with friends from all over the county. Sure did have a full day of shopping and looking, knowing full well that I would be in the exact same location next Saturday and do it all over again.

This picture is on the South side of the square which housed the bank, Kroger's grocery store and Montgomery Wards to name a few. There was also an appliance store and several offices as well as a drug store on the end but was places that I very seldom if ever entered the door because they were pretty boring places. Montgomery Ward did have a basement that was filled with hunting and fishing equipment and aisle after aisle of hand tools for the farm such as rakes, hoes, axes and hammers. Most of my time was spent standing in front of the fishing display and the leather ball gloves. The ground level floor was stacked with clothing with the upstairs at the back of this floor that housed all of the boys and men's clothing.

Next is of the West side of the square and the most important place here was on the end that housed J.C. Penney Company. Like all other stores the main floor was racks and racks of women's dresses and coats, upstairs the men and boys work clothes and downstairs was the really interesting things of outdoor tools and hunting and fishing equipment. In the middle of the block was the toy store that had the really great candy counter and caramel and red hot covered apples.

Pictures taken about the mid 1930's and is exactly what Mexico was like when I was spending Saturdays during the late 40's. This was the East side of the square facing west toward the court house. F.W. Woolworth was on the corner and was what we called a 5 and dime store which housed every kind of household goods, huge assortment toys, ready made clothing and a food and candy counter that held a soda fountain and served sandwiches and had massive amount of bulk candy behind the glass cases. At the end of the counter was a heated peanut roasting display behind a lit glass enclosure that had a lazy Suzan going around with different types of hot roasted nuts available all day long. This store was the first store in Mexico to install air conditioning but the trouble was that the temperature was so cold it nearly made you sick when you walked outside into the summer heat of the day. Above all of the stores were rented apartments that had a stairway entrance between each building which led to the many apartments of which there were dozens.

This little service station sits about 200 yards outside the city limits of
Mexico on the North side. Whenever Uncle Jody and I made a trip into
town with grain or whatever we always stopped at this place on the way
home to enjoy a Grapette and a candy bar. It was not unusual for me
to sit looking out the window with the little awning on the right side
of the building for hours while the men visited and spit tobacco out
the front door. Life was going at a much slower pace back in the day.

Memorable Moments Flashback
School and 4-H Field Trip to Mexico

When the mention of Mexico, Missouri, comes up, the thoughts of a really young kid from Santa Fe recall visits and trips to the big city. At the time, Mexico was not all that huge, but when you come from a country town the size of Santa Fe, then "huge" takes on a totally new meaning. A highlight took place two different times when the elementary school planned a field trip to see firsthand how things were made in a factory. One of the most interesting and one that has remained vivid over half a century was the tour of the Holsum Bakery, which was two blocks south of the main square. There was about thirty students and a dozen drivers making the trip to the city with plans to see at least three factories each trip. When we arrived and got out of the car at the bakery, the entire city block smelled like Mama's kitchen when she was baking fresh bread. I consider freshly baked bread smell as being wonderful and make your mouth water, thinking how great warm bread and melted butter tasted. If you thought it smelled good outdoors, then you can imagine how wonderful it was inside the building. To a country boy, this place was one of the greatest places we had been in this lifetime. In the first room, there were four mixers in a row with four men dumping in flour, buckets of eggs, and whatever else it took to make bread dough. Huge beaters were mixing round and round the flour and other ingredients until there was a huge ball of dough. This was dumped into a wagon-type thing that was then rolled into the next room. Here you could see dozens of bathtubs lined up side by side. The man pushing the wad of dough tipped the wheeled wagon up, and the entire ball of goo hit the bottom of a tub with a splat. On the other side of the room were many more tubs, but they were brimful to the top and nearly running over with dough that had risen from the glob like we just saw in the starting room. A guide told us a story about what we were seeing and made a remark that our mamas always told us not to run in the house while the dough was rising as it would make it fall and ruin the bread. With this said, he stood beside one of the tubs and drove his fist into the top of the mound, and all of a sudden, the entire mass let out a quiver and sank nearly out of sight. He said to remember this tub when we returned and will check to see if the bread dough is ruined or not. The next room, the tubs were dumped into another machine that turned the dough over and over for about three minutes. It was dumped into a large hopper where a stream of dough was pushed out, and a man chopped off a blob, which then fell into a bread pan like Mom used at home. The pan proceeded down the line and entered an oven. When it came out the other end, it was a golden brown. A few minutes later, the pan dropped the loaf of bread on a belt that took it through a machine. When it came out, it was sliced and in a plastic bag with a twist tie that held it shut. Thus was born a loaf of bread; in fact, a lot of loaves of bread, right in front of our eyes. As we exited the oven room, we proceeded back toward the tub that the man had destroyed, but lo and behold, there it was right back up and popping over the top of the tub. I guess that meant that we did not have to stop running through the house when Mom was baking bread.

Another trip was that of going through the Armour Packing Plant outside of Mexico. This actually was a slaughterhouse that had been at this site for as long as I could remember. However, going through the plant and seeing what actually was taking place was for sure an eye-opener. Having been around butchering on the family farm, it was not all that different than what was being done at the packing plant, but the lines and lines of cattle that were being killed and processed were unbelievable. Doubt if I will ever forget the kill line and for sure will remember full well the room where they were making Vienna sausage and hot dogs. Up to that point, those two meat products were two of my favorites when going to the river but could not look at a can of Vienna sausage without remembering the scene before us for years to come.

Our next was a tour of the soybean plant that was on the east side of Mexico but must not have been many negative or positive factors. I can hardly remember anything about that factory other than the smell of soybeans being cooked. This same smell was available to anyone driving into or through the entire town and could smell it almost year-around. That same factory was operating since the early thirties and is still in operation today.

Another plant we visited that day was the Coca-Cola plant that was just across the street from Uncle Johnnie's Night Hawk Café. The building covered nearly a complete block with the entire front open glass, so you could see the people working the lines and lines of soda bottles going single file through the filling process. We saw the room where there were huge stainless-steel vats where water and syrup ran together to make Coca-Cola. From there, hoses took the mixture into another room where the fizzy was put into the liquid, and then it went through hoses into another room where bottle after bottle went around in circles until they were filled. A cap was shoved down on the top. Full bottles were place in a wooden case that held twenty-four bottles and then proceeded down a running belt to where the trucks were loaded and disappeared down a ramp to be delivered. Another room had several men standing about head high on a platform that was next to what looked like water spraying all through the glass case. When a bottle came through upside down, they were scrubbed with a spray of soapy water then rinsed with a spray of clear water. The guide told us that this was the place where all germs were soaked and destroyed so no one would get sick from drinking from a bottle that others had touched with their mouth. At the end, we all had a bottle of Coca-Cola for refreshment. While we were drinking, the guide told us when we finished the drink to turn over the bottle and check the bottom. Molded into the glass was a city and state that told us where the bottle was first filled. From that point on, I found myself always turning over the bottle and reading how far away the bottle had come.

Our next stop was a tour of the radio station KXEO. It did not seem all that interesting with people sitting around behind their desk and one guy doing all the talking while sitting in a very small room with switches and plugs and cables surrounding him. It did help a little to explain what and where my country music came from while sitting on a tractor at the Kendrick Brothers' Farm many years later. This station is also operational today and has been for at least sixty years.

The last visit was at the newspaper office of the *Mexico Ledger*, which was a daily paper of which my parents subscribed to for at least sixty years. Most amazing thing that I remembered was the size of the press and the huge paper rolls that fed the machine. The speed of the papers being printed and folded was almost faster than the eye could recognize. I can also remember seeing Aunt Martha's father sitting at a huge machine that melted lead and then poured the lead over letters and numbers he had typed. They said the machine was called a linotype machine. He said hi to me and called me by name as we walked by because he knew me well from being at his house many times in the past. It made me feel pretty special to have someone call me by name in front of all the other kids and parents.

Blackberry Picking with Mom and Helen Sharp

I n the early months of summer, tradition had it that the women and kids of several families in the community left the house early in the morning with several buckets. They either walked or drove to one of the many known locations where the wild blackberry patches were located. In our case, it was usually in the presence of our next-door neighbor, Helen Sharp, and at the time her two girls. Caroline was about three years younger than me, and her little sister was about three years younger still. So someone had to be responsible for staying back at the car and watching the little girl and brother Jim, and that person was me. Actually, I very much hated to pick blackberries and very much dreaded when the berry bushes became loaded with red fruit that would in the very near future be turning into ripe shiny black fruit of the vine. Usually, the patches would cover an area of about a half acre, be located in the center of a wooded area, have grass around the entire patch about knee-length, and early in the morning would be covered with morning dew to where the water actually dripped off the blades and soaked the ground. Along with this heavy layer of grass came an infestation of ticks and chiggers that would lie in wait for weeks on end until some blackberry-picking person came along and rubbed against the plant and immediately picked up one or a dozen bloodsucking insects. The procedure at the time was to wear heavy pants and boots, tuck the britches into the boots, and tie a piece of twine tightly around the top of the boots to try to prevent an easy access from the grass to the tender skin of the picker.

Another problem that was present when picking blackberries was the ever-present plant standing about six feet tall and draped downward because of the heavy load of berries on each branch. Mother Nature was very wise to protect her seed-loaded berries from becoming jelly and preserves by putting very sharp and curved thorns about every two inches apart on the entire shoot. It was totally impossible to reach for the berry without coming into contact with virtually thousands of needle-sharp briars that seemed to reach out and hook your skin from several different angles at the same time. To prevent this, a person wore a pair of leather gloves on each hand and a long-sleeved denim jacket covering the entire arm. Because of this protective covering from head to foot, it was extremely important that you get to the patch very early in the morning so as to have your buckets filled before the sun rose over the top of the trees. If not, then it was known for the temperature to go from sixty-five degrees to eighty-five degrees in a matter of minutes. Deep inside the woods, no air would be moving, so the blackberry pickers heated up to an uncomfortable level in a matter of minutes. With all this in mind, you can easily see why I was willing to do anything to prevent having to be standing next to the briar bush if at all possible. That is why I volunteered to stay by the car and entertain the little kids for as long as it took for Mom and Helen to return with full buckets. It was during one of these warm and wet mornings I noticed that Susan Sharp was really turning red and seemed to be coughing a lot for a little kid but thought nothing of it. When the pickers returned, Helen said something about her little girl was really red and splotchy and seemed to have a bit of a fever. The next day, it was pretty evident that the little girl was more than little splotchy; in fact, she had a full-blown case of measles, which we all caught in the very near future. Really did wish that I had been picking blackberries this one time instead of being around to catch a case of the dreaded measles. No matter how bad the berry picking was, it was nearly always worthwhile. It helped remove the memories of hating to pick the berries the moment Mom took a blackberry cobbler out of the oven or removed the top of a pint jar of blackberry preserves on a cold winter day later that year.

Dangerous Farm Animals and Race with Bull

We were taught from day one to look ahead for animals and any other moment or movement that could prove dangerous on the farm. It could be said that there were many times when nothing of any consequences was within sight when all of a sudden there would loom before you a sudden change of your surroundings that could and many times did spell catastrophe. When working with animals that you have been around since they were born, a false sense of security often takes the place of safety. On the whole, nearly 100 percent of the hand-raised cows, hogs, and sheep were totally docile; and very few of them ever caused any concern for one's safety. Notice I said almost? It was the 1 or 2 percent that made up the almost-total percentage that you had to watch out for. This was especially true with the hogs and sometimes true with the cattle. It was an understanding that any animal with a newborn was not to be trusted nor let out of your sight. In the case of having to move the new arrival because of location or any other problem, you kept one eye on the baby and the other eye on the mother. This was proven to be a fact one afternoon when we came back from Sunday dinner at Grandpa Burl's and found a sow making bed in the middle of the hog lot. There was a stand-by-itself movable shed right beside where she was making the bed. Would not have been any worry; however, it was beginning to look like there was an inevitable thunderstorm approaching from the west. It seemed a good idea to move the shed over the sow so that, when the babies arrived, they would not be subject to drowning if a toad strangler hit as she was giving birth. I drove the tractor with Dad standing on the back drawbar. Drove up to the end of the shed where the chain could be attached. Dad stepped down to hook the chain to the drawbar, and I was to pull it straight ahead until it covered the newly made bed. As Dad stepped back away from the chain, he saw out of the corner of his eye a movement. That movement was the sow coming around the corner of the shed about two steps from where Dad was standing. She hit him with her mouth open and clamped down on his upper leg and threw her head up, and Dad did a complete summersault in the air, landed on his knees, and was digging with both hands and feet to get away from the next attack that was sure to come. The sow made a leap toward him but missed completely, turned, and rushed into the shed without a look back. After taking inventory of what damage had been done from the hog's teeth, Dad found that the only damage was torn overalls and some bite marks that had not broken the skin. His only statement was "Never would have guessed that ole girl would have done that. She is one of the most even-tempered sows on the place." I took it he was saying most of the words for me to learn a valuable lesson about just what dangers can arise from even the gentlest animal on the farm. An incident that occurred just down the road from our farm happened when our neighbor had turned the male boar hog in with the sows for fall breeding. He was riding his horse through the pasture where the hogs were located when, out of nowhere, the boar hog came at a dead run. He hit the horse in the gut with the tusk on the left side of his jaw and ripped a gash almost halfway up the horse's side. So much damage was done that the horse had to be put down as there was no way the damage could be repaired. From that time on, whenever a boar hog was present, Jim and I had direct orders to never go into the lot where the hogs were kept no matter what the need for climbing the fence. After the sow hit Dad, I did not have to be reminded of the danger of being around hogs.

Another sure danger is that of a mean bull or a bull that has the trait of aggression but had not really carried out any assault. We always had an Angus bull with the cows during the spring and fall season for calves to be born the following fall and spring. As a rule, Angus bulls were pretty docile and did not possess the trait of making a move to hurt any individual that happened to be in the pasture at any given time. Fact is we never had a problem with any bull over all those years, but it was drilled into us over and over that you never take your eye off a bull no matter who it belonged to or where it was pastured. Another rule was that you never pat a bull on the head. Several times, we owned a bull that was very tame and easy to care for and really enjoyed having his back scratched with a corncob. This was deemed permissible, but the rule always applied: do not rub the bull on the head. Really did not know why this was to be, but Dad knew why, so this always was that rule. Another rule in place and for good reason was to never get in the pen or pasture with a Jersey bull. They were the worst, meanest, and were forever seeking ways to hurt anyone not paying attention to their presence. It just so happened Henry Heckert, our neighbor to the west, owned the land directly between us and the best fishing holes on Salt River. Our place ended at the river, but it seemed that this hole of water did not have the potential for great fishing, at least not as good as what skirted Henry's place. Henry had a small dairy operation, which consisted of about a dozen Jersey cows and, as you would guess, a really large Jersey bull. That sucker made it a fact of life that if you walked along the fence line beside the pasture he was kept in, he would come to the fence and look you in the eye and paw the ground while making some really low-tone sounds that sounded a lot like a locomotive with too much steam built up. I always imagined that in bull talk, he was saying, "Come on little, boy, crawl over this fence, and I will roll you up into a little ball and stomp you flatter than a week-old roadkill." One summer when I was old enough to go to the river by myself and having fished our holes of water and caught only rather-small and nonbragging fish, I walked down the riverbank to Henry's part of the river. Sure enough, each time down, I caught some really big catfish and carp. This happened nearly every time I made that long walk down our side and then the longer walk along the river to the best fishing holes. After about six trips back and forth, it seemed that there was no real need to go all that way around when the shortest distance between two spots is a direct line. One morning with pole in hand along with stringer and can of worms in the other, I stood on our side of the Jersey bull fence and looked long and hard in each direction. There was not a cow or bull in sight, so I surmised that they were in the barn for the day, and it was located a long way from where I was standing. Those cows and the terribly big and mean bull probably would not be back in the area for hours or maybe even days. Putting the rod and reel and all the fishing gear under the fence, I climbed over the five-strand barbed wire and landed on the other side. Gathered up my equipment and surveyed the vast bare pasture and surroundings carefully. All seemed at peace, and knowing that the big catfish were waiting for me, I started across the pasture with quick long strides. At least as long a stride as a kid standing four feet tall could make. About halfway across the pasture, I started to feel much more at ease thinking that all that time before I had wasted steps going the long route when everyone knows the closest distance between two spots is a direct line. Being a lot less nervous about the situation, my mind drifted toward the river and was trying to decide which hole of water would be the most productive and was laying out my plan of assault on that big set of whiskers waiting at the end of the pasture. Suddenly, there was a feeling and a sound that bought me back to reality in the blink of an eye. The sound that I heard was not a low-tone sound that I had heard so many times before when on the other side of the fence. The sound that I heard now was a rumbling loud high-pitched roar that echoed through my entire body like a clap of thunder. No need to turn and look to see where that roar came from, and needing to know how close it came from was a waste of time. The ground was actually vibrating from the rapidly approaching mountain of beef. They often say that in moments of danger, your life goes by before your eyes. This I can attest to because my entire eight years did not take long to complete in a flash. Dropping the pole and all other equipment, I started looking for the fence on the other side of the pasture. It wasn't even in sight, and the sounds coming from behind me were definitely getting closer and closer with each step. There in front of me arose a small oasis of trees that had been left there by the owner to provide shade for the cows.

As I arrived at the first tree, it took about two seconds out of life to shinny up like a squirrel. Halfway up the tree were several very sturdy branches of which I chose one to become my perch. I was just out of reach of what I saw as one of the largest heads of any bull that I had ever seen up that close. As I hung onto the trunk with a bear hug effect, the bull was uttering those same low rumbles of a killer sound and began pushing on the tree trunk as if to bulldoze its roots out of the ground. Luckily for me, I had chosen one of the sturdier trees as it only shook with his head-butting efforts. From this point, I cannot tell you how long I hung on and how long that bull stood beneath the tree and pawed dirt while making those killer bull sounds. You can almost bet that if that tree is still standing today, there will be several fingerprints embedded into the limbs just above the bull's head. Little doubt was the fact that, if it had not been for the presence of that tree, this story would have been a lot shorter. Once again, while holding on for my life, the words of Dad came back with much more meaning: "Don't take your eyes off a bull." My dad had sure become a much smarter person than he was before I crawled over that barbed wire fence. Cannot tell you how long I was sitting on that limb, but it actually was a very long time before the bull became bored with this game and disappeared over the hill to check on his girlfriends. I'm sure he left with a total satisfaction of knowing that he had taught this little kid a very valuable lesson. Retracing my steps back to where I dropped my pole and stinger of what seemed ages ago, I picked up the equipment and quickly got back over the fence on my side of safety. Fishing really was not all that important at this second but knew now why it was a good idea to make the long trip around the bull pen even if the shortcut was more exciting.

Dumb Move: Climbing the Bluff

As a person grows older, one often wonders why certain aspects of his life have become prevalent and why the abnormalities exist. It is a proven fact that many things that have happened within our life span have a strong meaning as to why we think and behave the way we do. I feel that what was presented to us by our parents' teachings and our parents' lifestyle will manifest itself in us throughout our entire life. There is no doubt in my mind that nearly all the moments of discomfort today were established well before we reach our fifteenth birthday. One such feeling of uneasiness can be noted each time I find myself high off the ground, which presents a feeling of terror and fast heart palpitations. Most people call this a fear of heights, which I would agree wholeheartedly that it is a true fear whenever the surface below me is over four feet away. Thinking back, there are two moments of what I would construe as being scared literally stiff.

One was when the 4-H club was attending a wiener roast on the river behind Herb Moore's house. After scarfing down at least three hot dogs and an uncounted number of toasted marshmallows, we found ourselves sitting around on logs, making small talk and becoming bored with every second that passed.

This was when one of the older boys—I am pretty sure it was Dale Bridgford—stood up and said, "Bet you I can climb that bluff and be on the other side in less than ten minutes." Suddenly, there was a chorus of voices agreeing with him and betting that they could climb it quicker. Having never even paid a moment's notice of what the bluff looked like made the mistake of turning around and looking up the side of the smooth sheer rock surface and saw a mountain going straight up into the sky. I can remember watching Dale, Darryl and Doogie Roberts, Earl Miller, and Bruce Berthold, who were mostly in their middle teen years while I was much younger, stand up and head toward the base of the cliff. As I stood staring toward the bluff, they started climbing straight up by holding on to rock outcrops and small tree sprouts that were growing in between cracks in the rocks. Suddenly, I realized that Bob Moore and J. C. Kessler were at the bottom and beginning the climb slightly behind the older guys. To make matters worse, they were a year younger than me. Looking skyward to the top of the ridge, I heard myself say something to the effect they could climb all they wanted and that I was not about to get myself on the side of that mountain. Suddenly, I heard my name being called from somewhere on the side of the bluff and heard the words "sissy" and "chicken" directed toward me. At that moment, all eyes turned toward me, and I realized that all the eyes were located on the face of girls, some of which I thought were the prettiest persons on the face of the earth. For certain, I was the only male person standing at the bottom of the bluff, and all those others were looking at me with eyes that tended to burn into my very soul. There was no way I would be classified as a scaredy-cat nor a sissy, so with a large show of courage, I made a wild run to the bottom of the mountain and began to climb straight up. I had to catch up with Bob and J. C. and most certainly, I had to beat them to the top so as to maintain my status as not being the youngest male on the bluff nor be called sissy ever again. The first few feet up were not all that hard to achieve, and the fact that all those others had gone on before me made the task less frightening. With most of them almost to the summit, it did not seem as difficult or fearful as I had imagined it while looking from the ground up. Using the fact that others had safely made it almost to the top made it seem that there was not all that much to fear in the first place. I found that being the last to start up the mountain presented some hazards that those ahead of me had not encountered. One was the fact that the rocks and dirt holding the little trees in place were now pulled loose, which made for a particularly weak handhold or foothold with which to pull oneself upward. This dirt and rocks also were raining down on my head from all the feet and hands above me in a steady downpour of debris. Once I got past Bob and J. C., it did seem that there was less falling on my head as the older boys going over the top of the ridge helped the situation a lot. It dawned on me that this was really not all that difficult and that we had made lots of progress toward the top in the few minutes that we were hanging onto the side of the bluff. Just maybe I would be over the top and into the safety of the level ground just beyond the edge in a few more seconds. I could hear the two behind me and wondered just how far they were and what would be the chance that they may catch up with me. The next move I made was the worst decision of my life. I looked over my shoulder to see where they were located. I did not see them as they were directly below me, but what I did see was a scene that made my heart stop, my butt to pucker, and had the worst rush of total terror my body had felt since the Jersey bull came over the hill and was trying to kill me. I shut my eyes and tried to blank out the memory of just how far up that mountain I had made it before the mistake of looking down occurred. I did remember that, way below me, the people that usually stood a head and shoulder above me now looked like little ants or really small dots on the ground below. To this day, I can remember not seeing anything between me and the ground a mile below other than a massive amount of air and space. I came back to reality instantly when Bob Moore hit me on the foot and yelled something about get out of the way. Now was when I notice just how loose the little trees and sprouts had become from so many feet and hands having gone before me. Nothing about that last eleven or twelve feet of climbing holds even the vaguest memory of the feat accomplished. I do remember crawling on hands and knees away from that bluff until my body was a minimum of forty feet of level ground behind me. My legs and arms were so weak from the tension and fear that I could hardly rise from my kneeling position to an upright position. My legs felt like rubber bands that had lost their stretch. The memory of the scene below me as I looked down on the side of that bluff is forever burned, or branded if you wish, into the innermost section of my brain. All it takes is to shut my eyes seventy some years later and see vividly what the lack of solid matter in space looks like. You can be certain that I was proud of myself for having conquered the raw brutal surface of that bluff but that I will never again put myself into a like moment of danger. They can call me sissy or whatever else can portray me, but I will not ever allow myself to be that far off solid level earth. You may surmise that this episode may have lots to do with me not being comfortable away from the contact of solid ground.

Second Dumb Move:
Retrieving the Arrow

Another incident may well have added to this so-called fear of heights. For sure, it did not take away any of the discomfort of being in the air several feet off the ground. It all began when I received a super set of archery equipment for Christmas one year. It came with three target arrows and an arm guard, everything needed to become an accomplished archery person. I practiced hours in the shed by putting an ear of corn in the crack between two bales of hay and, standing thirty or forty feet away, practiced the stance and release like listed in the direction manual. Having become fairly proficient with target practice, it came time to hunt the elusive rabbit. After hunting for and seeing several rabbits up close and personal, it was evident that this was not going to be an easy task to successfully provide meat for the table. After each shot, it was immediately evident that when you missed, the arrow would continue on and invariably go under the layer of grass that covered the entire farm. The three arrows were lost in a very short time, and no matter how much one would search, seldom did the arrows reappear. I now had a bow and a quiver that I made out of a rolled-up newspaper with binder twine but was missing a very important item—namely arrows—to complete my hunting equipment. It cost forty-nine cents to replace one of the arrows, so saving up egg money and allowance to buy three of them would take a great deal of time. As you can imagine, the arrows purchased with my own money was much more drastic than the ones that came free from Santa Claus. Several weeks later,

I purchased three arrows and spent many entertaining hours practicing archery. The problem all began with the thought of just how high one of these arrows goes if you shoot it straight up into the air. As it happens, they really go high when you pull the bow all the way back and release it straight up. It actually almost goes out of sight. I quickly found that the old adage of what goes up must come down and found that, when it appears, anyone directly under it must move quickly to keep from being arrow struck. Trying again, I learned not to pull it all the way back, and with this shot, the arrow only went a short distance up, but when it came down, it hit and stuck in the top of the huge oak tree in the front yard. From the ground, I could see it about fifty feet up and was lying in full sight among the limbs but was a long way up from where I was standing. So as not to have lost another new arrow in such a short time, the task of getting it back was very important. The tree was an ancient piece of wood and was about four feet in circumference, and the first limbs were way off the ground. So far in fact that there was not a ladder on the farm that would reach the first handhold. Made a trip to the toolshed to find a way to get to the first limbs and found on the workbench a box of sixteen penny nails that Dad had been using to build a lean-to for the hog pen. Grabbed a handful and a hammer and went to work driving a nail about two feet off the ground and another nail farther up the trunk until I had a stepping nail up the entire tree. Started climbing and found that my weight made them bend, so I started at the first nail and drove in a second one beside the first, and sure enough, it bent slightly but did hold me up. Scaled the side of that huge tree in a matter of seconds, swung over the first big limb, and proceeded upward to retrieve my lost arrow. Got nearly to the top when it suddenly dawned on me that the limbs I was perched on were now getting very slender and was bending toward the ground from my weight. Did not take long to realize that I could not go farther up, and when looking down, I did not want to go farther down. Suddenly, I realized I do not want to be here any longer. That arrow is not as important as it was half an hour ago. With a death grip on the limbs before me, I looked down and saw brother Jim playing in the sandbox a long distance below me. Let out a meager yell that came out more like a squeak for him to go get Mom and bring her to get me down. Jim said that he was playing in the sand and did not want to go get Mom, and I couldn't make him. That was for sure the truth; I could not even scream at him from the position I was in, let alone make threats that could not be carried out. After several minutes, he did crawl out of the sandbox, went to the well to wash off his arms and legs of the sand, took many minutes to dry off, and then stuck his head in the door telling Mom, "Kennie is way up in the tree and can't get down." Mom appeared instantly while drying her hands on her apron, made a dash to beneath the tree, and saw in a blink that her oldest son was certainly way up in the tree and certainly could not get down. What she said next was what I figured out later was not nearly the words that she was thinking. After being a parent, it is easy to see how a son can get into these predicaments but just not that easy to get out. She said something to the effect of me needing to crawl back down very slowly the way I crawled up. To my way of thinking, it was really much more serious coming down than it was going up. She said that she would catch me if I fell, so just be careful and come down slowly. Finally, after many minutes of creeping downward, I arrived at the huge limb that was just above the first set of nails. It dawned on me that swinging up off the nails was much simpler than swinging back down to the first set of nails. This appeared to be a great deal more difficult. Was now about twenty feet off the ground, so I felt fairly certain that Mom would catch me if I fell. By gripping the limb with both arms and swinging down, I felt the first set of nails touch the bottom of my shoes. Reached down and grabbed the nails and stepped to the next set, and in a few seconds, I was back on solid ground. Would guess that the time elapse from the bottom limb to solid earth as being approximately four seconds. Once again, I had experienced the thrill of being suspended in space and still did not have a broken bone or cracked skull to show for it. Mom must have been a little relieved as she hugged me and said something about do not ever get into a tree that high again. Being that far off, the ground definitely be a problem from this time forward as now my fear and appreciation of heights was a 100 percent fixation. About the arrow, I stood looking at it from the ground, thought of shooting it out with my BB gun, went inside and got the gun, and shot at it and hit it on the third BB. Arrow slid out of the top of the tree and stuck in the ground about three feet from where my dangerous mission began slightly less than two hours before. Did have a little dent in the shaft from the hit of the BB but was about as good as new. Not sure my nerves will ever be good as new but certainly a far wiser kid.

Jim and Kennie: The Cowboys

This is another story starring Kennie the cowboy and Jimmie the wrangler. This started midmorning during early spring when the weather was making the turn into warmer air and dryer dirt. Dad was plowing the field behind the Big Pond, and Jim and I were going through the granary, looking for something of interest that may turn into entertainment. Sure enough, we found hanging on a peg a dandy lariat, just what we needed to while away a couple of hours. We both had previously become acquainted with the lariat and had both gotten fairly proficient using it to lasso a fence post or at times had lassoed each other. We figured it was time to move up the ladder and begin roping live critters, so the first victims were the bird dog pups that was lying asleep under the locust trees in the yard. Didn't take long to tire of this as about all they did was sit there and wag their tail, so they were not much of a challenge. Jim came up with a great idea: why not go to the corral where Dad was feeding steers and do some real roping and calf tying like we saw at the county fair each year. Over the fence we went. I stationed myself in the center of the pen and told Jim that his job was to make them run past me as they circled the pen. Now this was about as close to real cowboy work as we had ever been.

Having ten or twelve head of feeder calves with some of them weighing around two hundred pounds and the biggest about eight hundred pounds, the actual calf roping began. After several throws with the calves running around with Jim right behind them, it appeared that lassoing was not as simple as it seemed when the cowboys did it on horseback. Just as I was catching on how to keep the lariat circle open and how to twirl it above my head and release it at just the right time, there came a voice above the pounding hooves that caught our attention almost immediately. It sounded a whole lot like Dad, and for sure, it sounded like he was not particularly happy with our roping session being conducted at the present time. He said that we were to stop running them and stop right now. He said that the reason the calves are in the pen were to be fed heavy grain, so they could gain weight rapidly and be ready to ship to the slaughterhouse in St. Louis. We were not to run them as this would wear off the weight gain and take longer for them to be ready to ship. His tone and words left no doubt in our minds that what we were doing was to come to a rapid halt, and right now was the right time. That pretty well put us back to where we originally were when starting to look for entertainment and back to throwing the lasso over the fence post. This really did not have much appeal after the rodeo had ended. As it was time to head into the house for a bite of lunch, we knew that when we returned about the most exciting thing we had to look forward to was watching the grass grow. Thirty minutes later, we heard the tractor start, and the sound disappeared over the hills until quiet and boring was happening everywhere on the farm. Jim said out loud what I had been thinking, "Who would know if we ran the steers just a little bit as there was no one around to notice and Dad would not return from the back field for at least several hours? What little harm could come from using the steers a few minutes? Besides, we needed the practice on a real critter if we were going to learn how to lasso properly. Once again, I was in the center, and here Jim came running behind the steers whacking them on the tail with a long stick. Coiled the lasso, whirled it, and let go. And would you believe it caught a little calf the first time around? Turned it loose and prepared for the next run, and once again, the loop was perfect, and the calf was under my control. After doing this about three or four times, we were pretty much convinced that there was not a critter in the world that we could not lasso if we so desired. Kind of figured we should not push our luck too far, so I told Jim how about we do just one more so the calves could calm down and get things back to normal long before Dad finished for the day. Here they came again with Jim right on their rear, whirled the lariat, threw it with a perfect arch, and just as before went perfectly over the head of a running steer. Big problem, and I mean big problem, the lariat missed the little calf that was my intended target but did not miss the eight-hundred-pound steer that was running just to the rear of the chosen little one. Noose tightened around the huge neck of the not-chosen mountain of beef. When the rope snapped tight, it took me off my feet and drug me face-first through dirt, dust, and the many huge piles of steer patties. As the smaller ones were no problem to hang onto and as they were no problem to pull in and take off the noose, it was very evident that this practice of calf roping was now taking a turn for the worse. We were about to find out what real cowboys have to go through when catching the running doggie. Every time I got hold of the rope and tried to get near the huge steer, it immediately took off around the corral with me either making leaps and bounds on my feet or getting the feel of what true grit actually felt like. After about fifteen minutes of getting nowhere near releasing the steer, I turned to Jim and said, "Guess you better go get Dad to help get this rope off this steer." Brother Jim did not take but two seconds to think about it and said, "No way I'm going to go get Dad. You caught the wrong calf, and you can go get Dad." Once again, all I saw was the rear end of Jim going over the corral fence and disappearing around the corner of the barn in the blink of an eye. Now there was only one lonely cowpoke standing in the middle of the corral, and to say that the feeling of impending doom was heavy all around would be an understatement. For the next several minutes, I stood trying to think of any way that I could get out of this predicament without going all the way to the back field and facing what could well be the end of my life as I knew it now. Oh well, better man up and get it over with 'cause that rope was not going to remove itself without help. I knew full well that I was not capable of ending this situation and getting the lariat back on the peg in the granary. I have never taken such a long and slow walk through the pasture as I did that afternoon. Even by walking slow and going the long way around, I still ended up at the end of the furrow with Dad stopping the tractor and asking what was the problem. I very quietly asked him if he could come to the house and help me take the rope off one of the steers. I wanted to add that Jim had a lot to do with the rope being where it was but thought better of it as being caught in a fib would not be of much value at this moment. No further words were spoken as we rode the tractor over the hill and stopped by the corral. Dad entered through the gate, reached down, took hold of the rope, snubbed it around a post, and drew the steer in.

Took off the lariat, coiled it up, looked me straight in the eye, and handed me the rope. He turned and went through the gate of the corral, got on the tractor, and disappeared over the hill. As I stood there with lariat in hand, the only thing that came to my mind was "What just happened?" The second thing that went through my mind was, from this moment on, the only roping I will be doing will be over a fence post. I for one will never go through what I just went through by roping a post. It was never mentioned again, and I never roped anything live again, not even one of the lazy bird dog pups, just in case I would have trouble getting the rope off their neck.

Memorable Moments Flashback
Dinner at Aunt Hattie's House

Back in the good ole days, mainly the late forties and the early fifties, very seldom did a family not eat dinner at home, and each meal was served in the kitchen with the entire family sitting at the table. Immediately after, the prayer was given that consisted of a two- or three-liner memorized by each child from the time they were old enough to speak well enough to be understood. The bowls were passed around the table, and each person took as much as they wanted of what was presented. An unstated rule was if you took it, you ate it all. If it were to be served today, the type of food available would be classified as totally organic, consisted of fried meat, always a serving of potatoes, and with it at least one and usually two fresh or canned vegetable. Adults had a choice of tea or water, but all children up to age fifteen were required to drink a glass of milk. The rule was that if there was Kool-Aid or tea, then the young part of the clan could have a small glass after the milk was drunk. This caused many a kid to chugalug a glass of milk immediately upon sitting down and then hold up their glass for the much sought-after adult drink. Mealtime was usually a pleasant time of day, and everyone was too busy enjoying the great-tasting foods to say much until the bowls were empty. This was not always the same at other households, and I will never forget what I saw at the dinner table of my aunt Hattie and uncle Billie's house when we were invited to stay over for supper one evening. To explain the difference of our family and theirs was the fact that Aunt Hattie had fourteen kids. Their ages ranged from five months to seventeen years or somewhere close to that and all living under the same roof. In the kitchen, there were two stoves, three tables sitting end to end with benches on each side, and while Aunt Hattie was preparing the meal, the older girls would set plates, drinking glasses, and a ton of silverware that covered sixteen place sittings. That particular day, they had fried chicken, green beans, mashed potatoes, and a kettle of gravy. She put two platters heaped up with pieces of fried chicken, a kettle of potatoes, three pans of green beans, and at least three loaves of bread. All was reasonably quiet until Aunt Hattie beat a wooden spoon on the bottom of an old pan. At that moment, there was a rush and a noise that would have awakened the dead if they had been buried anywhere in the near vicinity. Within three minutes, the plates were filled, emptied, and taken to the double sink in the washroom where certain assigned kids did the washing and drying and putting them back on the table all stacked up ready for the next meal. I really cannot remember getting anything to eat but can recall the event with complete certainty as to how what seemed like a ton of food disappeared in less than four minutes.

Memorable Moments Flashback
Uncle Billie and the First Pizza Parlor

Uncle Billie was a construction engineer and built some of the more elaborate business buildings in Mexico. After an accident on the job and after a long period of convalescing, he tried to return to the job but found that he could not follow that occupation any longer. He was without work for some time and was looking for a new line of work when his son-in-law, Frank Bellow, came up with an idea that they should open a pizza house. Frank was a full-blooded Italian and looked the part with dark completion and black wavy hair. When first encountering Frank, I was in awe of his wit and humor as well as the fact that he looked and acted like a vaudeville comedian. He had the kids in stitches when he was around with his actions and witty talk. He also owned a pink Cadillac convertible that was about a city block long and had it decorated with lots of chrome and little statues of every kind. There also was a horn when he pushed the button that sounded like a train coming down the street, which made everyone within a block look up to see where a train would be in the middle of town. The time was about the midfifties, and anything new was questionable, so when they said that they were going to open a pizza house in the old hotel restaurant and kitchen, everyone said that they were crazy to even consider such an outrageous venture. They remodeled the kitchen and began the introduction of pizza to a mid-Missouri crowd of skeptics. Surprising to all the people that had enough nerve to try it found that it was outstanding, and nearly everyone that tried it came back again and again. They were really making a name for themselves, and the entire area tried the pie, and nearly all returned to Bellow's Pizza time after time, so the crowd was growing by leaps and bounds. Tragedy struck when the kitchen caught fire late one night and gutted the first floor of the old hotel, making it totally destroyed. Everyone thought it was the end of Uncle Billie and Bellow's Pizza, but they were very much mistaken. He purchased a block building on the east side of town and turned a century-old building that needed to be torn down into a first-class pizza house.

This was where I tasted my first pizza pie that was sausage and mushrooms, and from that point on, that was to be then and is now my favorite pizza order. It was totally different from the ones we have available today as this one was about an inch-thick, deep dish crust, a special sauce that was laced with a tiny seed that gave it the best and original flavor. Once you tried it, you never were satisfied without it. It truly was an original Italian recipe and had a special taste that none can nor had duplicated since that time. They did buy out Frank, and the entire Dolans family worked the parlor for years and years. They even started making the pizza pie and froze it and then delivered it in the back of a pickup truck hauling a huge deep freeze. So began the first "bake your own pizza" to be found in grocery stores all over central Missouri. Of course, whenever someone comes up with a revolutionary idea, all the Johnny-come-lately greedy people steal the idea and do their own thing so that, after a few years, the throw-off pizza pies ran Uncle Billie out of business. This was probably for the best, however, as the entire family was getting on in age, and Uncle Billie and Aunt Hattie as well as their fourteen kids had gotten to a stage of family life that changes were being made. Thus ended the original Bellow's Pizza Parlor. It can be said for certainty that if you were old enough to have eaten one of these pies, then you will never forget it nor will you ever find one that can take its place.

Working Team of Horses

Nearly every kid raised on a farm either had a horse of his own or dreamed of having a horse during their early years. I was around Dad and his working draft horse team almost as soon as I drew my first breath and was riding on the wagon from the time I learned how to walk. When I was five years old, I would go with Dad walking behind the team from the barn to the field. He would let me hold the reins and actually drive them to where the plow was left the night before. When he started plowing, I would explore the area, but with such a short attention span, I usually headed down the dirt path and headed for home. When evening was getting close, I would walk back to the lower field and wait for Dad to unhook the plow so I could drive the team back to the barn. Problem was when the horses were going to work, they plodded along rather calmly, but when the day was ending, they knew that they were heading for the barn, so I now was picking them up and putting them down way too fast for a little kid to keep up. Dad held them in check with me holding the end of the reins until we reached the barn. Whenever I asked if I could have a pony or riding horse, Dad always said that if I had walked behind as many horses' butts as he had in his lifetime, I wouldn't even want one. That did not, however, stop me from asking. One of the mares was named Mable, but I am not sure of the second one's name, but think it was Dolly. I have a picture of me standing behind the mountain of horses holding the reins by myself, but truth is, Dad was about one step behind just in case they decided no one was in charge. A couple of years later when I was nearly eight, I actually did sit on the grain wagon seat and drive the horses up and down the cornrows while Dad was walking along beside the wagon shucking the corn ears and throwing them one by one into the wagon bed. My job was to keep them going in a straight line and, when reaching the end of the row, turn them to head down the next row to be harvested. Thought I was pretty big stuff being in charge of two tons of horseflesh, but truth is, they were being directed by Dad on the ground through voice commands. However, that did not stop me from thinking I was a farmhand and doing what farmhands did best, and that was to drive horses.

It was amazing how fast Dad could walk along beside the huge wagon and break off an ear of corn from the stalk and throw it into the wagon all in one motion. Many times, I tried to shuck the ear and found that it was really solidly anchored to the stalk. After pulling and twisting the ear, I would finally break loose, but by then, the horses and wagon were already ten feet in front of me. I found it much easier to ride on the wagon seat and let Dad do the leg and arm work, so once again, I was in charge of the team. There was a reason Dad made it look so simple and easy to shuck, and that was because of a leather strap he wore on his wrist and hand. It buckled on like a glove, and in the palm of the hand was a metal hook that when used correctly cut the ear loose from the stalk, so it was almost effortless. It was amazing how fast a wagon would fill up when throwing one ear at a time that eventually ended up with thousands of ears thrown into the bed. When the wagon was overflowing with ear corn, it was time to head for the granary, pull through the alley in the center of the building, and have the horses stand patiently resting while Dad scooped the corn into one of the several bins that lined the wall on the east side. By the time the fields had been harvested, the bins would be full to the top with corn or milo and was ready to feed to the livestock in the coming months of winter. A task that Jim and I were assigned to was shelling the corn from the cob. There was a machine standing beside the bin of corn that stood about three feet tall and had a flywheel on one side and a rotating crank on the other. Inside was a set of gears mounted on a circular disc with steel teeth on one side. The wheel was very difficult to start moving, but when the heavy flywheel was rotating, it made short order of removing the grain from the cob. I would get it going at a rapid speed, and Jim would drop an ear of corn into the machine small end first. In about ten seconds, the cob came shooting out the rear, and the loose kernels dropped into a bucket beneath. It was expected to have a full bucket of corn available for feeding time the next morning. This was a task that even Jim was expected to assist with, and he did.

Black-and-White Pony

Time went by and I reached my ninth birthday. Still in the back of my mind, I wished for a riding horse of my own. One Sunday when we were at Grandma Willingham's for lunch, I said something about wishing I had a horse like cousin Donnie so that I could be pulled around the farm in a buggy like he did. Donnie said that, if we were interested, we could take his horse home for a while because he was working a full-time job in Mexico and was not really able to keep her busy as she should be. Dad did not say that we could not, so I took it that it meant that I could. The next day, I started getting ready for the horse by pulling sack after sack of grass from the pasture around the house. Not knowing that the purpose of curing hay was to keep it from molding, the natural thing that happens to green wet hay happened to the sacks of grass that I had worked so hard to pull and stacked in the loft. Did not take long to smell there was a definite amount of green grass that had molded and heated in the hay barn. Just about broke my heart thinking that now I would not be able to bring the horse home. After dragging around the house for several days, Dad realized that I was really taking the loss of my horse pretty hard. One morning, he said that maybe we could go over to Kenny Moss's place and see if he had any small horses or pony that we could afford. Kenny Moss was the best-known horse trainer and horse trader in the entire central United States and was known to deliver horses or trade for horses all over the country. There usually were more than a hundred heads of horses on his farm at any one time. Dad honored his word, and the next weekend, we drove over to Kenny Moss's place where Dad

One of my favorite stories is on page 246 when my dream came true that I could have a pony. For the next two and one half years I was almost joined at the hip with this black and white gelding. I began my search for a picture of this little horse to put in the book but after several hours of none found decided there was not one available. Really never got over the thought of having a story without a picture but the book went to press. One evening recently while having dinner with my wife's High School class reunion one of her classmates tapped me on the shoulder. It was my neighbor from across the pasture, Carolyn Sharp, that I had not seen for forty five years or more. She handed me a plastic envelope and what did I see but a picture of her and me with my little black and white pony. My world and my book was now almost complete. My black and white beloved pony will live forever in the middle of my book, "Life in the Country Through the Eyes of a Kid."

explained that I was in need of a small horse or pony to work with for the summer. I can remember exactly what Kenny Moss said word for word, "Hell, there are a dozen horses out there you can work with all summer if you want to. Take any of them home and keep them as long as you want." Looking over the corral, we saw every color, every size, every breed of horse known to mankind; and I could have any one to take home and ride. After studying the herd carefully, my eyes fell upon a smaller black-and-white pony that was in the very center of the corral. Kenny threw a rope over the pony's neck, put a halter and bridle with a bit in its mouth, led it out of the gate, and handed me the reins. I was so happy I was almost dumbstruck, and all I could say was "Thank you" about a dozen times. We walked to the road, and Dad got into the car and told me he would see me when I got home. What a terrible feeling hit me in the pit of the stomach. Would see me when we got home, for crying out loud, home was miles down the road, and Dad was disappearing down the road in a puff of dust. It was a fairly small horse, but it was just about all I could do to get mounted, and after several jumps and pulling of horse mane, I was seated and ready to hit the road. After the first several hundred yards, to my surprise, the pony was very well trained and not at all difficult to ride. Making it down the road for the first mile thinking that I truly was a cowboy, we approached the bridge just below Herb Moore's house. Bob Moore and I and several others spent many hours swimming under that bridge, but now for the first time, I was about to ride across the bridge. Going at a crisp gallop, we headed down the hill toward the bridge and got within twenty feet of the wooden planks, and the pony put down the brakes and came to a sliding halt just inches from the bridge floor. Flapping the reins, using the heels of my shoes to poke him in the side, making noises that always got horses to proceed forward all failed to produce any amount of forward movement. Turned him around and headed back up the hill about two hundred feet, turned his head toward the bridge with the plan to race down the hill and race across the bridge before the pony realized that there was a bridge under his feet. Same results, pony sat down on his back feet, dug in his front feet, and came to a sliding halt exactly where we were the first time around.

OK, I will get off and lead him across as riding across was not going to happen. Hated to dismount what with all the trouble it took to get on in the first place, but standing in the middle of the road looking at the bridge was not getting us any closer to home than we were fifteen minutes ago. Pulling with all my sixty-five pounds produced very little results; in fact, he was still standing in the same spot as when I got off. Led him around in a circle, headed for the bridge, and came to a complete stop. Getting nowhere fast was a reasonable sum of what was taking place. As I stood there for several minutes wondering what my next move would be and knowing that the next move was not to be going across that bridge, I noticed a tiny path going off the road and down the riverbank that had been used by countless raccoons and other critters over the years. With nothing to lose but a few more minutes of my life, I got back up on the pony and turned his head to the side of the road, and to my amazement, the pony skidded down the road bank, jumped across the water riffle, made two lunges up the far bank, and ended up standing in the very center of the road on the opposite side of the bridge. Lesson learned, unless you want to stand in the middle of the road for the rest of your life sitting on a pony, when it does not want to go across a bridge, it is not going to go across a bridge. In case of finding oneself in such a predicament, look around; there may be another path available that is much less stressful and may provide an avenue of escape much easier than the original plan. Thinking ahead, there were no other bridges to cross, but there were three wooden trestles between where we were and our home pasture. It was amazing how fast that pony could go when the open road ahead was nothing but gravel and also amazing how fast the wooden floor of the next bridge appeared. True to form, the paint pony would run like the wind until a few steps away from the floor, and there we came to an abrupt halt. Being much wiser now, I turned the pony's head toward the ditch, and he shot down the creek bank, jumped to the other side, made two lunges up the other side, and continue on as if there had not been an obstacle of any kind behind us. What a relief when we made it to our driveway without any more stops, and as I looked back over the past hour, I found that we had made a really super trip from the

Moss's farm to my house. The little black-and-white pony was fast and provided me many hours of riding pleasure over the next two years. One little quirk that did appear about the third day we were at home was a ritual that we went through daily. He was very easy to catch, accepted the bit without any problem, allowed me to grab his mane, and swing up onto his back without so much as a wiggle. This was where the easy part ended. No sooner than my butt hit his back, he would take three steps forward, stop suddenly, and lower his head, and I would depart with a single flip and land on my backside looking up into the heavens. He never ran way, never tried to step on me, never made a move of any kind, just stood there looking down at me. It seemed he was saying, "Yo, dummy, you knew this was going to happen, but still you end up on the ground." I would get up, dust myself off, climb back on, could easily ride for the next six hours, and never is thrown again. Next day, same scenario—crawled on, flipped off, got up, mounted up, and rode the rest of the day. I made up my mind that if I could afford to buy a saddle, this one horse would never throw me again. Never did get a saddle, never stayed mounted for more than five seconds the first time on each day.

For sure, that little pony was fast. One day, I rode him back to where Dad was chopping trees in the hedgerow to make fence post, and after stacking the limbs for a couple of hours, it dawned on me that this was Saturday, and Saturday was extra special because *The Sealtest Big Top* came on at eleven o'clock. It was one hour of the most amazing animals and clowns and aerial acts that a country boy could imagine. You just did not miss that one particular hour, and if you did, you felt that something was missing in your life during the next week. I asked Dad what time it was, and he said it was ten fifty-five. The pony was standing half asleep about twenty feet from where we were working. Grabbed the reins, leaped up on the pony, and hoped that just this once he would not flip me to the ground. I guess once a day was his limit 'cause we hit the dirt path at a full run, and when he felt the reins go slack, he went into a gear that we had never ridden in before. Wind was going past my ears at what seemed to be sixty miles per hour. The thought ran through my mind just what would be the damage to my body if while going at this speed the pony decided to stop. Actually, I did not have to worry as it did not happen, but we did make it to the house in record time. Took off the bridle, threw it over a fence post, and ended up in front of the TV with nearly a minute to spare.

One episode with the pony happened one afternoon when I was riding down the hill behind the pond that led to the hog pen. After making several runs, we ended up back at the fence by the front lawn and were both stopping long enough to catch our breath and get ready to move on to another location. Suddenly, little brother Jim appeared from around the house. He began yelling that he wanted to ride the pony and wanted to ride the pony right now. Knowing full well that he would not want to ride very long, the best thing was to get it over with and let him ride a few minutes, and then he would go on to bother someone or something else. I put him on the pony and gave him the reins, and the first thing he did was hit him in the side with his heels and let out a yell that woke up most of the sleeping animals for miles around. The pony jumped straight ahead, took off down the hill at a dead run, got halfway down the hill, and did a half buck and half kick. Brother Jim went airborne. He made a complete summersault in the air, came down on his feet, shot forward, lit on his face about ten feet farther down the hill, and scooted on his nose for another five feet. It was the funniest thing I had ever seen, so I started to laugh, but that was not the thing to do at that particular moment. Brother Jim got to his feet and was screaming at the top of his lungs as if he were mortally wounded. Knowing that he would tell Mom that it was my fault, I would get into big trouble and maybe take away my ride. The wisest thing was to get him to stop screaming and get some of the dirt and grass stain off his face and nose and act as if nothing happened. After making promises that I knew I would never keep, Jim did stop screaming, but when we went to the pond and washed off the top layer of dirt, I saw that the missing skin on his nose was going to be a dead giveaway that something had happened to poor little Jim. Cannot remember just what happened when Mom and Dad saw the bloody nose but must not have been too serious because I never did have to stop riding the pony, and the good part was that brother Jim never did ask to ride again.

The real problem with the pony arose the second summer he was on the farm. It all started toward the end of August when the family made the yearly trip into Mexico to attend the Audrain County Fair. The fair was the highlight of the end of summer where all the families looked forward to going at least one day, and if you were real lucky, you would be going two days. Mom would get up real early in the morning and prepare a huge picnic basket of fried chicken, homemade bread, beans, and usually a cake of some kind. All through the morning, we would walk through the livestock and horse barns and watch Drew Umpstead—our next-door neighbor—compete in the horse-pulling contest. We looked at all the displays and people trying to sell everything from horse liniment to the latest in household gimmicks. About noon, we would make our way back to the car that was parked under a shade tree on the north side of the racetrack and watch the racing sulkies go flying by while we quickly woofed down the picnic lunch. After lunch, we headed directly to the carnival where we were allowed to ride the huge merry-go-round at least two times and get some cotton candy and then go to the plastic duck booth that had dozens of little ducks going around and around in a trough of water. The dream was to pick a certain little duck with a number stamped on the bottom that matched the number of one of the huge stuffed animals that was hanging on the tent wall. Never did win a huge stuffed animal but usually got a little plastic whistle or a set of Chinese finger cuffs or some other little pieces of junk that were hidden below the counter. We then headed to the top of the amphitheater where most of the Willingham, Creed, and Towns clan would gather and visit, drink Coca-Cola, and watch the horse show that was taking place in the arena in front of the grandstand. This was where the problem with my pony got its beginning. The magnificent horses would go around the arena under the watchful eyes of the judges, and they would go through a maze of poles that had really high poles lying sideways. Each horse would go to the poles and jump over them with speed and grace that made them look as if they were flying. This was where my dreaming and thinking what it would be like to be a rider in the arena and be able to fly over the poles and hear the crowd cheering began. The next day, it was all I could think about, so when breakfast was done and the chores completed, I started to make a jumping platform just like those at the fair. First drove two poles side by side into the dirt in the garden that was now bare of all plants. Put two more poles about six feet from the original poles and then laid a long pole horizontal between the uprights. Very quickly, I put the bridle on the pony and led him up to the horizontal pole and stepped over the pole, and the pony followed right behind me. Did this twice and then got on his back and rode over the pole two more times. Found that the pony was a natural. Placed another pole on the first, and he jumped it as if he had been born to be a jumping pony. Within the next couple of days, we were jumping five poles high, and with every jump, he was getting smoother and higher. When Dad got home, I had my folks come out and watch while we made jump after jump, and all was amazed at how high the little pony and rider could go. Could not have been prouder if I had been at the fair jumping with the big horses instead of the little pony with me riding bare back in the garden. Next morning, I got up early and was planning to put on another pole to see if he could go higher than before. Little paint was standing in the garden waiting for me to put out his rations of oats as I had done for many months before. Had the bridle thrown over my shoulder the same as dozens of times before and was ready for the fun-filled day ahead. As I reached for the mane of the pony, he stepped sideways so as to be just a few inches from the reach of my hand. Took another step toward him, and the same thing happened. This was totally unexpected and was totally out of character for him to be moving away from the bridle. I quickly stepped toward him and reached out to his mane when he made two or three quick steps past me, ran beside the fence for about five feet, launched himself into the air, and cleared the fence by a good twelve inches. Wow, it was amazing how high he had jumped and looked like a trained horse at the fair that was actually flying for a short period. To make a long story short, that was the last time I was allowed to catch the little paint pony, and no matter how much corn or oats I bribed him with, he would wheel, take several steps, and jump any fence in the area without effort. After about a month of him jumping the neighbor's fence and chasing the cattle next door, it was almost written on the wall that I and the pony were about to become a separate team. Dad tried to catch him several times but to no avail until one day Dad had a dog tied in front of the barn and the pony was pestering the dog. Dad jumped out from behind the barn corner, which surprised the little paint that made the mistake of jumping straight forward into the barn. There he stayed until the weekend when Dad caught him and rode him over to Kenny Moss's farm and returned the little black-and-white pony and bridle that had served me as riding gear for the past many months. All I had left of the little paint were the memories of the hundreds of hours we had raced around the pastures before that first ill-fated training session of teaching him how to jump in the garden.

Quail Hunting with Dad and the Uncles

A huge part of free time, either on the part of the adults or on the part of the kids, is pretty easy to see that it was spent either fishing or hunting. On my part, fishing was the ultimate sport to be utilized as much and as many times as time would permit. Within my many days of being a child born and raised on the farm, hunting really did not have much allure to me. For generations before me, hunting was the preferred activity, and fishing was to be done when the hunting seasons were closed. When the quail and other game birds were attending to their nest in the early spring and as they were busy tending to the new hatchlings, there was a period of about three months where all bird hunting seasons were closed entirely. To keep from overhunting the bob white quail, the season was open only from the first week in November to the middle of January. When this season opened, it seemed that all thoughts centered around waiting for the next weekend so that the hunters and dogs could hit the fields the moment clocks said it was sunup. In the same accord, they stayed in the field no matter how bad the weather until the moment of sunset. Back in the day, the limit was fifteen birds per shooter, so at the end of the day, seldom did they come in with anything short of the limit. Do the math; figure three hunters shooting two days each week, which means that they took home ninety birds each weekend for the entire season. It is almost unimaginable how many birds it would take to keep the population going with that large a kill during any one season. Today the limit is eight and sometimes six depending on the hatch, but the mind-boggling stats back in the good ole days was so successful because of the number of quail coveys available in Missouri. Dad had at least five places to hunt within thirty minutes' driving time as he knew every farmer by name in all of central Missouri as customers of the grinding mill. It was nothing unusual to release the dogs and have found four coveys within the first one hundred acres. If they did not find ten or twelve coveys a day, then they thought it was a really slow day. Today if you're hunting the bob white quail, you will be lucky to find three coveys, and if you did, one would consider himself to be lucky. I personally saw many birds come up from a flush and would guess them as being fifteen to twenty birds in each covey. One of the secrets of why Dad was so successful in finding his limit day in and day out would be the fact that he bred and trained some of the best English setter bird dogs found in the state of Missouri. Over a period of ten years and after working with a half-dozen dogs during off season, he would find one or two that were exceptional. With many hours of onsite hunting, many turned out to be some of the best hunters could find. The best combination Dad trained was a female named Blondie and one of her male pups named Champ that was born on the farm when I was about eight years old. These dogs hunted for Dad almost twelve years and, in that period of time, proved themselves over and over to be two of the best trained in Missouri and surrounding states. Even when Dad's brothers bought along their dogs to hunt, it was totally recognized that Champ and Blondie outhunted them four to one. The two dogs were a thrill to watch in the field. Champ ranged out and when found birds came down on a point, and Blondie, who was always two steps behind him, would honor his point. And both were as if frozen statues when dead on a point. When Dad walked beside Champ on point, the dog did not so much as move a muscle, but when the bird flushed, Champ jumped into the middle of them, and for a second, the sound and sight of more than a dozen quail took to the air with the roar of the wings and dozens of high-pitched chirps announcing the flight was underway. The shooters would usually get three or four, and this was when Blondie was at her best. If she did not see them fall, she knew what direction they flew up, so she made circles until she found everything on the ground. If Dad knew another one was down, all he had to do was call out, "Blondie, dead bird, dead bird," and she would search until she either found it or Dad decided to move on and called her by name. Champ, on the other hand, did not pay any attention to finding dead birds. As soon as the shotgun blast died down, he was heading directly toward the direction the flying birds disappeared. He was deadly on finding singles and knew exactly which direction to go and about how far they would fly before coming down. Occasionally, they would be hunting in tall grass when Champ came down on a single, and it was almost impossible to see or find where he had set on point. It was a fact that when he found a live bird, he would not move no matter how long it took the hunters to catch up to him or find where he was down. It was not unusual for a bird to stay frozen for several minutes when they thought they were in danger. You could lay book on Champ staying on it until someone walked up and flushed the bird. The tale of Champ staying on point for more than twenty minutes was not exaggerated as many hunters have seen it happen. All would be amazed at how really super a dog named Champ really was.

If I was allowed to go along on the hunt, it was understood that I was to stay in the rear, and no matter how hard the walking or how deep the grass, never did I ask to rest or go back to the car. There was no acceptable reason that they would slow down the hunt for a tired kid, so I knew better than to complain or ask to retreat to the car. Several times, I was assigned the task of carrying Mary's movie camera to record the working dogs, and in this instance, it was me that went in front. As soon as one of the dogs came on point, then I was to get back to where I could see one or more hunters in the camera sight before they walked in on the covey. When watching the tapes, it was easy to see when Dad said that his dogs were two of the best, it was hard to disagree. One of the signs of a highly trained dog in the field was when they were hunting quail, then that was all that they were allowed to search for. A real sign of a dumb bird dog was when they were hunting along and happened to flush a rabbit out of the cover and made the mistake of running after the cottontail barking and trying to catch it. As there were way more rabbits in the thick brush than quails, the opportunity to smell a rabbit was happening about every few seconds. Many times, the other dogs would not be able to stop themselves from taking off after a fleeing rabbit and would find themselves in bad trouble when they returned from their run. All dogs, except Champ and Blondie, would at one time or the other slip up and take off, but Dad's dogs would not even look in the direction of a rabbit, let alone chase it. The no-nonsense attitude of the two dogs was what made them two of the most talked-about pair of bird dogs in Central Missouri. Some hunters as far away as St. Louis heard about Dad's dogs, and occasionally, he would take them on a short hunt to the back of our farm to show them off. As usual, anyone that saw them work was totally amazed. It was told and told as the truth that, after one of the hunting demonstrations, a man out of St. Louis offered Dad five hundred dollars for Champ but was told that the dog was not for sale. That amount of money back in the late forties or early fifties was an unheard-of amount, but Champ was at home on the farm, and here he was going to stay. It also was a fact that Champ would really only hunt for Dad and give 100 percent to the hunt. If anyone wanted to take him out by themselves for a trial run, Dad would tell them it would not do any good as Champ would not pay much attention to any commands other than his. I did take them out several times after I became old enough to carry the twelve-gauge pump, which made me about eleven or twelve, but always stayed on our farm where the dogs were totally familiar with the surrounding grounds. They both did a great job finding birds, and on one trip as we were going through the middle of a corn patch that had corn shocks stacked over the entire field, the hunt instantly became more exciting. Champ came down on a solid point, and Blondie backed him up about ten yards in front of me. When they both came down like this, it was definitely because of a covey, and being out in the open like this was a dream come true. Just like Dad taught me, I clicked the safety off the shotgun and began carefully walking up beside Champ, and when I was slightly in front of his nose, he remained solid as a statue, but nothing appeared to be heading for the sky. Thought bummer they must have been here and now are gone. Took another step, and the ground around me exploded with a roar of wings and a solid chorus of frightened quail becoming instantly airborne. Was so surprised and spooked I almost forgot why I was carrying a gun. Champ made a leap and clipped my leg, which instantly brought me back into the realization that I had a gun and was supposed to shoot at the fast-disappearing flock of birds. Shouldered the gun and leveled it at the outside bird, and when the gun sounded, the bird dropped like a rock. Pumped the chamber and fired again when, to my complete surprise, another bird fell. Maybe this was not all that great a thing for hunters that expected to hit birds, but for me, that was right next to a miracle that the first one fell, let alone the second one. It was a fact that I was not a very successful hunter when it came to quail due to the fact that the element of surprise always caught me off guard. I knew that Champ had a bird or birds in front of him, but knowing when they ignited directly under my feet, it never failed to startle me, and I forgot that I was supposed to shoot them. Too often, I found that by the time I came back to my senses, the covey was at a distance and way out of buckshot range. I did have a better average with the singles as they did not make nearly as much noise as singles and usually went away in a straight line, so my average of hits was somewhat better than with a covey. It was a bit difficult to miss a bird and have the dogs come and sit at my feet looking up at me as if I had let them down. It did not take them long to forgive me as they both would quickly turn and proceed with the hunt. Blondie was instantly on dead birds in seconds and, after two trips, laid both of the birds at my feet. After she saw Champ making a beeline toward the fencerow, she took out after him like a rocket. In a matter of seconds, they were down on point again with singles just at the edge of the grass. We got up no less than a half-dozen singles, and after many shots over the top of the dogs, I found that I did not have a single bird to add to my pouch. That evening as we sat around the dinner table, I told the tale of the double several times but failed to mention how great a job the dogs did on singles and that I had missed every one of them. I actually felt that the misses were not nearly as important as the fact that I did a double for once in my life.

Bird Dogs and Rabbits at
Helen Sharp's House

As previously mentioned, the sin of a bird dog running after a rabbit was totally unacceptable and was not tolerated from any self-respecting trainer or bird dog owner. To show just how exceptional Blondie and Champ were in the world of quail hunting, it was a fact that they neither one ever chased a rabbit while on a quail hunt. What we did not tell Dad for the longest time was about what Jim and I did with the dogs after quail season ended. When the dogs were just laying around and almost as bored as Jim and I were, it was discovered that we could really have fun chasing rabbits at Roy and Helen Sharp's place. We would tie onto the dogs' collars and walk them across the pasture. When we arrived at Helen's place the first time, we found their garden had grown waist-high with weeds and that several families of rabbits had taken up residence in the dense weed bed. When we first entered the area with the dogs and started through the tall weeds, the rabbits began running through the underbrush. The dogs just sat on their haunches and looked up at us as if to ask what was it we expected of them. A short time later, they caught on to the idea that it is actually fun running through the garden trying to catch the furry critters that kept circling in every direction. They quickly recognized that Dad was not there to impart firm warnings to the dogs, so they began having the fun of their lives by jumping high above the weeds and coming down right in the center of the rabbits. It was really fun holding on to the dog leash while they were dragging us through the garden and chicken yard. The rabbit-chasing game lasted for about an hour before the rabbits noticed that their private lair was not as private as before the kids and dogs arrived, so they headed out away from the tall weeds to a place that was much quieter. When the kids and the dogs had pretty much worn themselves out and there seemed to not be any more movement of rabbits, the entire group sat down under a tree to regain their breath. As we were sitting under the tree in Roy and Helen's front yard, what did appear but Helen with two quarts of grape juice that she had canned last summer and was kept cool in her cellar. Its original intention was to be made into grape jelly, but we found that chasing rabbits really worked up a thirst, so when tall glasses of juice was passed around, we all enjoyed grape juice that tasted almost like juice fresh off the vine. I had seen Mom put up gallons of grape juice before, but it was different because Helen had lots of juice but also had half a jar of whole grapes floating around on top. This trip turned out to be a really great adventure that was much more than we had ever imagined. It was so much fun, in fact, that we returned the next Saturday with the dogs and found that the rabbits had returned and now was just as much fun as it was previously. Helen even had another jar of grapes that she shared with the kids, so we all decided that we would make the trip over to Sharps a regular event of which we did. At least we did until Jim was talking at the dinner table and explained how much fun we were having chasing rabbits with the dogs. When Dad asked a couple of questions about what dogs and about what rabbits, it was then that some new rules and laws involving his sons and his dogs were pretty well established. Not real sure, but I do not remember going to the rabbit patch with the dogs ever again. This was like the understanding that we were not to lasso the fat calves anymore. It was well understood that we were not to chase rabbis ever again with Blondie and Champ. So began another phase of our education about what not to do on the farm when seeking entertainment.

Memorable Moments Flashback
Electric Fence and a Hog's Memory

This memory comes to mind of working many years with hog production and finishing out many tons of pork. We were never without one boar hog and a dozen breeder sows, which in turn produced on the average eighty-five piglets twice a year. When a litter was finished out, they would usually weigh in at two hundred to two hundred twenty-five pounds per hog. The real story is what happens with these stupid critters between the time they are born and the time they were shipped to St. Louis. It has been said that hogs are among the most intelligent of all animals, but to my way of thinking, that is a stretch of the truth to the breaking point. I was expected to be around and care for and work with these so-called smart animals and found them to be completely against you from the first squeal until they disappeared down the road in back of Russ Bishop's truck. I actually tried not to hate the sight and sound of these stinking critters but would have to admit my attitude was really close to despising everything about them. One such instance was when Dad planted a huge plot of a leaf vegetable that looked a lot like a turnip and was called rape. This grew rapidly, had really huge leaves, and—when the herd was turned into the new patch—was dearly loved by the hogs. To keep them enclosed in the portion of the feedlot that was to be consumed, we installed an electric fence that was one wire encircling the plot stretched between metal posts driven in the ground about ten feet apart. On each post was attached a ceramic knob where you attached the wire so that, when electricity was applied, it did not provide a short circuit. When the wire was activated, it was totally harmless until a person or a hog touched it while standing on wet ground. This completed the circuit, and the jolt was quick and severe enough to make the touching individual rapidly back up or, in the case of a hog touching it with his wet nose, let out a surprised squeal and leap backward. Seldom if never did a hog walk up to it and touch it a second time; in fact, they never forgot the first encounter. When the leaves were devoured, which took about ten days, the hog herd would be moved from this bare patch to a new area so they could eat this while the previous one was growing back. Problem occurred that when you removed the wire, there was a distinct line where the old plants started and began, so the hogs would go to that point and stop and view the new plants, but not one of them would cross the imaginary line where the wire had once been. Once shocked, always shocked was their theory. You could not push them across the line; you could not carry them across the line. In fact, you could not get them to cross over for the rest of their natural lives. You had to drive them through a gate that was nowhere near to where the wire was, or you had to load them into a wagon and drive them to the new spot. Once they were on the other side of the line, they were very content to eat and live their lives as if they had no care in the world. You for sure did not have anything to worry about them ever going back to the old plot because their memory was forever. The same was true of all other animals as any that touched the wire did have a lot of respect for it but not to the same degree as the supposedly smart pig.

Fun on the Farm

The time we can refer to as preelectricity and pretelevision occurred during the first twelve years of this farm kid's life. During that period, life seemed to be totally in balance with each day being met individually. Adults had their days work ahead of them starting about daybreak, and the kids during the summer months were up and out of the house as soon as breakfast was over. There were no cartoons nor any educational television, no music videos, and in fact, there were no sounds heard other than birds calling and roosters crowing and an occasional bang from Mom connecting two pots or pans while cleaning up after breakfast. As there was no electricity in the house, the music from the radio was only heard in the evening on certain days of the week and was never played during the day because the battery used to power the radio was too expensive to purchase, and the life span was short. I guess we could have sat around the living room and looked at the four walls or could have read the three books we had already memorized from going through them over and over. If not sitting around, maybe we could go out the back door and find a world that was full of mystery and wonder in every direction you looked. Jim and I were masters of setting up camps and had dozens of them in all directions of the front yard. We constructed lean-to shelters made of rag weed stalks and cut dozens of oak sprouts over the years to build walls and roofs for make-believe houses. We were not allowed to build fires, but we had rocks set in circles with roasting stick over each fireplace where we did imaginary meals of buffalo and deer meat or any other type of food our imagination desired. We did have a place at the edge of the garden set up as a campsite where we were allowed to build a real fire when one of the parents was working in the area. A pile of corncobs and a bundle of sticks were stacked carefully at the site just in case an adult was around, so we could be prepared to light the fire and proceed with our for-real cookout. When the fire was going, we checked out the laying boxes in the henhouse to see if any left an egg or two in the boxes after the eggs were gathered. Our cooking kettle was a tin can hanging from the stick across the fire where we actually did fry eggs one at a time and pretended that it was a lot more than a half-raw egg. The fire would not produce enough heat, so we used coal oil from the shed to keep the flames hot. Problem with the coal oil was the aftertaste of burned oil, so the eggs really were not all that tasty. Occasionally, Mom would give us a can of Vienna sausages that we could roast over the flames. That produced a right down good-tasting play meal of which we could actually enjoy in our make-believe world.

Another flat spot area in the garden was where Mom planted her huge flower bed each spring. As there was not extra water available, it usually died off the first hot spell that hit. This was a bare ground flat spot that we utilized as a roadway between cities. By using a garden hoe, we made roads and hills over the entire area and set up little towns by using cigar boxes and cans we scavenged from the many dump sites located around the neighborhood. A single board made bridges and rivers that ran through the entire countryside. Most years, Santa Claus gave us a toy truck or a toy tractor, so we had several of these that we drove through the country to visit people and places in our imaginary country. My favorite was a little tin bulldozer that was running on rubber tracks that looked and roared almost like the real thing. It was powered by a coil spring inside the hood, and when the key was wound, it would crawl up and over mounds of dirt or twigs that had been tied together. One of the saddest days of my life was when the dozer was crawling along and suddenly stopped. The motor had been wound up recently and should have gone for many more minutes before running out of power. This was a really bad sign and got a lot worse when I wound it a little tighter. Suddenly, from within came a huge twang such as had never been heard before nor has been heard since. The little dozer was quiet and remained quiet from that moment on. When it rained and washed away all our roads, we spent many hours putting them back just as they were.

Going to the Movies at
Perry and Mexico

There was an unlimited amount of free time down on the farm especially when you were between the ages of five and ten years. Every day was a new adventure within itself as nothing happened the same way twice on the farm. What with the big barn to explore, the granary filled with mice and other types of critters, the chicken house full of eggs, and the livestock barn with all its corrals and hallways and hay stacked to the ceiling on the second-floor hayloft. There were acres and acres of woods in all directions and hills and hollows running through the farm and the farms next door along with the dozen or so mud ponds located everywhere. Seemed a miracle that we had time to come home for lunch or to return as dark settled in over the homestead. We did not have television to fill the void of killing time, but we did not worry very few minutes about being bored or looking for something to do to entertain ourselves. It seemed that new and different adventures followed us no matter which direction we went once the kitchen door slammed shut behind us. It was easy to see Jim and I did not find the days to be boring; in fact, we were never still a second because of all the adventures that surfaced from daylight to dusk. Killing several hours in front of a TV from days on end was never a part of the equation of us growing up on the farm.

One of the greatest memories that we did together as a family was when looking forward to making a trip to Perry to go to the theater. Long before the coming of the television, a super delight was when our folks said that maybe tonight we should go to the movie theater. Mom made it a habit of not telling us of the plans until well into the middle of the afternoon because, had we known the possibilities of such an exciting evening, then we made life miserable hanging around the house waiting to go. Long before the sun was beginning to set, we three kids were washing our face and hands, putting on clean clothes, and waiting beside the car for the moment to load up and drive down the driveway toward Perry. When we walked into the door of the theater, it seemed that the entire world opened up with new sounds and smells that only could be found in a dimly lit little room in the front that led into the huge room with a massive number of seats that appeared to go on forever. We had tons of popcorn at home because of the corn we planted to be used during the winter months, but the popcorn that you got at the theater was way beyond better than the home-grown kernels we popped in our kitchen. Suddenly, the lights dimmed, and the music began, and on the screen flashed a picture of newsreels and short features that were happening around the world. It was years later that we found that the news we were watching, which we thought happened either yesterday or today, were actually things that had happened at least a month earlier. One really sad story was the one about a little girl that had fallen down a well shaft, and as we sat motionless, we felt that we were right there beside the machines and rescue squads. When they showed the moment they reached her and brought her to the surface, they wrapped her in a blanket, handed her to her mother, and said that they did not get to her in time and that she had died a few minutes earlier. That scene played on my mind for years, and when I found out it had happened half a year before we saw the newsreel, it really did not make any difference how it affected my young child thoughts. After the newsreel came my favorite part, the cartoon. The ones that were in color were awesome, and the music and characters made you laugh even before the cartoon started. The most popular was *Tom and Jerry*, so when the first picture appeared of them standing there, it was all we could do not to start laughing and talking out loud. The funniest scenes were where Tom would chase Jerry around the corner and then meet up with a baseball bat or a rocking chair or whatever it took to make Tom have stars spinning around in front of his head. Another was *Popeye the Sailorman*, but it never did keep up with the excitement of *Tom and Jerry*.

As for the movies themselves, anything that was cowboy or horses or animals was always good, but the ones that I remember the most was the ones with Maw and Paw Kettle and the stories about them raising the huge bunch of kids and the trouble they always got into. The funniest one was "Maw and Paw Kettle Goes to Town." It was by far the funniest of the many we saw. We could compare them all as we saw every one of them as soon as they came out. Another movie we always looked forward to was anything with Red Skeleton. He was also our favorite character when television came around and was one of the shows that the family hardly ever missed on Tuesday night when the *Red Skeleton Show* came on at seven o'clock in the evening. Francis the Talking Mule was always a funny one, and when it played, there were very few seats empty in the theater. Lassie movies seemed to come out about two movies each year, and when the papers showed it at the local theaters, we always started making plans to see it soon as it appeared. The one that I most distinctly remember was when Lassie was living in an orphanage with about a dozen other kids, and their bedrooms were located on the second floor of a really old and really big house. An accident happened when one of the kids tipped over a coal oil lamp, and the bedroom caught on fire, and flames were shooting everywhere, and kids were screaming and calling out for help. Lassie was standing on the roof above the porch barking so someone would come and save the kids. I got so hysterical Dad had to take me out of the theater and walk me around the shops until the movie ended. I remember almost like it was yesterday that we entered a drugstore, and Dad sat me down at a glass-top table and put a dish of ice cream in front of me. He was standing by the counter and was asking the guy behind the counter that was wearing a white coat what was good to put an animal out of their misery when they were sick and dying. He gave Dad a little bottle and a needle, which he put in a bag. We sat at the table until people began leaving the theater. I knew that Poochie, Mary's little dog, had been really sick and had injured her belly so pretty well I knew what they were talking about. I never asked Mom or my brother or sister what happened in the fire, but Mom did say that everything came out safe. As far as I was concerned, that chapter in my life was over. On the way home, Mom assured me that it was just a make-believe fire and that Lassie had saved all the kids. That fire maybe was put out in the movie, but in my mind, it would be burning for the rest of my life.

A few years later, my uncle Bob and Aunt Shirley married and moved into a house on the southwest side of Mexico. It had a front yard about the size of a postage stamp and a backyard that was a little larger and had a fence around it. I got the job of mowing the grass about every two weeks with a push rotary mower, and my pay for the task was one dollar. We always arrived in Mexico early every Saturday morning, so I would make a beeline to their house and mow the grass as quickly as possible. When I received the one dollar, I would walk directly to the Liberty Theater and lay my money down. It was located about ten blocks from their house and just in front of the bread bakery. After tearing my ticket at the door, I would buy a box of popcorn and go directly to the middle of the theater and get one of the best seats in the house. Nearly every Saturday, there was a cowboy movie, but it did not really make any difference what was playing because just being in the middle of all the activity was sheer delight. I always stayed after the movie ended and would wait for the cartoon to come on again so I could watch it the second time for free. Would have watched the movie again, but the afternoon was pretty much shot by the time the cartoon was over the second time. It was a rule that I was to be back at the car sitting on the north side of the square before the families departed for home. One time, I went to the movie with Aunt Odell, and she asked if I had seen the man working on the tall ladder just to the side of where we were sitting. After my eyes got used to the dark, I did see a man standing on a ladder that reached way up nearly to the ceiling. He was dressed in white bib overalls and had on a white hat with a bucket of paint in one hand and a big wide brush in his other. Aunt Odell asked if the guy looked familiar, but it was so dark that I really could not make out anything about him other than the white clothes that he wore. At that moment, the screen lit up and bathed the entire area in light, and by golly, I did see what she was talking about. On top of the ladder was Grandpa Burl painting the fancy scrolling and scallops that made up the ceiling. She said he had been working there for nearly a month and was just about done with the job. It entered my mind that maybe this was a job that I would like. I really did not like to paint anything larger than a swing board seat, but if a person could get paid to do this and watch all those movies day in and day out, then that must have been a really good job to work at. One Sunday, I asked Grandpa if he really had fun doing the theater, and he said that it was actually a really terrible job. It was dark and then light that he could not see where he had painted or had not painted; the ceiling was about twenty feet off the floor, and they played the same movie over and over two or three times a day for a solid week. As I got to see a movie occasionally, I just figured that there was a new movie about every day. After talking with Grandpa Burl, I figured that maybe painting theaters was really not all that good a job after all. For certain, the entertainment of going to the movies was a huge addition to the life of a little boy that lived outside of Santa Fe. Each movie I watched bought thoughts and images of a new world and place that was totally different than life in the country. It established a section in my brain that produced information, which was stored for later development. Through the movies, I knew there was another world outside of my realm that someday in my later years I may experience firsthand and not have to read about it in the *World Book Encyclopedia.*

Clothing for Kids: Then and Now

Recently, we were watching our grandkids while shopping for clothes to start school. It seemed there were thousands of choices of shirts, tank tops, pullover T-shirts, just to name a few. There was every color or combination of colors imaginable that would boggle the mind. They had to make the choice of what words or pictures they wanted printed on the front or back or collars or pockets or whatever. It took hours to make the choices and to try on for just the right size and feel.

At the end of the shopping ordeal came the final assault on the mind, a cash register tape that seemed to take several minutes to print out and show the final grand total. As the cashier handed me the tape and I saw the final figure, it rushed through my mind, "For crying out loud, I bought my first car in 1958 for slightly less than the clothes for two boys totaled at today's prices." We know that little boys will outgrow the stack of clothes before they wear them out and know that none of the kids today will accept a hand-me-down from an older sibling. This would mean this scene will be taking place at least twice during the twelve-month period or maybe even more often.

Now let's take a moment and go back in time to about 1950. I was about the same age as my two grandsons, and like them, we started school in the fall just as those did decades before and decades after me. I'm sure we got ready for the first day of school, but my memory fails me if we got new clothes at that time or just wore what we had and did not know the difference. I do remember that, all summer long, we wore a pair of cut-off jeans, no shirt, and no shoes

271

unless we were going to Mexico or Santa Fe, and that only took place on Saturday and church two hours on Sunday. This meant that we did not have shoes on for days at a time, and the pair of shorts usually was the same pair until we put on shoes to go off the farm. In this case, we put on another pair of shorts that were identical to the ones taken off but about four shades lighter in the absence of a layer of farm dirt. Best part of wearing out the skin on the bottom of the feet instead of rubber off the bottom of sneakers, the skin grew back and did not cost anything. For sure, a person's feet became just as tough as whit leather by the end of the first month of spring. It was a rule that Mom used that we were not to go barefoot until the first day of April because anything earlier may cause you to get the croup from walking on cold and wet dirt. I personally did not have feet that were tough enough to walk on rocks without taking caution as to how much weight one would put on each step. Jim, on the other hand, was really tough when it came to treading on any type of surface. He made it a practice to come up behind me and grab whatever I was playing with or having a snack in the middle of the afternoon and then run like blue blazes to get away. He knew that if he made it to the gravel path or the road, there was no way that I could catch up with him while he devoured the treat we had halved. He acted as if the rocks did not cause him any pain but with me following behind him at a much slower pace knew that it had to hurt.

When summer ended and school began, we had to go back to wearing pants and shoes, so the easy life of unbound freedom came to an end. I was pretty lucky to have been born the middle child, and by being a boy with an older sister, I seldom received hand-me-down clothes. Jim, on the other hand, was directly behind me, and no matter how worn an article may have been with a little bit of yarn and a patch, everything was made ready for another school term. Dad would sell a hog or a steer about the middle of August, and we would all go to the Missouri Brokerage store in Mexico and buy what bare essential we needed to get through the year. That usually meant a new pair of Levi's or bib overalls and a new set of underwear along with four pairs of socks and two or three flannel shirts for when the weather took a turn toward winter. Mom many times said, "You kids may have patches on your clothes, but you will be clean." That was a promise we heard frequently and always knew that the promise would be carried out. I remember that Monday was washday and come sunshine or driving rain, the laundry was done and hung out to dry no matter what the condition of the weather. It was hanging until it either froze dry or dried from the wind whipping it around. There was no such thing as dryers, and even if there was, the absence of electricity would have made them pretty useless. If the sun was not out, it took a long time to dry while hanging on the line. In the wintertime, Mom would hang the clothes out early in the morning and about dark would bring in the entire wash load and put it behind the heat stove in the living room. I can remember distinctly the times during the middle of winter when the overalls and Levi's would be standing behind the stove frozen solid and standing up, like a ghost was wearing them. When they thawed out, Mom would drape them over chairs and whatever was close by to use what heat was available to finish the drying job. Surprising enough, most of the underwear and shirts were dry from the freezing air tossing them about during their stay outdoors.

Thank goodness for Christmas because every Christmas, it was a well-known fact that we would all get some heavier socks and heavy shirts as part of our Santa Claus gifts. One of the best surprises came when we got up at daybreak on one Christmas morning, and Jim and I both found a pair of combat boots under the tree. These boots were highly sought-after, and only the kids with money were known to have them, but here they were under the tree, and they were brand-new—meaning that no one had worn them before. Several years in a row, we got new combat boots, and as I grew older, one year, I got a pair of engineer boots, which was a tremendous highlight in a young man's growing years.

Washday on the Farm

With the subject of Mom and washday, I can just remember in the farthest corner of my mind her having to use a scrubboard and a tub. I can remember very distinctly the first washing machine my granny Edwards used back in the early forties. It was a wooden tub built of stave barrel lathes that made a tub sitting on legs. There was a top on it that was hinged in the middle where half the top would raise up giving access to the wash water. On the outside was installed a pump handle that was connected to a gear that turned the agitator inside the barrel. I considered the machine a dream for women as it took away the backbreaking task of the scrubbing board. Many years later, she got a wringer washer and turned the wooden tub into a rain barrel that caught cistern water she used to water her vegetable garden. Mom, on the other hand, went from the washboard to the newest model of self-propelled wringer washer. It was set up permanently on the screened-in back porch so, when washday rolled around, all that was needed was a half-dozen buckets of boiling water, and all was ready to go. Before electricity had arrived at the farm, the power was provided by a really little gas engine connected to the bottom of the tub. It held about a cup of gasoline and was started by raising a pedal on the side of the engine and then placing your foot on the pedal and pushing down rapidly. When the engine was running, Mom filled the tub with clothes and kicked it into gear starting the paddles to agitate the water and clothes back and forth. After a few minutes of whisking around, she would turn on the set of rollers on top of the machine, snag a piece of clothing with a stick, and push it directly against the moving rollers. This fed the clothes between the two rollers and squeezed the water out of the material, which then fell into a basket setting behind the machine, and the water returned into the tub to be used again for the next load. This procedure continued until all the laundry was done and three loads were taken outside and hung out to dry. When the tub was used, the chore of dipping out the water and carrying it outside was replaced by the new washer that had a hose connected to the bottom of the tub. When the hose was lowered, the water automatically emptied and flowed out the back door and onto the ground. This made the Monday morning weekly task of cleaning clothes we would wear for the next week a much easier task. Strange how a family of five would have three loads per week when today a family of this size would go through six to eight loads per week. Maybe the fact of each member of the family today has way too many clothes and probably changes two or three times per day compared to the good ole days when the same pair of pants and shirt was good for a couple of days. With the installing of electricity, the washday ritual took on a totally different outlook. First off, the washer used an electric motor, which eliminated the gas and oil smell; the hot water was produced by filling the tub with cold water and inserting a piece of equipment that was called a donut heater. It was constructed of an aluminum circle that resembled a donut but much larger. Drop it in a tub of water and plug it in, walk away, and come back in about forty-five minutes, and the water was wash water hot. It did work well for some time until the cord became a bit frayed or the heater coils became loose. When you walked by the machine and accidently brushed against it or touched with the hand, one would find that not only the water was getting warm but also the person touching the metal. Occasionally, one would receive anything from a slight tingle to a teeth-clicking jolt. There were no written warnings about the dangers of electricity, and no one mentioned the potential hurt of an electric shock, so most found out the hard way that the available lights and running motors was truly a blessing but could have consequences. Occasionally, electricity could impart pain and/or knock you on your butt without as much as a slight warning. My first run-in with electricity having a mean side was about a month after we got our first lights. Mom came up with a funny-looking iron tube with a flexible hose sticking out of it that was called a vacuum cleaner. Dad decided to vacuum out his car one afternoon. He handed me a long piece of cord and told me to run to the porch and reach inside the door and plug into one of the outlets. Doing as I was told, I strung it out from the car to the house, plugged it into the outlet inside the living room, ran out toward the car, and picked up the end while reaching for the vacuum cord end to plug together. All of a sudden, I got a jolt that went from my bare feet to the very tip of my rooster-tail hair. There are no words to explain the surprise and feeling that hit me other than being kicked by an invisible mule and being knocked down while still standing upright. Seemed like an awfully long time between the first hit until the time Dad jerked the cord from the outlet inside the house. About all that remained a memory was not being able to let go of the end of the cord and just what great amount of pain can be derived from something as innocent looking as a braided wire lying on the ground. Definitely, there should have been instructions and warnings given to the family when they first received electricity. The only training I remember when it first arrived was when Jim was flipping the light switch off and on every time he walked by.

Wooden Ice Box we used before electricity was installed. Bought 50 pound blocks of Ice in Mexico each Saturday, lasted a week.

After electricity we got a modern ice box that did not utilize a block of ice.

This ringer washer was like the one Granny owned. We helped her pump the dasher and then turned the rollers to wring the water.

Maytag on insert was like the one we got when moving to Santa Fe, used gas engine for power. Next move was to get a wringer washer with Electric motor.

Attempted Murder in
the Neighborhood

Thinking along the lines of what an electric shock feels like reminds me of the most important set of events that almost caused the first murder that Santa Fe had ever become acquainted with. To explain a little geography about our area, there were five houses sitting between our house and the Salt River Bridge and about less than a mile of gravel road. The last house toward town was the home of a bachelor that was well-known for spending much of his time going to Perry, a little town about ten miles from Santa Fe. It had several bars and dance halls of which we were not to even talk about, let alone look in their direction when we went to Perry for a movie or a haircut. He was what everyone referred to as a drinker and a carouser, was tall and thin, dressed a lot nicer than the average farmer around Santa Fe, and did what I considered strange—carried an open stick of cologne in his pants' pocket. I did smell drink on him occasionally, but the cologne stood out above all other odors, which hid a large variety of smells that little kids would not have been aware of. Early one morning, the phone was ringing off the wall about daylight, and whenever that happened, all phones were picked up immediately. When Dad hung up, he said that we were all to stay inside the house the rest of the morning and that our neighbor, Ervie Scoobe, was found a little earlier lying on his porch nearly dead. Immediately, we noticed there were cars going down our gravel road going really fast and then a few minutes later would come flying back again. Now on a road that may have three cars a day go by, you got to admit that this was a really strange happening. A few minutes later, a sheriff's car came up the driveway, and two men got out and approached the front yard. Dad went to meet them with me about six inches behind him with Jim about three inches behind me. The story told by the officers was that someone had it out for Ervie because he had been seeing this man's woman in Perry. The man had made several threats to do bodily harm if he did not quit messing with his woman. During the night while Ervie was chasing the ladies, this guy came to his house and strung piano wire between the wooden posts on the front porch of Ervie's house. One was about shoulder-high on Ervie and two more with one about his waist and the other wire about his knees. He then threw one end of the wires over the high line wire that was on a pole beside the house and the other end over the bottom high line wire, thus making a direct connection to about two hundred thousand volts. When Ervie came home early in the morning and having had a bit more drink than the average person, he stepped onto the porch and ran directly into the three wires at exactly the same time. One wire hit him across the throat; the second hit across his stomach and the third just above his knees. According to the sheriff, it cut his neck almost like it had been hit with a razor blade, and two other wires did just about the same amount of damage. According to the doctor that examined him, Ervie was killed instantly, but when he fell through the wires, he broke the connection, and when his body hit the floor, it brought him back to life. He was taken to the hospital and was alive but in bad condition. What the sheriff was worried about was that there was a set of footprints that went from the porch directly south along a plowed field and looked to get into a car or truck just several feet from Henry Heckert's house. That put the killer less than a quarter mile by gravel from our house and about six hundred yards as the crow flies. When the officers left, we went into the house, and Dad said for us to all stay in the living room while he did the chores. As he left, he was carrying his shotgun and had on his hunting vest, so at that point, we all felt safe. Good a shot as Dad was, there was no way a killer would dare to come to our house. Got to admit I was about as spooked as I have ever been, and thoughts that went through my mind that entire day was about Ervie and the killer being so close to our house. It has been decades since this happened but, all this time, has not erased the feelings of fear and dread that we went through that day. After it was all over and the guilty man was arrested in Hannibal the next day, you can just imagine what it was like to stop in front of the house for the first time. In a kid's mind's eye, I could see all that unheard-of hurt and pain that went on a mere twenty feet from where we were parked in the car. Caught the attention of an awfully lot of other people as there were no less than thirty cars parked on the side of the road that led up to Ervie's place. We did go see the footprints later that day, and sure enough, they seemed to be just a stone's throw from the side of Henry Heckert's side door. It was said that the car turned around in Russ Bishop's driveway, but no one really know if that was true or not. Many months later, we were sitting in front of the general store of James and Mac's, and who got out of his sister's car but Ervie Scoobe. He had to use two canes and did not look like the ole boy that used to drink and carouse around and had his neck totally wrapped in white gauze. I did notice that he did not smell like the stick of cologne anymore, so I guess he gave that up because of the accident. Later, he was featured in an article out of New York or Chicago from a detective-and-crime magazine. We all got to read a copy of the article about his electric shock that was the main feature that month. It carried a front-page picture of Ervie with the title "I took 200,000 volts in the neck and lived to tell about it." Never did hear what happened to the bad boyfriend, but they said that he got life in prison somewhere for attempted murder. Saw a lot of the victim after that as he hung out on the benches in front of the store for many years. Never was able to drive again but did walk from the rider's seat to the bench by himself with a cane, so I guess he was pretty lucky with the outcome.

Guess I got a little off the subject of school clothes, but what the heck, this is about things a person can remember about being a kid. Nothing will remain any more a vivid memory than seeing that house every time we drove past it to get to town or return home. Another bit of irony, my uncle Roy and aunt Martha bought the farm from Ervie many years later and lived in the house until they acquired enough money to tear the old house down and build a new one. The house they built is still standing in the original spot the attempted murder occurred, and the electric poles may be the original ones used as a murder weapon.

Member and Activities of 4-H Chapter

O f the many activities I participated in during my youth, that of belonging to the Santa Fe 4-H Club was some of the most interesting. You could join the club when you were seven years old and remain a member until reaching the age of sixteen. Each year, you received a pin that designated the year that you completed. I still have all nine pins stored in a piece of silk wrapped securely and safe in my ring box. When I first became a member, our leader was Mrs. Hanna, mother of a buddy of mine that was a year older than me, and we met in the basement of her house. The number of members grew so rapidly we moved into the elementary school in Santa Fe for our monthly meetings. After the third year, there were so many new members that Sharon Poage's mom and dad helped split the group, and the older ones met separately from the younger kids. We started out with a community projects, but the one that was most awesome was when Mrs. Hanna gave two acres on the blacktop to be made into a public park. It was located about a half mile down the Molina blacktop and was really close to town but out in the country enough that it seemed a part of the great outdoors. Ernie's father had recently passed away, so Mrs. Hanna donated the plot to the 4-H group in his memory.

When we began working on the picnic area, there was nothing on the lot but dozens of scrub oaks, thorn bushes everywhere, and grass so high one could not walk through it. Right next to the road was a huge very old pine tree. Must have been there for dozens of years or longer as it reached toward the sky by at least sixty feet. What was unusual about the tree was the fact that it was the only pine tree growing wild in the county but was real special to be right at the entrance of the soon-to-be picnic park. The entire club met at the plot to work many days during the first few months. With the help of a donated tractor and blade, the ground was cleared of all the briars and thorn bushes, so when the grass seed was sown, soon appeared a rich green carpet of new grass that covered the entire park. The extension office in Paris was very interested in our project and volunteered to provide seedling trees and at the time was pushing for the use of multifloral rose plantings for fencerows and windbreaks. We must have planted thousands of the seedlings around the entire park. Within two years, the tiny plants we put in the ground became sticker bushes that were four feet tall and growing thicker. They put out millions of seeds, and many bushes came out of the roots, so what started out as a protection for wildlife became a threat to our entire picnic area. After the club got control of the rose bushes, the little trees flourished, and with the help of the community who donated picnic tables, we had a super play area and club meeting park for years to come.

4-H Contest on the Radio

Another activity I remember vividly is that of practicing for hours to perfect a demonstration that was to be presented at the county seat in Paris at the main office of the extension center. We all thought this organization was the lifeblood for the 4-H Clubs around the state, so when they asked us to participate, we usually did. I do not know how I was convinced that I was the one that should give a demonstration on the proper method of and the rules behind the proper setting of a table for dinner. Before I knew what was taking place, this presentation became one of the biggest nightmares of my childhood. The number of hours spent memorizing the five-minute skit and showing how to precisely place the plate, spoon, two forks, knife, and the napkin became a terribly painful ordeal. To make matters worse, Mom volunteered me to give the demonstration in front of her ladies' club one afternoon at Mrs. Macalhnes's home. There were no less than a dozen women all sitting around the screened-in porch on the back of her house and me in the very center standing beside a wooden table with all my utensils stacked in front of me. The lady before my performance was showing how to make some kind of flower arrangement. It was a lifetime before my name was announced. I stepped up to the table to recite the most embarrassing group of words that I was ever again going to speak forth. Talk about humiliating, there could have been a thousand things I could have talked about if I had my choice, but forks and spoons would not have been one of them. Mom was all smiles when I got through, so I guess it was worth something to make my mother proud, but I imagine she too was relieved to get me through the past five minutes. She could not have been nearly as relieved as I was to put that room behind me in my file cabinet of dreaded moments. I also gave it in Paris about a month later but have no memory of anything that happened at that meeting, so I must have gone through such a traumatic show at the ladies' meeting that anything else was like a walk in the park.

Another highlight was when Stanley Poage signed us to compete in the annual knowledge of history and procedures of 4-H. This contest was held each year in Hannibal through a local radio station located on top of a hill just outside of the city. The program was emceed by Cactus Jim who was also the star of *The Cactus Jim Show*, shown every afternoon on television at channel 7. At this show, little kids in the area could be seen on TV where they ate cold hot dogs and sipped a carton of milk while cartoons were being shown. He also was in charge of the 4-H contest on the radio, which took place every Saturday morning for several weeks. Two teams competed, and the winner would return the next week to meet another team from another club. We met at the Poage house at least four evenings a week for about a month and was drilled and drilled on information about being a 4-H chapter and member. There were four of us on the team, but Sharon is the only one that I can remember for sure was a team member beside me. Strange that I cannot remember the faces of the other two, but no matter how hard I try, there is no return of memory of who they were.

Only good thing that came out of the hours of study and practice was when it was over, Louise brought out homemade cookies, Pepsi, and Kool-Aid for refreshments. I really was not into the study part all that much, but the chocolate chip cookies made it all worthwhile to pretend that I gave a hoot about giving out 4-H information. Finally, the big day arrived that we were to go to Hannibal and meet at the radio station and meet Cactus Jim and the other team that had come to beat us. There he was, Cactus Jim himself; he had on a cowboy hat that was about the size of a Mexican sombrero and a bandana tied around his neck. The entire combination made his skinny face, sharp nose, and big ears all stand out like a comedy show instead of a cowboy. He did have a really nice set of cowboy boots on though of which I could hardly take my eyes off. That did make him appear a little more like a cowboy but not so much. We sat in chairs facing the other team with Cactus Jim seated on the right side of us and a lady beside him with a chalkboard to his left. Each side had a microphone on a long cord, and each of us had our first name written in large letters on a string around our necks so that Cactus Jim could call us by name and not have to remember who we were. He had a handful of little cards stacked neatly and asked a question of each team back and forth, and if any team member knew the answer, they were to hold up their hand, and he would call their name. They were handed the microphone and gave the answer, and if they were correct, they got a point written under our club name. The first questions were really lame, and any seven-year-old could have answered them correctly, but it did not take long before they became more difficult. It was a good thing that Louise and Stanley had made us do all that drilling from the get-go. I cannot remember who the other two on our team were, but we all answered the first set of questions. It became pretty evident that the harder ones were coming, and thinking was pretty much required. I answered several questions, but toward the end, it seemed that when our question was read, Sharon would look at us for a second to see if we had an answer, but usually, we were sitting there with a blank look on our faces. She would raise her hand and recite the correct answer, which gave us the point. It was also pretty evident that the other team had not worked nearly as hard as was required. We did not have much working against us; therefore, our score was a great deal higher than the other team's score at the end. I actually did know a lot of the answers, but when it came from push made to shove, it was all about the mind of Sharon that gave us the win at the end. When all the questions had been read, the top score was announced, and we were invited back for next Saturday to meet a new team. When it was all over, it was about noon when we turned to go down the hill. When we reached the highway, Stanley turned to the right, which took us by surprise as we needed a left to head back to Santa Fe. In a few minutes, we parked in front of a really tall three-story hotel that was right in the middle of Hannibal. We entered a door that was going around and around in circles so that when a person got into an empty chamber, the person in the first chamber was already inside the hotel. Was not like any door that I had ever seen in my short but well-rounded life. Stanley led the way into a big open room with many, many tables and a whole lot more chairs all sitting empty. On the tables were fancy cloth covers and a flower sitting in the center of each table. We were told that we could have a choice of hamburgers and fries or open-face roast beef with gravy. Being a person that had lived most of his life on gravy, there was really little choice as to which one I would pick. There was a lot more on the plate than I should have eaten; but being a great fan of beef, potatoes, and gravy, there was no stopping until the plate was empty. The lady came to the table and asked if we wanted dessert, and most said that they wanted a dish of ice cream. I noticed there was a picture on the counter of a dish of strawberries heaped up with whipped cream on top. I asked if the dish on the picture was also dessert, and she said it was, so I asked Stanley if it was OK, I would rather have the strawberries instead of ice cream. He said that if I would rather have the strawberries, then that would not be a problem. Now I had eaten strawberries all my life, but with them sliced and sitting on a soggy piece of cake with a huge mound of whipped cream on top of it was for sure a first-time thing and one that I would remember the rest of my life. As I was scraping the juice off the bottom of the dish, Louise said that she thought that it was empty. I for one knew that there were just a few drops left, and it would be a shame to leave anything as good as that had been.

To make a long story short, we practiced another two nights the next week and once again made a trip to the top of the hill the following Saturday, and just as before, we won the match. When we went to the hotel for lunch, the lady brought me another roast beef plate, and before I was done, Stanley had strawberry shortcake put in front of me without asking. The next Saturday, we ran into another team that had two Sharons sitting across from us and, at the end of the contest, was just barely ahead of us in points, but we did go down in defeat. With another trip to the hotel and with the same menu as twice before, I found that being beaten was not all that bad when you had super strawberry shortcake to take your mind off losing.

It actually was a relief not to have to go back to drilling for another visit with Cactus Jim. From that time, the Poage family would always mention how good it was to see a person enjoy a dessert as much as I had enjoyed three Saturdays in a row. With this many years later, I always see Sharon at our class reunions, and she never fails to ask if I am still partial to strawberry shortcake, and my answer is always the same: "You can bet on it."

Memorable Moments Flashback
Price of Products during the Late Forties

If you're a senior citizen and are reading this moment flashback, it will not surprise you that the information that follows sounds almost like fantasyland. The prices we paid for entertainment and food staples were thought of at the time as being plenty high. If you're thirty years old or younger, then it seems that stores were giving their products away, but ironically, they were making a profit at these prices.

loaf of bread	12 cents
milkshake	25 cents
shredded wheat box	18 cents
potatoes (ten pounds)	35 cents
ham salad on bun	30 cents
pork and beans (three cans)	25 cents
candy bar	5 cents
jar of baby food	10 cents
new car	$2000 to $3000
gasoline	20 cents
sliced apple pie	15 cents
movie ticket	35 cents
movie popcorn	10 cents
hamburger with chips	25 cents
hamburger (three pounds)	89 cents
chuck roast (one pound)	59 cents
grilled ham and cheese	50 cents
bacon (one pound)	29 cents
doughnuts (one dozen)	15 cents
Coca-Cola	5 cents
large candy bar	10 cents

The prevailing wage during the early fifties was 80 cents per hour and toward the end of the fifties was about $1.00 per hour. At the end of a ten-hour workday, wages came to approximately $10.00 per day. During my first farm labor job working away from the home farm at age thirteen on May 1956, wages were $6.00 dollars per day or 60 cents per hour. Workday started by reporting to work at seven o'clock in the morning and quit at six o'clock in the evening.

First Moneymaking Schemes

I f there was anything my parents taught me during the first fourteen years of my life, it was the value of the meaning of a work ethic. Along with this ethic, I was also taught that if you wanted some of the fun things in life, then you were expected to get out and earn enough money to pay for your wants. Never in my lifetime at home was I ever with a need not met, but early on, I found that I had several wants that were not going to be provided by my parents. We never worried about not having enough money or food to meet our everyday needs, but when it came to buying enough fireworks for the Fourth of July, then that was another serious problem that had to be met by the individual kid. In June and July, the issue was to have enough money to replenish fishing equipment, like sinkers, hooks, new line, and other items that would occasionally be taken by a big fish that did not make it to our dinner skillet. A real problem was acquiring enough coins to purchase a sack of fireworks large enough to keep the bang of the Fourth going for many days after the holiday was ended.

My first recollection of earning money began when I was about five or six when Mom and I reached an agreement that I would be responsible for keeping the fly population at a low number in her kitchen during the spring and summer months. With animals and chickens along with dogs and cats just a stone's throw of the back door to the kitchen, there was always a ready supply of flies working around the back porch trying to get inside. They were attracted to the odor of cooking, frying, or any preparation of food items that was constantly being made ready for one of the three meals each day.

Seldom could a person open the screen door and be quick enough getting it shut to stop at least one or two flies to enter. It was my job to swat the flies and stack them in piles of ten, and when the counting was over, I would receive one cent for each pile of ten. On a good day, it was reasonable to have a nickel or slightly more in my coin purse. The real problem was that the Fourth of July was fast approaching, and it was well-known that a nickel or two would not buy many firecrackers. After chasing flies for many hours and with the supply of flies unpredictable, it was essential for a better supply to be made available. When Mom was out in the garden or doing laundry on the back porch, I would quietly open the door and walk out very slowly, then close the door, then open it again, and slowly go back in. After about ten minutes of this procedure, it became rather tiring, so what the heck, just holding it wide open was much easier and a lot less tiring. With the supply of flies rapidly increasing, it was easy to swat enough to make at least eight to ten piles, so the money just kept rolling in. Mom said something about why in the world were there so many flies all of a sudden. I explained that brother Jim was crawling and starting to walk a bit more now and probably he was holding the door open; thus, more flies were getting in. Even with the large influx of flies available, it just did not seem to meet the need of a firecracker addict. Once again, I began thinking of ways that would increase my income. It dawned on me that my parents always got money each Saturday from taking cream and eggs to Blacks Market in Mexico and received money for their pockets. I approached Mom with the idea that maybe I could share the eggs with them so as to increase my income. She told me that they used that money from the cream and eggs to buy groceries, but if I would search the granary and the hay barn, then I could have any eggs that were laid outside the henhouse. Most of the ole hens would lay their daily egg in one of the laying boxes in the back of the henhouse, but sometimes a few would get to wandering and move outside the chicken house. Their journey usually took them to the barn where they found a comfortable spot in the hay to deposit their one egg. The reason they turned to the hay barn was to make a nest away from people and animals to have a place that they could over the period of several days have a clutch of eggs numbering six or eight. They then would begin incubating to hatch out their children so to speak. When the nest was full, they turned from a laying hen to an old setting hen where they did not lay any more eggs but sat on the nest for twenty-eight days before the hatch began. During this time, every one of the hens that turned into a setting hen took on a completely different attitude, and when approached from the outside, they would literally attack a person whose intention was to gather her eggs and turn them into firecracker money. Thus came the saying, "Mean as an old setting hen." And believe me, it was a fact that when they were laying eggs, they were easy to get along with, but the second they changed over to a setting hen, they became dangerous fighting machines. It was a well-known fact that the eggs had to be gathered daily during the spring season so that the nest never held enough eggs to turn the hen from a laying hen to a setting hen.

Returning to my moneymaking venture, I knew full well that there were at least two and maybe three hens laying in the hay. I made it a point to watch carefully to see when any ole hen left the safety of the chicken yard and headed for the hay barn. In an hour or less, there was a cackling sound coming from the barn, and this was a sign that the ole hen had laid an egg. Whenever they produced an egg, they bragged about it to tell all the other hens what and when they had made a new egg. After a few minutes, the cackling would stop, and the hen would fly out of the loft and go back to the chicken yard. This was the moment the egg gatherer had been waiting for. With a quick and quiet trip to the nest, the newly laid egg was removed. Often, another hen would hear the first hen say that her work for the day was done, so she was replaced by another that had been waiting. This was pretty lucrative moneymaking scheme, so each day, I would take the freshly laid eggs and place them gently in an empty rolled oats carton in the kitchen pantry for safekeeping. Next Saturday, I would deliver the eggs to Blacks Feed Store to collect my twenty-nine cents for each dozen collected. Problem was the eggs were not coming in nearly as rapidly as the weeks were rolling by, so the Fourth of July was going to get here long before enough coins had been saved up. What to do to make more money? Could not get more ole hens to leave the henhouse than what was their own idea, so the next best thing would be to get the eggs to go to the hayloft without the ole hens. Knowing that taking the eggs from the henhouse was not in our original agreement and thinking that it may be a kind of stealing, I made a solemn vow that I would only take a few eggs each day for the present time. When the Fourth of July was over, I would take the eggs from the barn loft and put them back into the nest until the borrowed ones had been replaced. The plan worked like a charm, so I make a trip to the henhouse, transfer two or three eggs to the barn loft, leave them in a nest that may or may not have one in it already, return later in the day, and gather the eggs. Carefully placed them in the rolled oats box in the food pantry, cash them in on a Saturday, and start all over again come next Sunday. By the time the Fourth of July came around, my savings plan had over two dollars in it. When lady fingers cost fifteen cents for a one-hundred package and bottle rockets were twenty cents a gross, one can only imagine the feeling of walking out of the store with a paper sack crammed full of fireworks. True to my Christian church upbringing, I did start returning eggs to the henhouse from the barn loft just a few days after I purchased the bag of fireworks. Cannot remember for sure, but I planned on putting back more than had been taken out, or at least that was my original intention. Mom never did catch on to the switch, or at least I never heard anything from her about the lack of eggs for a month and then the increase in eggs just a little while after the Fourth of July. I was ready with an explanation about having seen a black snake hanging around the henhouse for some time and that it had not been seen lately, thus the possible increase in hen fruit output. Best as I can recall, this method of borrowing and return took place for several years and always happened about a month before firecracker time.

Another business adventure was introduced to me just before Christmas one year when I was about nine years old. When it was time to start practicing for the program presentation for the parents, it was also time to begin making crafts to give to the parents after the program as a gift. One really popular item was the sculptured wax candles that we made by bringing a quart milk carton from home, taking a block of ice and chipping hunks of ice into a bucket then filling the carton to the top with the ice. Taking a stick that had a notch in one end placed a wick end into a groove in the stick, pushed the wick through the middle of the ice until it reached the bottom of the carton. While this was taking place, Mrs. Martin was heating a big pan of wax on the heat stove until it was turned into a pan of liquid wax. That was then poured over the ice until the wax was about an inch from the top of the carton. In a few seconds, the ice had melted, and the wick was left sticking out of the center of the carton surrounded by wax. The carton was then placed in the playroom next door until the wax was solid, which took about an hour to complete. When the carton was removed one side at a time, the water would tumble out into a pan. When all sides had been removed, there stood before us a candle that was filled with holes where the ice had once been was now pockets of air. For some, Mrs. Martin would put a lot of food color in the melted wax so that the candle would either be red or purple, but my choice was white because it looked so much more like a column of white snow standing there.

It should be mentioned that the white candle was really a nice gift but was not anything that looked like a moneymaker.

I must explain that while some were working with the candles, others were using a square metal loom and a wire hook to make pot holders for their mothers. The loom was about nine inches square with little rounded pegs on all sides. On the table were seven or eight plastic sacks of cloth loops, and each was a different color. With the loom lying flat on the table, the row of pegs was standing straight upward around the loom. The pot holder was started by stretching one end of a loop from one side to the other until there was a solid layer of loops stretched tight. Then take the wire with a hook on the end and place a loop of cloth in the hook. With the other end, we weaved the wire under a loop and over the next until it was completely through to the other side. Before pulling the loop through, one end was placed over the peg on one side, and the other was stretched over the peg on the other side. Again, the wire was weaved through the preinstalled loop but starting over the first loop whereas the first loop was weaved under the preinstalled loops. When the second layer was completed, this left a solid mat of loops that looked a lot like a rug that Mrs. Williams had made in her basement, but this was only about an eight-inch square. Using the wire hook, the first loop end was removed from the first peg, and the second loop end was pulled through the first loop, which was continued the entire outside length of the loom. Now there was a border around the pot holder that held it together. This was a completed cloth pot holder ready to give to my parent as a Christmas present. It was quickly evident that when you used one color for the first row and then a second color for the second row, the design was by far more appealing than a holder of one solid color. When we gave them to the mamas in the crowd the night of the program, there were much uuuuuuuuh-ing and aaaaaaaaaaaw-ing over the pot holders. The apparent pleasure that was projected by each lady in the audience suddenly made a light come on in my head. If every woman in the crowd liked the pot holders so much, they would probably be willing to buy them if they were available. When we returned to school after the holiday break, I asked Mrs. Martin where a person could find the little metal loom, and she said that they were available from Woolworth's five-and-dime store in Mexico. From that moment on, I was on a mission: get a loom and get a sack of loops and start manufacturing as soon as possible. The next time we were in Mexico, I had my entire lifesavings in my pocket and was headed for Woolworth's the minute Dad turned off the engine. Forget what the loom cost, but the huge bag of loops was twenty-five cents each bag. I began my venture with four colors—red, white, black, and blue. The next day, I started making pot holders and, by the end of the afternoon, had twelve completed. When we headed for school the next morning, the pot holders were carefully packed in a brown grocery sack. By moving the books around in my desk, there was just enough room to have a safe place to keep them for the day. When school was dismissed, I made a mad dash to the row of houses down the road from Grandpa Burl's, and first houses to hit were the biggest and whitest ones in Santa Fe. The price was twenty cents each or two for thirty-five cents, and by the time I knocked on the fifth house, my inventory was completely gone, and I had over two dollars cash in my pocket. When Dad got off work from the mill that evening and we had done the chores and cleaned up after supper,

I set up a card table in the living room and, under the light of the coal oil lamp, began the manufacturing of pot holders. With a little trial and error and with only four colors to work with, I spent each night for the next several days putting together various combinations of colors. It seemed that the combination of red and white and black and white was by far the most popular, so in short order, the bag of white loops was empty. Next trip to Mexico and now carrying a stash of over two dollars in my blue jeans' pocket, it was time to invest. I spent the next hour carefully studying the many colors available. The trip home had us kids sitting in the back seat next to eight bags of loops crammed in between us. Next several evenings were devoted to making every color combination possible with the many colors of loops that now were available. When the brown paper sack was filled with completed holders and the weight was about all a short kid could carry by himself, it was then time to once again hit the streets of Santa Fe. This time, I did not only hit the rich families but knocked on every door down every street and was delighted to find that it was not only the ladies in the big white houses that bought out the quarters. Nearly all of them would buy at least one or more from the huge selection that was available. When I hit Tommie Hendrick's house, it was a total surprise when she kept going through the stack and pulling certain ones out and placed them in a pile on the kitchen counter. When I left her home, I had in my pocket a great deal more than what the entire bags of loops and the loom cost altogether, so with a little math thinking, it was pretty easy to see that everything else I sold or would sell was to be clear profit. It was the jingle in my pants' pocket that had real meaning as to whether the venture was successful, and right now, it seemed that it was really going well. By the time I covered the entire town, which took three afternoons after school, and by working up a new batch when I got home, my Sir Walter Riley tobacco tin can was filled, and my desire to make more pads had dwindled to almost zero. Lost count of how many I made and sold, but nearly all the loop bags were near empty. This would mean that I was almost out of business and was completely out of the desire to make any more pot holders, so retirement was inevitable. Several days later when I was at Dad's mill barn waiting to go home,

Tommie asked if I had any more red and white ones left over. I did not but promised her that I would make her some in the very near future. She wanted a half dozen, and when they were delivered, it was at that moment my business venture of pot holder manufacturing came to a complete halt.

Jim and the Outhouse Pit

When writing about the good ole days and remembering how great things were during the forties and fifties, it is seldom that things that were not all that good come to the surface. I would classify the presence of the little shack out back with the half moon carved in the door would fall into the category of not all that good. Not that it wasn't a very essential part of our lives, it just so happens that it was there for such a short period of usage that we overlooked it being a part of a way of life way back then. The ones that I was familiar with were all two hollers, and usually each hole was of two various sizes. Not that you could not use either one you chose; butt size was very important to the person visiting the facilities. Everyone today thinks that there has to be a least two bathrooms in any given house, but back then, one was totally sufficient as the amount of time sitting behind closed door was quite minimal. This was especially true when the temperature outside was well below freezing and the temperature inside the shack was just as cold. It was a matter of fact that the little building was not in the immediate area of the living quarters of any family. It was in fact about as far away from open windows as could be arranged especially in the summer months when the air was heavy and the aroma of bygone visits drifted with the wind. With warmer weather, one would find the trip heading due east of our house not much of an ordeal, but with deep snow and a freezing wind whipping around the corner of the little shanty, it was much more of an absolute necessity that it not take more than a few minutes to get there, make a deposit, and then make a mad dash back to the house. One never found a waiting line outside the little building, and for sure, no one was waiting during the months of December through March.

Several stories come to mind involving the little building, and one of the worst was with little brother Jim when we were visiting Grandma and Grandpa Burl on a Sunday afternoon in Santa Fe. With several kids of all ages wandering around the house and looking for something to do, it was mentioned let's play hide-and-seek. One was selected as "it" and hiding their eyes behind their hands began counting to twenty-five. The entire bunch of kids scattered like a covey of quail flushing out of a weed bed. Little brother Jim made a mad dash across the backyard, ran directly behind the outhouse, and came to a sudden stop. It seems that Grandpa Burl had dug a deep hole in his backyard years before and placed the open bottom shanty over the hole. After many years of heavy usage, the hole was about flush with the top of the ground. He dug a hole in front of the little building and moved the outhouse forward over the top of the new hole.

After covering the previous pit with a foot of fresh dirt and planting new grass, little thought was given to any problem that would arise from this old pit as it was completely covered. Brother Jim made the turn around the corner of the little building when he suddenly found the ground beneath his feet giving away to a very moist, very deep, and very stinky liquid that went over his feet and above his knees. What the grownups sitting in the front yard under the shade trees heard was a high-pitched scream from a child that sounded like the devil had taken hold of him from behind and was loud enough to have been heard throughout the entire city of Santa Fe. When the adults pulled him away from the grip of the mixture around his legs, he lost his shoes, his socks came off, and in their place was a coating of stink that had most of the bystanders gagging and choking. I guess his shoes must have been pretty much worn-out 'cause no one tried to get them, and Jim was without shoes until the next trip to Mexico.

Another memorable episode was at Aunt Naomi's house one summer when the clan had gathered for dinner and was sitting around the backyard under the big oak trees after all had eaten much more than they should have. At the corner of the yard was a big chicken house, and just beside it was the little privy. Not sure which lady it was but think it was Aunt Martha who, after drinking lots of ice tea at lunch, needed to make a trip to the little building. No one paid any attention to this happening as it was nothing out of the ordinary for people in despair to disappear behind the closed door and appear in a few minutes walking much more relaxed. However, this time, the person behind the closed door remained only a few seconds when there was a banging and yelling and stomping around on the wooden floor.

Suddenly, the door flew open, and out came a lady with her undies around her ankles and making a rapid exit away from the little building. After getting her drawers back to their original position, she let out a stream of words that was about half mad, half scared, and totally in pain. Just so happened, a nest of wasp had set up housekeeping just under the right hole beside the opening from above. When a fleshy white portion of a lady appeared very close to their nest, there were several guardian wasps who took exception to this invasion. They did what wasp do best when irritated by placing several stingers in a very tender portion of the intruder. I would have to say that it was a very effective method of getting rid of potential danger. I did feel sorry for Uncle Jody having to replace the door as it was now in several separate pieces scattered around the yard. The family tried to be serious about the matter, but there were several muffled chuckles heard from the crowd.

Along the same line but not nearly as well witnessed was the time I hastily made a journey toward the little shanty. Barely making it in time due to waiting for the last second to make the long trip, I did not take time to notice anything out of the ordinary. Unbeknownst to me, the back boards of the little building had come loose and fell down leaving the area under the seat wide open to the chickens. As it was midspring and with warm weather came the changeover from laying hen to setting hen throughout the hen population. All of the older hens were seeking a quiet, out-of-the-way, secluded spot to build a nest. One such hen found this to be a comfortable out-of-sight location away from people and predators. She made her nest and deposited several eggs over the past week and was now patiently incubating them.

If you've been raised around old setting hens, you know that it takes very little for them to become hostile and very aggressive once they start the hatching process. After hours of sitting quietly and peacefully, the old hen was very happy with her choice of nesting places. Suddenly, something appeared directly above her and within inches of her newly acquired nesting area. Her first instinct took over, and that was to attack the threat, and attack she did. Wings flopping, bill pecking, claws scratching, and squawking like a screech owl, she changed what was usually a quiet nonthreatening atmosphere of the privy to a hellhole of unexpected pain and noise. It did not take long for the little boy with his pants down to stop what he was doing and evacuate the building and be twenty yards away in less than a heart-beat. Having sat on that one particular hole dozens of times without so much as a whisper, I am now convinced to check out any and every open area before ever sitting down again.

Along the same line and in the same building was the story of the metal wastepaper bin. To eliminate buildup under the outhouse, there was always a basket or bin sitting in the corner to receive used tissue or catalog pages. One day while sitting on the little hole, a slight movement caught my eye, and the previous encounter came to mind. There in the basket all snuggled down in a comfortable nest was another ole hen looking straight at me just daring me to make a move in her direction. Not wanting to go through another attack like previously, I very slowly pulled up my overalls and quickly eased toward the door. No doubt, one wanted to be cautious around a set-ting hen that has taken up residence in the hall of relief.

Childhood Medical Problems

It is very easy to write about fun memories going back to my really early years because of the great times encountered daily. The time has come, however, to look deep into the moments when trials and tribulations of growing up became memories that remain vivid but ones that have been shoved into the background. It started when, at age of eight years, I heard Mom and Dad talking among them about how thin one of their kids had become and seemed to be getting thinner. With a little bit of looking and watching the other two kids, it was pretty easy to narrow down which one they were talking about. Mary was becoming a very pretty young woman and beginning to develop into a lady, so that pretty well put her out of the picture. Then there was brother Jim. Kid was bouncing off the walls, throwing tantrums, going everywhere at a dead run, and knocking down everything and everybody that got in his way. Pretty much could agree that it was not Jim they were discussing. Now that narrowed down the field drastically of who was the subject.

Thinking back, it all began to dawn on me that I was really not the kid that was here a couple of months ago. About noon each day, it seemed that my energy had just about disappeared, and taking a nap was the only thing that I could do and do well. I remember Mom saying, "Suppose we need to get him to the doctor and see why he has become so thin and pale all the time." Two days later, we found ourselves sitting in Dr. Nieshum's exam room on a table with hardly any clothes on and a really bright light that did not seem to be putting out any heat for being as bright as it was. Made me wonder why it was so cold in this bright room. With several "stick out your tongue and say aaaaawwwwww" request and poking around on my neck with hands that were colder than the bench I was sitting on, the doctor said to Mom and Dad, "Nothing serious, he has a bad case of tonsillitis, and soon as we get them out, everything will be just fine."

Everyone seemed relieved, and the way he said it, I kind of figured it would be about like taking off a pair of overalls so we could get back to the farm and take up with fishing and things like it was before. As procedures went back in the good ole days, they took a blood sample and scheduled the taking out of the tonsils for next midweek. We returned home that afternoon, and everything was almost back to normal by the time we pulled into the driveway. Phone rang a couple of days later, which was a long ring and two short, which meant this call was for the Willinghams. There were four families or parties as they were called on each line, so when it rang, it depended on what number of rings were as to who was to pick up the phone and answer. There was little doubt that when the phone rang, there would be the click when we raised the receiver and four more clicks when the other "parties" clicked in. Was less than amazing how quick the clicks signaled someone was snooping on the other end to see what the one certain party that received the call was about to hear. Those people must have been standing beside the phone that was attached to the wall to be able to pick it up so quickly and be ready to listen in on the conversation. For sure, the one long ring and two short was certainly for us, so with a polite "hello" from Mom, the discussion began. Was not hard to tell it was Dr. Nieshum from the loud voice on the other end and not hard to tell that the news being delivered was not about the weather, so with several short answers from Mom, the call was over. Nothing was said until Dad got home that night and Mom said that we all needed to sit down for a few minutes and talk; it became apparent that there was more to be said than one wanted to hear. The short story was that we could not do the operation as quickly as we had originally planned because the blood test came back positive for something called Undulant Fever. Mom got out the medical dictionary, and there in a short paragraph was something about a blood disorder obtained from drinking whole milk from a cow that had not been properly vaccinated for some big word that no one in our family could pronounce. The short of the story was that this germ got into the body and started spreading out to the important parts of the body and made the person with the germ grow sick and weak and lose weight until the parts quit working. The tonsils would have to wait until the germ was killed and the body began to gain weight and the kid had more energy. In short order, I was sitting on the cold table again but in some kind of robe that was loose in the back and had cold air going all around my body. Dr. Nieshum said that we were to be at the hospital, which was down the road from his office, four times a day to get a shot, and this was to take four days. Being young, the math was way over my head, so Mom said that we would start today and be there four times a day for four days. As we lived about thirty minutes from Mexico, it was almost impossible to drive day and night from home to the hospital, so Dad called Uncle Roy who lived about six minutes from town and told him about the problem. Aunt Martha said to just move me into their house and they would get me to the hospital when needed and would not be a problem. It entered my mind that, as much as I loved Uncle Roy and Aunt Martha, it just did not seem that good an idea that I go anywhere close to that scary hospital without my mom and dad or both. As it was, Mom made the trip in with me every six hours during the day, and Dad would come up in the evening after working all day on the mill and after doing the evening chores. Not knowing just what six hours consisted of, it seemed every time I turned around, we were heading into town, walked into the side entrance to the hospital, and became engulfed with the smell of alcohol and disinfectant and occasionally a heavy choking smell of ether. First trip in, I remember being so scared that my legs would not work, so Mom had to help me and sit me on the table. Good part was that I did not have to put on that half-open gown to get the shot. The first visit to the hospital was early the next morning. As I sat on the table, a mountain of a woman entered the room. She had dark skin and huge arms and hands sticking out from under a bleached white and heavy starched nurse's uniform with a little funny hat sitting on her head. She had in her hand a tube and needle that looked no larger than a darning needle that Mom used to knit holes in our socks. It dawned on me it was because the size of her hand that made the needle looks so little. As she was coming toward me, it seemed the closer she got, the bigger she became. I guess I was crawling up Mom's arm trying to put some distance between the nurse and myself when, all of a sudden, she pulled out a huge red sucker from behind her back. She said in a really low voice something about having a treat for me, and if I would let her give me a shot, I could have the red sucker all to myself. Well, being scared of a needle and giving up the chance to fill my sweet tooth with that huge sucker suddenly made that needle and that huge nurse not to appear nearly as dangerous as before she showed me the candy. To be truthful, all Willinghams have a really large sweet tooth, and the next thing she said was "Now if you be a really brave big boy and take all the shots Dr. Nieshum wants you to take without crying, I will have a really big sack of candy after it is all over." Heck, I was not really paying any attention to the needle or to the pinprick that came with the shot. I was totally overpowered by the hunk of nurse that was carrying the needle and had that big red sucker in her other hand. The part of not crying was a piece of cake because it really never did hurt all that much. Was more of an inconvenience than painful. The nurse and I became really good friends over the next several visits and even got to looking forward to her coming into the room with the needle. Got to wondering did she work all day and night because she was there to meet me almost every time we sat down among that terrible odor of alcohol, disinfectant, and ether no matter if it was around noon or two o'clock in the morning. There was another really nice nurse a few times but not many. I thought that I would never forget the name of my favorite nurse, but to this day, I can shut my eyes and see her just as plain as if she was standing in front of me but cannot remember her name. Did get a little sore after a couple of days of shots as my arm was about the size of a badminton racket handle. After the sixteen shots and half-dozen pricks to draw blood, it did hurt but did not hurt enough to cry or get in the way of seeing that sack of candy I was promised. True to her word, the last shot was sometime in the early morning around three o'clock in the morning when she handed me a brown paper sack. It was so heavy I could barely hold it off the chair. Inside was everything that I had dreamed would be inside a sack of candy. It looked nearly as good as the candy counter of the general store in Santa Fe where Mr. Williams peeked down at us while we tried to make up our mind of what a nickel would buy. I really thought a lot of my special nurse after all that we had gone through. Figured that after the last shot and receiving the sack of candy, my nurse would fade away into the hospital. We were in the hospital many, many times after the round of shots, and seldom did I go there that she did not see me and give me a big hug. I bet she is still working in a hospital somewhere this nearly seventy years later, and you can bet that she is one huge lady with a heart twice as big as her arms, and that would be a big heart.

Now that the series of shots were over and the last blood test was drawn, we had to wait another day for the results to come back. If they were negative, then we could go home and wait for the hospital to call and give us a date to have the tonsils out. This meant that we had one more day to stay at Uncle Roy's, and that meant one more day to be around the five kids that belonged to Uncle Roy plus brother Jim. They were all staring at my bag of candy like a bunch of circling buzzards. All the time we were upstairs playing with the model train set that belonged to cousin Donnie, I held on to the bag for dear life. I knew that the moment I let my guard down, the candy-eating critters would be in the bag like a hoard of hungry hyenas on a fresh kill. When cousin Donnie yelled up the stairs that he was going to hook up Dolly to the buggy and go across the river to get a load of watermelons, we all made a mad dash down the stairs. We all wanted to be first in line to ride shotgun and maybe even get to hold the reins and drive Dolly. Away we went across the river when, all of a sudden, a moment of panic hit me. I forgot to bring the sack of candy. Looking around, it quickly dawned on me that brother Jim and cousin Richard were not seated on the buggy with the rest of the crowd. Along with that knowledge, a sinking sensation hit me in the pit of my stomach. We had gone too far to ask Donnie to turn back, so the only thing to do was get the load of watermelons back to the house as quickly as possible. After what seemed a lifetime, we were back at the house. With a mad rush, I ran up the stairs, and as you would expect, there were Jim and Richard with chocolate on their faces and candy wrappers scattered all over the floor. I launched myself directly toward them with a shriek that would wake the dead. Two of them made a dash for the stairs and were out of sight within seconds. Surveying the damage, I could see that they had eaten several bars, but the worst part was that they had eaten my Crackling Bar. This was my favorite and one that I was saving for a time at home where I could enjoy it at my own leisurely pace. Was trying not to cry, but when Donnie came up the stairs, I was sobbing out loud. Donnie surveyed the problem and, with great compassion, told me that if it would make things any better, I could have the train set to take home for my very own. That for sure made a turnaround from a terrible loss and made it a lot less earth-shattering.

Even better, Jim and Richard had eaten so much candy in such a short period of time they both became sick to their stomach. Even better, Mom and Aunt Martha gave them a swift whack on the rear for doing such a mean thing to a kid that was deemed not well. If the truth be known, there was way too much candy for any one kid, so probably it was a good thing that I shared with others. The fact that I got the train set to take home made me come out on top of a bad situation.

Hospital Visit and Tonsils

It is true that time goes slowest when you are anxiously awaiting an event to occur. In the case of an eight-year-old, there really isn't anything about time that makes a huge difference unless it's your birthday or Santa Claus is coming. Occasionally, time means looking forward to Saturday and wanting to go to Mexico and be among the crowds and fast-moving traffic. When waiting for the phone to ring and hearing from the hospital to have a final date and time for tonsil removal was not all that important. Whether it happens today or tomorrow or next week would not keep a kid from doing his own thing down on the farm. There were too many things to do that a kid understands, let alone having to worry about tonsils, which never occurred up to this moment in his lifetime. There it was, one long and two shorts, a sure sign that someone was on the other end of the line awaiting someone to pick up the phone and say hello. With very little too do and not more than ten words spoken by Mom, it was all said, and the time was set. She said that we were to be at the hospital next Thursday no later than nine in the morning and was scheduled for the operation at one that afternoon. What she said really did not mean much to me as I was barely aware of time being important, let alone worry what day it was that had us at the hospital at one o'clock. Several days later, it was pretty evident that this was the day as Dad did not go to work and Mom fixed us breakfast together like it was Sunday. I guess everyone was excited about this being the day, everyone except me. It did enter my mind that maybe my favorite nurse may be there, and after this tonsil thing was over, maybe there would be another bag of candy like the first one. Mom took a little paper sack and placed a clean pair of socks and a clean pair of underwear in it all folded neatly and handed it to me. She said that I was to be sure we got to the hospital with it, so I would have something clean to wear home in a couple of days.

Well, two days meant two suppers would go by before we were to be home, so now things were starting to make a little sense. Arriving at the hospital right on time, checking in at the front desk, smelling the same old strong alcohol, disinfectant, and hint of ether—all seemed to be just about as it was the last time we were here. Looked for my nurse but was very disappointed not to see her in her large white uniform with that funny little hat sitting on her head. We were told to go to the second floor and check in with the information desk, and they would tell us what room we would be in and about what time the tonsils would be taken out. Up the many steps we went, did what we were told, and sure enough, they took us to a room that had two beds and a couple of chairs. Mom took the little brown bag from me and placed it in a drawer beside the bed. A nurse came in with a big smile dressed in a white uniform and the little hat on her head, but she was a lot smaller, and the hat looked like it should have been on her head. It looked a lot more like it fit her than the hat on my favorite nurse because she was so little. Once again, a blood sample was taken just like the time and time before, so it was not a big thing. Nurse said something about being a really big boy and not bothered by the needle. If she had as many needle pricks as I had in the past few weeks, she would have known that it does not take a big boy not to pay attention, just one who was so full of holes another one was like old times. Thought about asking her if there was a sack of candy included with the needle but figured she was so young and little that she would not know what I was talking about. She told me to put on the gown, and when our turn came to go in, she would come get me to start taking out the tonsils. I had never seen this type of gown before. It was even more wide open and a lot airier than the gowns I used before. My sister Mary always wore a gown to bed, but this type gown was nothing like anyone would wear if they were in their right mind. Put it on and noticed that there was not a back in it and at no time did it stay closed no matter how much you pulled the ends around. As I said before, time did not make much difference to a kid. Well, that was before I put on the wide open-backed gown. With my rear uncovered and the cool air making goose bumps all over, it seemed that it was forever before the nurse returned. When she did finally show up, she said that the doctor was expecting me in the next few minutes. Dad picked me up and laid me on a cold table that had wheels on it, and the nurse put a sheet over me. She said to say goodbye to my parents and that we would be seeing them in a few minutes. There it was again: see them in a few minutes. Figured if the few minutes before seeing Mom and Dad again were as long as my rear was showing behind the gown, then it may be several days before that happened. Table ride ended in a big room with a ceiling full of really huge lights and a whole bunch of people walking around with mask over their faces as if it were trick or treat time. The only one I recognized was Dr. Nieshum, and that was mainly because he said my name and sounded like he did in his doctor's office downtown. He said, "Kennie, we are going to put a cloth over your face, and we want you to take deep breaths and count from one to ten. You will get very sleepy, and in a few minutes, you will wake up and be in the room with your mom and dad. Don't be frightened because I will be right here beside you all the time you are asleep. When you wake up, you will be a little groggy, and you will have a sore throat. Try not to talk or cry as this will make it sorer, so be very quiet, and it will go away. After that, you can have some Jell-O and ice cream to celebrate your tonsils being gone. They will be gone the rest of your life."

They did put a damp cloth over my face, so I started to take a deep breath. The smell of really strong ether almost took off my head. I tried to follow directions and count, but all of a sudden, the numbers would not come out, and the world was going faster than a merry-go-round, and I was flying through the sky in really fast circles. The next thing I remember was lying on the bed in the room where I left Mom and Dad. They were sitting in a chair beside me holding my hand and saying something about be very still and it will all go away. They were partially right; in a little while, things started to make a little more sense, and before long, the dizzy spell went away to some degree, and things were just as they were before.

Not! As the sleepy feeling began to leave slightly, there was suddenly a great big amount of pain in my throat. Every time I swallowed to get rid of the pain, the more pain came to my throat. Suddenly, I felt this hate come over me, the hate of the pain, the hate of not being able to swallow, and most of all the hate for that Dr. Nieshum for not telling the truth.

The nurse came in and gave me some little pieces of ice, and to my surprise, it did make the pain in my throat go away for a very short time. At the same time, I got so sleepy that I could not hold my eyes open, so in a few minutes, I was fast asleep. The next time my eyes opened, it was dark as night inside the room and dark outdoors as well. I finally figured that it was night and not just after sundown but way after sundown. Best part of having slept that long was the fact the throat was really sore but not nearly as painful as it was before I fell asleep. The nurse appeared and helped me sit up. She had a tray sitting on a little table across my lap, and on the tray was a small dish of ice cream and another of orange Jell-O. At any other moment in my life, those treats would have a life expectancy of a few seconds, but right now, the idea of eating anything was totally out of reason. After a great deal of coaxing, I did put a little ice cream in the back of my mouth and found not only was it good but it also seemed to rid some of the raw sore throat that was in the place where my tonsils used to be. After eating a small amount out of each bowl, the nurse laid me back down, and just as before, I fell asleep instantly. After a time of who knows how long, I woke up and saw Dad was lying beside me sound asleep and Mom was sitting in a chair at the end of my bed with her head on a pillow and was also asleep. The next thing I remember was waking up, and it was daylight outside. Mom and Dad were both sitting in a chair reading the *Mexico Ledger*. In the bed next to them was another boy lying asleep with his mom and dad sitting beside him. They became aware both patients were now awake and that both patients were beginning to realize how sore their throats had become. It was pretty evident that both were missing a set of tonsils and wishing that they could go back to sleep where there was no pain. Another lady in white entered pushing a cart with two trays on it. Once again, ice cream and this time a purple Jell-O were placed before us. Being a long way from painless but starting to feel hunger pains, sitting up and eating some of what was in each dish seemed to be a lot easier. After most of the tray was empty and being able to sip a little water from a straw, things seemed to be heading in a direction of feel better soon. A feeling of Mother Nature calling occurred, and the urge to pee was pretty serious. Dad bought over a little porcelain pan-looking thing that had a hole in the side, and the patient was supposed to go in that thing instead of the bathroom. Noticing the absence of underwear under the open-backed gown, I found myself wondering why Mom had me bring the extra pair that was folded carefully in the drawer beside the bed. The thought of no underwear was suddenly gone when, all of a sudden, a screaming pain began between my legs and rapidly shot upward through my entire body. This pain was just as bad as the one that shot through my throat after the tonsils were removed but seemed several degrees worse and a long way from my throat. Throwing back the sheet to see why taking a pee would produce such agony and having peed a thousand times before without pain wondered just what the deal was this time around. The thought ran through my mind just where were those tonsils actually located as they always checked my neck before. After a short period of time, the worst of the pain began to subside. Dad put the cover back over me and—in a very gentle and way-too-quiet voice for Dad—said, "Kennie, the operation you had that caused the sore throat was where your tonsils were taken out. The other sore place you have is where the doctor cut off the small piece of skin on your private that's called a circumcision. You had two surgeries at the same time, one above and one below so you can be healthier at both places. Dr. Nieshum said that you will heal in a few days and will forget about how bad it hurts right now." Yea, right, forget about it, my foot. After sixty plus years, I can still remember it like it was yesterday, and everything you have read in this episode was said word for word and fact for fact. One would wonder just how long it will take me to "just forget about it." The ole saying that time heals all wounds is pretty much a matter of fact, and sure enough, after the second day, the ice cream and Jell-O was swallowed with much less pain, and going to the bathroom was a lot like it was in the days before taking out the tonsils. When I was dismissed on the following Sunday morning, we loaded into the car very carefully and as it was Sunday close to noon and everyone was going to meet at Uncle Mike's for Sunday dinner just like they had for years before. As I got out of the car, I noticed all my aunts and uncles sitting or standing around on the porch awaiting our arrival. I very gently took steps toward the house, and everyone was saying how glad they were to see me and saying nice things about how brave I had been. Well, not all because there was Uncle Roy trying his best to be serious but not doing a very good job of it. He was laughing so hard he had tears in his eyes. When I got up close to him, he reached out and hugged me and said through rounds of laughter, "Boy Kennie, I bet you never realized that your tonsils would go that far down." To his dying day, Uncle Roy would bring up the story of how funny it was I had such a surprised look on my face. When he said this, he always broke down laughing. To this day, I feel good about giving Uncle Roy something that made his day a little brighter. Ironically, when we were cleaning out my parents' house many years after they passed away, we came upon the original hospital bill and paid receipt that Mom had kept all these years. The total cost for the hospital was thirty-four dollars and five cents, and the overall cost was an even fifty dollars. You can see how amazing the fees for surgery were back in the "good ole days."

Kids and Their Toys

As we were getting ready for the 2012 Christmas season, the wife and I were looking over the strange and unpronounceable names and logos on the long list of wants the grandkids had compiled. Looking through the many booklets of ads sent out with the daily paper, one can see that there are thousands and thousands of unique and totally mind-boggling toys and electronic games kids want. Their little minds are saturated with color, with flashing lights, with motion going in all directions with lifelike sounds. All this on a screen that can be either the size of a television or small as four inches held in the hand.

Kids today would have been totally struck numb and dumb if they had been subjected to the toys and gadgets that we played with in the late forties and early fifties.

One of my favorite toys was a gun cut from a board that looked like a piece of wood with a handle connected. It was kind of shaped like what a gun should look like, but you had to use your imagination somewhat to say this was a gun. On the back of the handle, a snapping clothespin was attached with a rubber band made by cutting a narrow strip out of an old inner tube. The ammunition was another strip cut a little thicker. By placing one end of the loop over the end of the gun and stretching the other end of the loop to the end of the handle, pinching the loop at the end, and snapping it into the jaws of the clothespin, it was now loaded. Aiming at the imaginary or real target and pressing on the clothespin, the loop would be released. If the target was within the short range of the loop, it would strike the target. The longer the barrel of the gun and the shorter the loop, the farther the band would go. The recycled tube ammunition would last forever as when in a shooting duel the person on the opposite end could use the same ammunition so neither shooter ever ran out of ammunition.

Corn shucking wrist knife

Old time corn sheller. One turns the flywheel and other kid feeds ear corn into the chute.

Cheap fun pair of stilts
sounds great on concrete
walks in town.

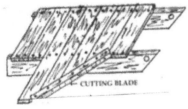

Corn cutter pulled by horse with
operator standing upright and
gathering shocks to be tied.

Handmade sling shot cut from
tree with two limbs attached.
We used rubber inner tube bands
instead of surgical tubing.

Another piece of equipment that was owned by every country boy and most girls was that of a slingshot. One could be purchased at the Montgomery Ward store in Mexico, but that took coins, which were in short supply for kids. Instead of buying one, they each would search through the woods for hours on end and examining no less than dozens of tree limbs until you found just the perfect fork. It needed to be a straight handle and a V with both sides of the V perfectly in line with the opposite side as well as the perfect size that would fit in your hand correctly. Again, the rubber inner tube was used to provide the firepower. Two strips were cut the exact same length; one end draped over the top of the V and tied in place with string. With both strips in place, a piece of leather was cut about the same length of the distance between the V top. End of the rubber band was placed through a cut in the side of the leather and once again tied with string. When both free ends of the bands had been tied off, this completed the manufacture of the perfect slingshot. The next chore was to walk down the road or the creek bed searching for the most perfect round rock that was about the size of a person's thumb. When the pouch was filled, the weapon was ready to fire. Put a rock in the pouch, pinch together the piece of leather holding the rock between the thumb and forefinger, pull it back as far as the arms would go or as far as the kid's strength would allow, sight through the V, and release the pouch making sure not to raise or lower the V. The rubber would snap back to its original length, thus propelling the stone forward at the speed of a bullet. The more perfectly round the stone, the farther and straighter it would travel. It was a given rule that you never aim the rock in the direction of another person or animal as the slingshot could actually be used as a weapon as in earlier times to kill or injure persons. If your parents caught you going against that rule, there were some pretty painful consequences to be suffered. Can't remember for sure, but I don't think the Ole Hateful Tom Cat in the granary was considered to be part of the animals excluded.

Another entertaining makeshift toy that was fun for a short period of time was the barrel hoop races. Was much more fun when there was at least two or more to compete but have actually whiled away several afternoons just running the hoop by myself. Barrels in those days were made of oak staves cut at an angle and held together in a circle with three bands of metal shaped into a large circle. When the wood eventually rotted away, you could find several of these bands in the dump below Santa Fe as they were seldom used the second time. By cutting a scrub oak sprout with a trunk about the size of a broomstick and nailing a flat board on the end, you now had a hoopstick. Each kid would have a hoop and a stick and would line up at the top of a gradual slop. At a signal, they would make the hoop roll out in front and keep it rolling by pushing it at the bottom of the hoop. One could almost guide the hoop by holding the stick sideways against the side, but control was pretty much out the window once you started down the slope. There was a turnaround at the bottom of the hill so that it was more difficult to keep the hoop going. Turning around at the bottom of the hill while rolling took skill and total control. Rule was that the only time you could touch it with your hands was if it lay out flat, then you could set it upright and try to get the stick under it for forward power. Most trouble came from the downhill run as the hoop would easily get ahead of you, and another real problem came from after the turnaround. The hoop did not want to go back up the hill as easily as it came down. It really did take some skill to keep the thing going in any certain direction, but the best part was that none of the kids got good at controlling the round piece of metal, so everyone was pretty much equal when this race took place.

Another nature-made tool used for fun was that of having a pair of stilts to walk around on. Kids five years and older were able to use a pair of stilts and instantly become a foot taller. Mary, Jim, and I would head out into the woods across the road in front of the house to search for the perfect tree that would provide a perfect pair of stilts. Usually, we were looking for a sprout that was about six feet tall, straight as an arrow, and had a limb fork about two feet from the bottom of the trunk. When you found one that met the requirements, the task was to cut it down and search far and wide for an exact replica of the first. The problem was there were three of us to outfit, so it may take several afternoons in the woods to find a pair for each kid. After the stilts had been cut to the correct size, we were ready to mount the sticks and walk around standing much taller than we were five minutes ago. To get up on the things, we laid them side by side against the side of the house or shed. Stood between the two sticks, placed one foot on the V branch stub, raised ourselves up with our back toward the wall, and then step up with the second foot. By pushing off with one's elbows, one could usually find oneself upright and ready to take one's first step. If all went well, then one could walk around the house by taking large strides by working the feet and legs in a stepping motion while picking up the entire stilt with one's underarms and hands. When having mastered the walking stage, the next step was to learn how to get onto the sticks without using the side of the house. As well as I remember, it was like pole vaulting except you used two poles instead of one. We would chase one another around the yard for hours, but as with all fun things, wear and tear would cause either one or both limbs that held the feet in place to split away from the trunk. My first big mistake was when I proceeded to take a piece of wire and tie the footrest up to its original position once it had split. I put my foot into the stirrup, took off at a rapid pace, but lost my balance and started falling face forward. Not a big problem usually as you just jumped forward when you lost your balance and landed on your feet. This time, my foot caught in the wire and fork, so instead of jumping forward, I was very stationary in my foothold, so I fell directly forward and landed flat on my chest and face with a really solid thump. Along with this thump, the stilt tended to follow me downward and cracked me across the back of the head with another jarring thump. It took several minutes for the shiny little lights and stars to disappear from in front of my eyes. That was the last time I repaired a stilt as I found that it was much safer to replace them from the forest and forget about the damaged one. Did try to make a stilt out of a two-inch-by-two-inch six-foot long oak board and nailed a block of wood where the fork was to be, but we did not have wood screws back then. The nails either split the board and block or worked loose after thirty minutes of walking around.

Another method of standing taller than real life was with the use of orange juice cans. By looking through the local dump, it was a snap to find several tall cans. These cans were about a foot tall and twice as wide as a regular can and made of a lot heavier metal. Seldom was the top or bottom cut out of these cans, so they were solid and in one piece.

By poking a hole on each side just below the top with a sixteen-penny nail, threading a long piece of binder twine or shoestring leather through the holes, and tying together the loose ends with a single knot, it made for a strong and handy handle. Stand on top of the two cans and hold the strings tight so that the cans pressed against the bottom of your shoes; you could now walk elevated above your true height. Walking on dirt was by far the quietest; but clomp, clomp, clomp of each step taken on concrete walks was far more enjoyable.

Along this same thought, especially in town where there were sidewalks and blacktop, kids would search behind the Ford garage for metal oil cans. At the time, oil cans were made of metal with a heavy rim around the top and bottom. One would lay the can on its side and then stomp on it in the middle. This caused the end to curl up on each side of the foot. By stomping several times on the concrete, the cans were clamped to both sides of the shoe. Do the same to the other can, and within minutes, you had what could almost be a set of horseshoes for the feet. When you walked or ran with these on your feet, it would make a really great clanging sound with each step. With a half-dozen or more kids running down the sidewalk, the noise was outstandingly annoying to anyone sitting or standing around the store or garage. The real deal was when you ran forward and turned sideways on the cans so that they came to a sliding halt. You could hear the scream of metal on concrete for blocks around. Most people around town had their teeth on edge. Most were very happy when the kids got tired of this noisemaking and moved on to other interest.

Another form of entertainment was found behind the skating rink. Here was a small pond about fifteen feet across and holding about a foot of water with an inch of green scum on top. Around the edges was a very strange plant that grew to a height of six to eight feet. It resembled the bamboo plant but was not jointed as such. When the plant finished blooming and making seeds, the stalks would dry up, and the blades would fall off the trunk. When you chopped off the stalk, you found the center was totally hollow inside. Measure off roughly a two-foot section and cut it from the stalk, and you now had a hollow reed that was straight as an arrow and hollow inside about the size of a pencil. When we were satisfied with the shooter, we headed down the street to the hammer mill. When farmers brought in a load of soybeans to be ground into meal, there would be little piles of soybeans on the driveway. Kids scooped up a handful of beans and put them in their pockets. The stage was set for a one-on-one or two-on-two or larger bean fight. Put a handful in your mouth, blow real hard through the shooter, and the beans would fire out the end in a steady stream of beans and spit. Any bean that found bare flesh would create a noticeable sting. If the shooter was fitted correctly to the bean, then it had a very long range, and with the more blow power from the kid, the farther it went and the worse the sting. Parents told us kids to be careful and not suck the beans down our windpipes, or it would make us very sick. Didn't find that to be a problem but frequently found a piece of dirt or small rock hidden in the mouthful of beans. Afterward, there would be a gritty sensation when your teeth came together.

Any time two or more kids got together, there was usually some type of war to be waged. In the granary, you would find a huge pile of corncobs stacked in the corner near the sheller, which always invited an impromptu throwing contest. Being only recently shelled corn, the cobs were not very hard or heavy, so getting hit with them really did not hurt a lot. On the other hand, when the walnuts began covering the ground beneath the trees, this was a horse of a different color.

When hit beside the head with a walnut, it felt about the same as getting hit with a rock or baseball. The walnut was only half the size but equally hard when it bounced off your skull.

It is easy to see there were many ways a kid could have fun. Usually, the amount of fun was directly linked to the amount of imagination a kid could come up with. We did not have electronic gimmicks to entertain us, but there seldom was a shortage of toys around to be utilized as entertainment.

Mom Dressing Chickens to Fry

D aily, a person reads about the dangers of E. coli, infections, pollutants, and many other dangers that can affect the health of an individual. You can expect there are bacteria and germs lurking around each bush and corner that may attack you at any moment. Thinking back to living in the country during the forties and fifties, we touched and ate everything that today would cause us to die an immediate death. There is article after article that says do not let raw chicken touch anything that other food would come into contact with. If it does, it says that this may cause us to become ill and possibly die. If a raw chicken touches the food preparation area, one must immediately mix one part of Clorox with ten parts of water and wipe the area down immediately. Now that in itself does sound like good advice, but think back to when my mom prepared my all-time favorite dish of fried chicken. The procedure she went through would have meant instant disease attack if it were done today. When the menu for dinner was announced to be fried chicken, the ability of going to the supermarket and getting an already plucked, gutted, and dissected fowl never entered into the menu equation. The task was accomplished by having one of the kids, namely the second born, go to the brooder house, pick up the broomstick pole that had a man-made hook on the end, and use it to snare the foot and leg of the nearest chicken. Going hand over hand along the pole until close to the wildly flopping and squawking chicken and being able to grab the leg that was loose would usually bring the fowl into a much calmer mood. Any time the chicken got one leg loose, then the gouging of the toenails and the hard surface of the two wings that were flopping around in circles would wreak havoc on the holding kid. This would bring blood to the surface of the person in charge of acquiring meat for the table. Knowing that coming back to the house without a chicken hanging upside down was not an option. No matter how much it hurt and no matter how much dirt and chicken poop were flying through the air at any one time, the goal of catching that fowl must be accomplished. Cannot ever remember not ending up with a bird in hand but do remember the distasteful smell and taste that stayed with the chicken catcher for many minutes after the successful hunt. In the early days of spring when the chickens were small and one bird would not fill the dinner plate, it took two to feed the hungry family of five at the dinner table. This meant having to go through the above-mentioned procedure twice. When the chosen fowl or fowls were delivered, Mom would go directly to the cherry tree in the backyard that had twin loops of binder twine hanging from a tree limb. They were about chest high to an adult; she placed the loop of twine around both feet, stepped back a half step, and held the chicken by the head. With the other hand, she whacked off the head with a huge butcher knife. It was very important that she move back quickly to avoid the blood splattering that occurred until the headless chicken ceased to flop. Was quite a feat to be able to have two hanging side by side and get both heads off and move a safe distance away and not get a drop of blood on the beheading person. I was lucky enough to never have to do the part of removing the head from the chicken that had just minutes previously nearly beat me half to death. Next came the feather removal portion of the making ready for the dinner table. While I was capturing the fowl in the chicken brooder, Mom was bringing a teakettle of water to a boil on the kitchen stove. After removing the dead chicken from the twine, she put the entire carcass into a three-gallon bucket head-first or first where there originally was a head. She poured scalding hot water over the entire bird and let sit underwater for a couple of minutes. Removed the bird from the pail and, holding it up by the legs, began pulling the feathers from the bird in huge handfuls. If there were two of them, one was handed to me. After several minutes of trying not to become nauseated from the putrid smell surrounding the entire area and after pulling and yanking wet nasty feathers with very little to show for my efforts, Mom would finish the first one and take the second from me. When they were totally featherless and devoid of most feathers, she returned to the house with the two nude chickens, turned on the stove burner, and held the carcass over the open flame. This is what she called "singeing the feathers." If you thought the smell of hot wet feathers was bad, you should have been there when the fire consumed the small little pin feathers that were left. Now came the butchering portion of the chicken. Placing the chicken in a pan of water, she dissected each wing and leg from the carcass. Now the pieces were starting to resemble parts that would in the near future be fried and placed on the dinner table. The gross part now took place when she cut out the pooper end and removed an amazingly huge amount of chicken guts. Out came the gizzard, which is the part that grinds the grain and bugs and anything else the chicken had swallowed during its last meal. This all was washed off clean in the same pan that held the other chicken parts. Cutting and turning the gizzard inside out made the task of cleaning this part much easier. There now was another smell that was vastly different from that which had previously filled the room. It took little imagination to know what had been released from the gizzard especially if you had been around the barn or the farm and witnessed the sight and smell of animal byproduct. After disassembling the entire bird, she rinsed the many parts in clean water. One could imagine that it was now germ-free and all the bad stuff was eliminated when the bucket contents were thrown out the back door to where the hogs would clean up the leftovers. When you think about it, one would wonder if Mom should have mixed one part of Clorox with ten parts of water to scrub down the countertop. Never did remember the distinct smell of bleach being in the kitchen, so I guess there were no germs left on the countertop where Mom was peeling potatoes, baking bread, boiling green beans, or whatever. Germs probably did not last long back then, which was the reason we did not all get sick and die. You can bet your sweet bippie that when Mom said, "You all wash your hands; dinner is ready," the last thing on my mind was if E. coli was present around my plate of fried chicken, mashed potatoes covered with cream gravy, slab of bread covered with the same gravy, and green beans floating around the entire plate. Dad and I each got a thigh. Jim got a drumstick. Mary got two wings because they were small, and Mom got a breast. The leftover pieces were split among the family the second time around. After cleaning up the leftover potatoes, wiping out the gravy bowl with a piece of bread, making sure there were no "crispies" left on the meat platter, everybody took their dishes to the sink. Now the argument began on who did the dishes last night and who was the one responsible now. You can almost bet that the youngest child was pretty much left out of the equation. Nearly everyone at the dinner table would tell you that a fried chicken dinner was one of the most sought-after meals that Mom would put before us.

Kids' Annual River Campout

I f parents are reading this and have children between seven and twelve years of age and knowing the dangers of today would allow a seven-year-old kid to freely roam the streets of Mexico or turn them loose for a day in the country, they should have their heads examined. When the years were 1948 through 1950 and later children were not concerned with harm coming from anyone in the human race. Our parents left the decision up to kids as to what was safe and what was of imminent danger. If we got hurt, it was because of action taken by ourselves that put us in a position of receiving cuts, scrapes, and bruises. Usually, a spot of blood produced because of not paying attention was all that was needed to educate the individual of cause and avoidance of future occurrences. If you took the time to read several articles written in this going back to bygone days of youth, you can see that I was left to my own devises to decide as to what was dangerous and in most cases activities that were fun and safe.

One activity that took place every summer after we were ten years old was the annual three-day campout on the banks of Salt River. After weeks of planning, a group of young men would load all the necessary items needed to exist for three or four days at a remote wooded site alongside the river. Our first campsite was below J. C. Kessler's house located a mile and a half from the city limits of Santa Fe. I and a half dozen of my most adventurous buddies chose a campsite just below the Salt River Bridge east of Santa Fe. We located a deep running riffle with an ideal flat dirt shelf and dumped all our supplies and camping gear ready to set up camp. First task was to stretch a rope between two trees and drape a huge canvas tarpaulin over it to provide a tent. We proceeded to stake down the sides and corners. It was a heavily oiled tarp, which we figured instantly had not been used for a long time because of the mold and choking oil aroma that made your eyes water. Spreading out sheets of plastic and rolling out our bedroll blankets and pillow was accomplished in a very few minutes so that we could evacuate the mold and get back into the great-smelling aroma of deep woods and running river. Next project was to build a circle of rocks for our cooking needs and fire safety, which was done with rapid success. All headed into the woods with instructions to bring in a load of firewood, so with the stack of dry sticks in place, the preparation of camp was complete. With the fire kindled and the snapping of burning wood, our attention turned to the river for swimming, and tubing was the next order of the campers. After hours of dam building across the riffle, same amount of time with water fights and races across the river, and all else that goes with camping, it was time to prepare supper and settle down for a quiet night of river living. My job was to peel, slice, and fry potatoes for the upcoming meal. Banked up the fire for perfect cooking coals, filled the pan with grease, and planned on having brown and crispy potatoes just like Mom made at home. Others got out hot dogs, prefried chicken that one of the Moms had sent, bread, crackers, and many kinds of mustard and ketchup. As the hungry crew sat around the fire waiting not all that patiently and after what seemed a long time of cooking in the grease, the crisp potatoes were far from crisp. The fire died down to just warm, and all around the camp sat guys with a paper plate and fork at the ready. Sure did not look like the potatoes that Mom made. Not to wait so long that the guys sitting around the fire started making rude remarks, I removed the potatoes out of the cooling lard. What appeared were not so crispy potatoes. A heaping portion was placed on each plate, and everyone dove into supper without paying a lot of attention that the potatoes were not restaurant perfect. Did not take long to figure the meal was a huge success. After the cleanup detail finished the cleanup work, all bodies rushed to the river and continued with the waterworks. Problem surfaced shortly after the soggy and greasy potatoes had been wolfed down. After about an hour of having great fun in the muddy river, there was a mass migration of bodies up the riverbank heading for the privacy of the nearest grove of trees. It was decided later that there was not anything much worse than throwing up greasy potatoes, but coming a close second was having the stomach cramps and outhouse runs that accompanied it. After stomachs and lower intestines calmed down, it was decided that sitting around the campfire and getting to bed early was not all that bad an idea. Cannot speak for the other guys, but for myself, I could say that I was worn to a frazzle. What with the dark outside the campfire, noises that were coming from far and near, splashing of water just a few feet from my pillow, sounds that could only be made by flesh-eating critters, and a host of mosquitoes making a steady hum, there were many thoughts running through my head. Stories told about the unseen dangers in the forest were suddenly up close and personal. It was hours before sleep finally took over my thoughts.

The second day began with preparing breakfast of scrambled eggs, bacon, and dried-out bread held over the coals that was supposed to resemble toast but did not even come close. After cleanup, the crew headed for the river to see what we had missed during the dark hours. Bob Moore and I walked the riverbank to check out the bank lines, and a couple of other guys headed out in the rowboat to check farther up the river. We had planned on having pan-fried fish for lunch, but as it turned out, the lack of catching fresh fish pretty well spoiled that part of the menu. By midmorning, out came the inner tubes, and swimming for the day began. Paddled up the river in the tubes, floating back to the riffle, paddled up the river, floating back to the riffle was the game plan. With all the excitement, we almost forgot that it was now time for lunch. With no fish on the menu, we dropped down to plan B. Out came the spam and canned sardines; out came the soda and candy bars along with crackers and bread smeared with ketchup and/or mustard. After the nutritious lunch part, the tribe set out in the boat to check and rebait the bank lines. Upon their return, we could not think of anything any more fun than what we had been doing since we arrived, so tubing and water fights were in order.

Supper was a lot easier this time around as the hot dogs and chips took place of the previous menu of fried potatoes. When asked if anyone wanted to have crispy fried potatoes again, they all chose potato chips instead. After supper was completed and camp cleaned up, the guys were sitting around, and the talk was about what to do next for excitement. One mentioned singing around the campfire, but the hoots and jeers he received about his idea pretty much put the damper on that possibility. Someone came up with the idea why not ride bikes up the gravel road into Santa Fe and check out what we had missed since we began our campout. We had almost forgotten about the bikes that Dad trucked to the camp as they had been stacked against the trees from day one. Really did not appeal to me as that would be a long pedal all the way back to the house and then all the way into Santa Fe on gravel road. I decided it would be easier to stay in camp and take out the boat and fish upstream where we had bank lines set. Ernie Hanna had the same idea as me about not making the long trip by bike. Ernie was pretty much a laid-back individual and not one to put forth a waste of energy, so staying with me was a good idea and one I appreciated. Over the hill, they did go, and with them went the talking and noise level that the entire group had been making for the past two days. Only then did it dawn on me how quiet it was sitting in the middle of the woods with dusk fast approaching. So quiet indeed that we could hear the water bubbling over the riffle, the whirl of wind produced from the wings of an owl, so quiet that you could hear leaves rustling and twigs snapping deep in the woods. As the sun began to set, Ernie and I decided that now would be a great time to get up the river and throw out lines baited to attract a couple of huge catfish. Loading the essentials for boating, which included a coal oil lantern, two poles, can of fishing worms, several candy bars, and two flashlights, we began paddling upriver. After rowing about a quarter mile upriver and finding the widest part of the river with a dirt bank on one side and a sheer bluff on the other, we both agreed that this deep water hole would be an ideal spot to seek out ole whiskers. We dropped anchor, set out the two poles, and both settled back into the boat to enjoy a relaxing leisurely fishing trip. In a matter of minutes, the sun sank below the horizon, and instant dark took over the riverbed. As there were trees hanging over the water on the bankside and a bluff straight up on the other side, there was very little if any way that light from stars or moon could penetrate the hooded waterfront. It was now time to break out the trusty coal oil lantern and light up the surroundings in an array of light. With the wick burning brightly, it was amazing how little light was produced and how dark the area around the boat remained. The quiet of the river ended abruptly with sticks snapping on the bank. It was amazing how loud the splashing of water along the riverbank became and how really close to the boat these sounds seemed to originate. Never had I heard so up close and personal what a bird of prey sounds like when flying overhead in total darkness. Dozens of times in my lifetime, I have heard fish splash when smacking the top of the water with their tails, but the sound takes on a totally new meaning when it is this dark and the splash is happening so close to where you're sitting. Not one to admit it, but this situation and location was beginning to spook me, and when Ernie said "Let's get out of here and let's go right now," I was in total agreement. Sounded like a great idea for us to get away from whatever was stalking us and find a safe quiet area to spend time until the crew returned from Santa Fe. About halfway down the river, the thought did occur that I wished that I too had made the trip down the gravel road and not stayed in this terribly frightening dark hole of the woods. When we arrived at the riffle next to camp, I was much relieved but then realized that the camp also was pitch-dark. When holding the lantern above my head, we looked in all directions and did not see any glowing eyes or hairy forms, so we felt somewhat safer. Built the fire quickly from the coals and did not stop putting on wood until it was light as early morning sunrise. Not sure how long we were on the river and do not know how long it took us to get back into camp, but after a seemingly long, long time, we heard voices coming down the road. Finally saw the little handlebar lights shining in the distance. I do remember mentioning to Ernie that it would probably be a good idea not to say much about how glad we were to be back in camp. Definitely not to mention how glad we were to see the guys back in camp just in case they asked why that was a big deal. Being scared on the river and frightened of the dark would be our little secret, and the less the others knew about it, the better things would be.

Big Day in History on the Farm: The Day the TV Arrived

One of the greatest moments on the farm happened the minute James Robert, the general store owner, pulled into our driveway one cool crispy sunny afternoon in mid-November. His journey to our house was to deliver our first television. He said that he would be at our house early afternoon, and to a twelve-year-old, early afternoon was right after lunch. Lunch was taken at twelve o'clock noon, so in what way would early afternoon be after three o'clock in the afternoon? At the time, Mom had a couch sitting against the west wall of the living room in front of the double windows. Immediately after lunch, three kids were hanging over the back of the couch with faces plastered to the cold and frosty window pain. Three little hot breaths were fogging over the view, and all three were waiting not all that patient for the deliveryman to turn into the driveway. Just beside the couch hung the wall telephone, so we each took turns asking Mom if it would be a good idea to call the store and remind them that they said early afternoon. Maybe he had forgotten that this was the day that he said the delivery would be made, so why not remind him just in case it had slipped his mind. After about the sixth request to call him, it was pretty evident that she was not going to. It seemed like a lifetime of waiting and staring out the window while the driveway was lonely and barren. After the longest time of waiting and at least three hours after early afternoon, there suddenly appeared a red truck cab with blue wooden racks turning directly into our road and headed for our house. It was well-known that the truck that James and Mac drove to Mexico each Wednesday to pick up supplies for the grocery store was the same truck that was almost ready to park beside our front yard. It finally was early afternoon, and the long-awaited moment of television arrival was about to happen. James and another guy got out of the truck. From the rear of the truck, they unloaded a cardboard box, and when they placed it in the middle of the floor, we knew that this was the moment we had been waiting for all day. They opened the box and placed the blond-colored console television set next to the wall where Mom said she wished it set up. What a beauty, it came in two pieces. The bottom was an open cabinet with a drawer in the bottom, and the top was a wooden frame with a glass front that covered the entire area from top to bottom. When James plugged the set into the cord, we three kids could hardly catch our breath from so much excitement. When he turned the set on, we could hardly wait for it to warm up and have our first TV picture in our very own living room. What the heck, nothing but snow and noise appeared where there was supposed to be a picture.

What a disappointment, a new television in our own house and all we could see was a snowy screen with a black line through it. Must have been fairly evident there were three kids with total disappointment written all over their faces. James Robert said not to get ahead of ourselves because they still had to put up the antenna before we could get reception. Whatever was an antenna and whatever was reception made no sense to us. What we knew was that we intended to see a television show by early afternoon, and at this time in later afternoon, there was still nothing to see on our new TV but snow. They returned to the back of the truck, and one of them carried a couple of long poles, and the other unloaded a huge cage-looking thing with rods sticking out of it on all sides and in all directions. It was reasonable to presume that this was the antenna, but we had no idea of what or where this monstrous metal thing had to do with making a picture on the new television. Jim and I put on layers of clothes and went out the back door into the washroom and out the back door to stand in the backyard and watch them put up an antenna. They connected a long black wire onto the metal box and then put the metal box on top of the poles. James had a block of wood with a bunch of nails sticking out of the block that were arranged in a circle in the center of the block. He placed the block on the ground. They lifted the really long pole into the air alongside the house. The bottom of the pole sat in the center of the nails. They nailed strips of metal to the side of the house and wrapped the strip around the pole and attached the other end to the house also. James said now we had an antenna, and now we would be able to get reception on the television screen. After drilling a hole in the side of the house, the guy poked the end of the black cable through the hole. The other guy went inside and pulled it through the hole until the cable reached the TV cabinet. When James hooked the wire into the back of the television, lo and behold, there was a picture on the screen, not a very clear picture but a big improvement on the snow and black line that we had before. James told his helper to go outside to the antenna pole and for me to go with him to see how to set the antenna to point straight north and for me to watch and remember how it was done. We had a better picture for the first time, so we now could say that we had a television in our very own home. James showed Mom how to change channels and how to adjust the sound, and now there were five channels that had pictures, but two were much clearer than the other three. I followed the helper back outside, and when I turned the pole and the antenna looked in another direction, I could hear Mom yell through the wall that the place we turned toward made a good picture. When the pole was facing over the big barn, we got St. Louis; when I turned it over the henhouse, I got Hannibal. A little more to the right and I got a Quincy station. With little to do and spending a few minutes going over instructions with Mom, the two men gathered up the big box and in a few minutes were gone. We were left with just the family and a brand-spanking-new television set in our very own living room. To say that the arrival of the TV set made little change in our happy household would be like saying Salt River was a little wet. Every second of peace and quiet of evenings in our living room was totally destroyed. When the box was turned on, there was little peace and quiet until it was turned off when Mom and Dad went to bed. We were still required to head to the bedrooms pretty early during the school term, but from this point on, there was no time for the kids to look outside for entertainment. The blond-colored box sitting in the living room provided filler for any need to seek outside activity. When we arrived home at the end of each day at school, my chores to tend to the sheep down at the big barn was still in place. It was amazing how fast a kid could scoop ground hay out of the wagon into the feed bunks in comparison to the time needed before the television arrived. As soon as possible, all three kids were sitting in front of the screen to watch thirty minutes of *Lone Ranger and Tonto*, thirty minutes of *Howdy Doody*, fifteen minutes of the *Little Rascals*, and thirty minutes of *Flash Gordon*. Only real problem with the TV was the fact that at the end of one of our favorite series, it was essential to go out the back door and turn the antenna toward another station. To compound the problem, when there was wind above a brisk breeze, the pole would turn, and one of us had to go out and correct the direction so that the snow screen with the black line would disappear. Mary and Jim did occasionally go out, but I do remember sitting there looking at a snowy screen hoping that someone else would venture into the sleet and snow. I usually gave in and did it myself as it seemed they could sit for an indefinite period of time while starring at a blank screen. After several trips to the outdoors to correct the antenna direction during the middle of a show, it finally fell upon me to figure a way to stop the block from turning. Got a handful of tarp stakes from the toolshed and drove them into the ground on each side of the block. It didn't eliminate the task of changing channels, but it did stop going outside while a program was on just to move the antenna a few inches. I suggested to Dad that we drill two holes in the side of the house by where the cable came in. After running a rope through the holes and wrapping it around the pole several times, we could move the antenna from inside the living room by pulling the rope. He said it sounded like a good idea, but there were enough holes in the side of the house letting heat escape, so we probably did not need any more holes. When the weather was really cold and snowing, we usually left the antenna turned toward Hannibal and Quincy and watched what was available on those two channels.

If you want to mention changes that the television made in our routine, you can really see the weekend changes that occurred. Saturday night was always spent at the general store in Santa Fe, but when the TV arrived, Saturday nights was notoriously known for live wresting held in St. Louis and was held in our living room. From this moment forward, we never headed anywhere but the living room to watch wrestling. There was at least an hour or more when wrestling matches took over the screen, and at no time did anyone take their eyes off the match in progress. The favorite was when Gorgeous George entered the ring. He had snow-white shoulder-length hair and wore heavy makeup on his face that gave him a really weird look. Anyone that watched him dearly hated this guy and would cheer and jeer him the entire time he was in the ring. Another wrestler was Farmer Brown. He was a rather big guy that wore bib overalls into the ring and carried a live pig under one arm. Another wrestler was a Chinese man that had a long pig tail but cannot remember his name but do remember that he was a really dirty fighter and nearly always wiped up on Gorgeous George in their match. Tag matches were a lot of fun when all four contenders got in the ring and were throwing punches and doing body slammers one after the other. Just when you thought they were down for the count, they would jump up and begin hammering on the other guy until he was lying on the canvas writhing in pain. The entire room would yell and holler when they really got going, but strange as it seems, what with all that slamming on their backs and all that pounding they took in the face and body, there never was blood or cuts on either wrestler. Now talking about the entire room yelling, I mean a room full of adults and kids as our television was the first in the neighborhood, and the only other one was on the icebox in James and Mac's general store. Every Saturday evening about dark, our kinfolks and neighbors came to our house and spent the entire evening watching western shows and wrestling. It usually consisted of Grandpa and Grandma Burl, Mike and Juanita, and whatever kids they had at the time, Roy and Helen Sharp with daughter Caroline, and sometimes Ralph and Minnie Bell Bridgford and a couple of their kids. Of course, this included Mom and Dad and we three kids, so sitting space was at a premium.

Mom would pop a huge kettle of corn, and each family would take turns bringing a carton of Pepsi while others would bring cookies and cupcakes and anything else to make a treat. I usually took in tons of popcorn, drank as much Pepsi as Mom would allow, but had to share with Jim and Mary, so they got a big share of my drink. This went on for months until slowly but surely other families got their own television. Eventually, it was just our family that sat in front of the television on Saturday night. No more did we sit in the dimly lit kitchen and listen to the *Grand Ole Opry*, and no more did we listen to *Fibber McGee and Molly* followed by Homer and Jethro because now our time was spent watching "The Hit Parade" and listening to the top hits of the week. We all enjoyed this music; that is to say all but Dad. He took an instant dislike to Gezzel McKenzie somewhere along the line and mumbled his displeasure about her singing every time she appeared in the spotlight. We would watch a little wrestling, but the western shows of *Gun Smoke* and *The Rifleman* would usually win out over Gorgeous George and the boys. When Sunday night rolled around, we were always tuned in to *The Ed Sullivan Show*, as everybody looked forward to seeing some of the best entertainers around the world. Dad did once again mirror his dislike of Ed but did like the entertainers that were on the show. We did all agree that the best show was on Tuesday night at seven o'clock and was *The Red Skelton Show*. Seldom did it come on that anyone in our family missed sitting in front of the TV for the entire time Red Skelton was on. It could easily be said that the era of the television did change our free time drastically, but back in that day, there was never any curse words said and never any real violence shown directly, and the family-type show was on the screen seven days a week. We did spend a lot of time in the evenings in front of the TV. The only time we were allowed to watch during the day was at ten o'clock on Saturday morning when the *Sealtest Big Top* circus show came on. It lasted for an hour, and when it was over, we went back to doing whatever we were doing an hour earlier. You can rest assured that we would all five be seated early each evening in the living room in front of the TV.

Memorable Moments Flashback
Grandpa Burl and the Fox Hunt

When talking about hunting and fishing, it seems that hunting was a way of life just slightly more popular than fishing. I began fishing at a very early age of four or five when our parents took me and Mary to the Big Pond behind our house. The ever-popular cane pole with a bobber was available to any kid that wanted to wet a hook, and age had nothing to do with going fishing. On the other hand, no matter what critter they were after, hunting had a different set of rules, and where fishing was relaxing quiet, the exact opposite was associated with hunting. My first memory of using hounds and hardware was the first time I went to the woods fox hunting with Grandpa Burl. That trip showed me what Grandpa was all about and for sure how serious he was when working with the hounds. Back in the midforties, the number of red foxes was at an all-time high. The damage they did to range chickens and turkeys totaled thousands of dollars in a single year. Many farmers were depending upon the selling of fryer-sized chickens to pay the bills and upkeep for their families.

There was no confinement building to house the birds the final six weeks of growth; therefore, there was no way to protect the flock. This time was known as the range period. The thousand or more birds were roaming free inside a chicken wire fence, which made them easy prey for any carnivorous critter that wanted a quick and easy kill. The foxes had a bad habit of killing more than they could eat, so many times, the waste of dead birds angered the owner to the point of hating foxes. This was where Grandpa came into the picture. He had three foxhounds that were lean and mean with only one thing in mind, and that was to chase the fox or coyote. The dogs were turned loose next to the farmer's chicken pen, and the race was on. The hounds could be heard miles away following a trail, and Grandpa knew exactly what they were doing, where they were, and approximately where the fox was coming from and going to according to their baying. Usually, the fox would circle and eventually come back close to where they started when the hounds took up the trail.

It may take an hour, or it may take half a day, but you could depend on the dogs staying on track until they came back to where Grandpa Burl was waiting. Eventually, they came within shooting range of where a load of buckshot was waiting, which ended their chicken killing days. At the end of the day, Grandpa may have one, two, or even three kills to skin and stretch hides on curing boards. The fox fur was sought-after for coat collars, fur coats, and often were made into winter hats. When a buyer purchased the hides, most of them were sent overseas where the furs were worth more than in the States. The coyotes at the time also had a county bounty of three dollars on each kill, so extra money could be made for serious hunters. Not always but often, when the farmers sold their flocks, many of them came by and gave Grandpa several dollars for helping them cut their losses because of foxes.

On the other side of the coin was the traditional raccoon or "coon hunt" that took placed about the time first frost appeared. When the sun set and the land and woods were engulfed in total darkness, this began the long-awaited signal that this was time for a group of men to gather at the river ford behind Henry Heckert's farm. The dogs, which numbered anywhere from two to six, was waiting patiently in their crates for the owners to open the door. This signaled the start of the long-awaited running of the raccoon. Each hunter carried a six-cell coon hunting flashlight, and some carried a coal oil lantern to provide enough light to see where the hunters were stepping when looking for the dogs. When the hounds were released, they started out in a dead run making ever widening circles down the riverbed until one caught the fresh scent of a passing raccoon. When the first hound picked up the scent, he opened up, and soon as the others heard him, they immediately went to where he was. They immediately disappeared into the darkness, each giving sound as they followed the trail down the riverbed and up the valley wall. The hunters either stood or knelt down to silently await a certain change in tone of the pack, which meant that they caught up with the raccoon and probably had treed. The individual dog's owners knew exactly which hound was baying, knew if they were on the trail, or knew the moment that they had treed just from the different tones of each hound. When they had treed, the hunters made a dash to where the dogs were sounding and arrived at the tree where all the hounds were circling below the branches. They shined the flashlights into the branches and could see the reflection of a set of eyes. In many instances, they may find several sets of eyes as raccoons are not a solitary animal and usually travels in groups. Usually, it was my dad's job to shiny up the tree and throw the coons out one at a time so they could be disposed of and quickly put into gunny sacks to protect them from the dogs. It was said that Daddy Clyde was the best tree climber in the county and hardly ever found a tree that he could not climb. I must say that I was not a good coon hunter. Running around on top of bluffs in pitch-black dark was not my favorite pastime nor was running down the river and fording streams to get to where the hounds were treeing. I did not want to say I was afraid of the dark but, to this day, can say that I am totally uncomfortable when the surrounding area is covered in total darkness. About the only thing I enjoyed about coon hunting was heading home at the end of the hunt.

First Full-time Farm Job
with Otti Roth

As the days rolled by and the years came and went, there was very little changed at the two-story house at the Willingham residence. Once I started the first grade, it seemed that I was almost instantly into the fourth grade, then into the seventh grade, and all of a sudden, we were at the end of the eighth grade. We were standing in a large group on the Paris High School gym floor singing, "Via Condios," which was made up of the entire eighth-grade students of Monroe County excluding the city kids. It was certainly a "dress the best" day as we were all in coats and ties and new shoes that hurt your feet while standing for hours during the festivities. Must have been the first dress coat I ever owned, in fact had to be, as I never wore anything other than a shirt and overalls or jeans for the first thirteen years of my life. Would imagine it took the biggest part of a hog to buy an entire set of duds such as I was decked out in. Ms. Acuff, the county superintendent of schools, gave somewhat of an address after we finished singing, and then we walked the length of the gym floor to receive our diploma. After it was over, the class of Santa Fe four stood on the steps outside the high school and had our pictures taken. Of course, Olive Willingham was there with her Hawkeye Brownie camera taking pictures so that we could all remember this moment for years to come. It really did not dawn on me that, in a few short weeks, I would be walking up these very steps on the first day of my high school career at Paris High School. It also did not dawn on me that life as I knew it was about to take a drastic turn for the worse. At the moment, my main thought was that summer vacation was now officially started, so the quicker we got out of this sports coat and tie and back on the farm, all the better. Nothing to do other than ride bike around the countryside and probably hit the "twelve-foot" swimming hole every single day for the foreseeable future. That was exactly what we did for the next several days until that ill-fated day on a Saturday when Dad was home. He said that we were going to build a hog house for the soon-to-be-delivering sows. While we were putting on the corrugated roof, there appeared a pickup truck coming up the driveway in front of a cloud of dust. It certainly was not anyone we knew because the pickup was a dark green and very shiny and did not have a dent or mangled fender on it. All our neighbors had old beat-up trucks with at least an inch of dust and crud over the entire body. For certain, they never drove anything that looked like it had come right out of J. R. Whites Ford showroom. We stopped what we were doing and watched an old man, probably somewhere in his forties, get out of the truck.

When he cleared the doorsill of the truck, he took a hat from the front seat and put on his head a huge straw hat. It reminded me of being more like an umbrella instead of a hat. As he approached, Dad said, "Hello, Otti. What brings you this way today?" He replied, "Hello, Clyde. I understand you have a young man in your family that just may be able to help me on the farm this summer." Really did not dawn on me right away that he was talking about me because number one, I was just a kid, and number two, I sure did not want to work on another farm this summer. Dad asked him what he had in mind, and the guy said that they needed help Monday through Friday and started work at seven in the morning and usually quit around six in the afternoon. If we wanted, he and his wife would provide room and board during the week and pay five dollars a day. Dad looked at me and asked something about would I be interested. I thought, *Heck no, I do not want to live with this guy and his wife and work on his farm.* Never saw him before in my life, and for all I knew, he may live in another part of the world from our happy home. Dad could see that I had not agreed to the offer, so he said how about he bring me over Monday morning to the farm on his way to work in Santa Fe and see how things worked out. The old man thought that would be workable, and if I did not stay with them, then he would pay six dollars a day. Now that part I understood. With a quick bit of math in my head, that would come out to thirty dollars a week, and that amount to a thirteen-year-old would be almost a fortune by the end of summer. The old guy shook my hand and said he would be looking for me next Monday and to bring a pair of gloves so that we could get started. It suddenly dawned on me; next Monday -was only a day and a half from right now, so my days of being footloose and fancy-free was just about to come to an end. As the guy drove away, I started to go over in my head just what had taken place here the past fifteen minutes. Just what kind of changes in my life would that handshake bring in the very few days to come? All Dad said was that we better go into town and visit Perry Davis's store to get a pair of gloves before Monday. Being Saturday, our schedule would get us there after the chores were done as we usually headed for Santa Fe some time during the weekend anyhow. Decided I may as well forget about what the future was to bring and just enjoy the rest of the weekend as if nothing new had happened.

Monday seemed to arrive quickly no matter how many other things I tried to think about to take the inevitable off my mind. Seemed it had only been minutes since I shook hands with the old man in the strange straw hat. All of a sudden, I was dressed in a pair of clean jeans and a clean button-up shirt with gloves in hand sitting in the front seat of the truck. Dad was heading down the road, going the complete opposite direction away from Santa Fe, going to a place only the good Lord himself would have any idea where we were to end up and what was about to happen. The road we took was one I was familiar with, so I easily recognized the corner where our mailbox was located, went past Skeeter Moore's tall two-story house, past the farm of J. C. Gibson, made a left turn on the farm to market road, and then a right, pulling into a driveway that I had never seen before. Dad stopped the truck beside a really nice two-story house with a front porch that was held up with fancy porch post. It looked like something you would see in pictures and not in real life. Our house had a porch, and our house had some post, but this place was huge and painted a really whiter than white. This place looked like rich people lived here. The guy that we had met previously was coming across the backyard and had that huge straw hat on just like the day we first met. He did look familiar, so I guessed this was where my first day of farming was to take place. After a bit of chitchat between the two men, Dad backed down the driveway and headed down the road to his job in Santa Fe, leaving me in a totally confused state of mind as a young kid out of his comfort zone. He said to call him Otti and that I should meet his wife who came out the back door of the house with a basket of clothes to be hung out to dry. Otti seemed a really nice old guy, and his wife sure did look out of place standing under the clothesline hanging out towels and whatever. Her dress was starched and ironed with an apron covering the front. Her hair was totally perfect with a blue gray color and not a strand of hair out of place. I gathered that she had a beauty parlor close by to look like she was going to church instead of doing chores on the farm. I was used to seeing Mom in a dress and an apron but never dressed like this. I would have guessed she was heading to the women's club and was about ready to leave. As I stood facing Otti and listening to what he was saying, I noticed that when he was looking at me, one eye looked at me, and the other one was looking up into the trees. Didn't know which eye was the one that I should be looking at or which eye was looking at me. Tried really hard to pay attention as to what he was saying but found myself looking at the out-of-whack eye instead of the eye that was like everyone else had. Never did get used to talking with Otti face-to-face or as I thought eye to whacky eye. When all was said or all that was going to be said was said, Otti turned and walked toward the nearest shed behind the cellar at the back of the yard. We went inside and found a sight to behold. There were two tractors, a combine and a corn picker housed in the machine shed. Along one wall was a workbench with tools all hung neat in a row and cans sitting on shelves also all neat in a row. It was a fact that everything in the building was all neat in a row. Otti got on the nearest tractor and backed the huge green-and-orange tractor out of the shed. He asked if I knew how to drive a tractor. Only answer that I could come up with was that I had driven a much smaller tractor pulling a hay wagon during the baling season. I got up on the seat of that big machine, and it seemed that I was sitting on top of the world as the tires were so high. He explained to me that this was an Oliver 88 and was used to do the heavy part of farming. He then proceeded to walk me through the steps of putting it in neutral and starting the engine. All this was kind of familiar but was a huge difference from the small machines I had been used to. To make matters worse, my legs were just barely long enough for my feet to reach the pedals. Only by semistanding and semisitting could I make the pedals get the machine to move forward. We drove down the path to the other machine shed where I had to move the tractor backward and forward until it was in position to hook up to a piece of machinery he called a cultivator. We headed toward the back of the farm past a feedlot of fattening steers, past the grass lots where another fifty or so heads of cattle were grazing and arrived at the cornfield that covered at least one hundred acres. The corn was about three feet tall and had rows that seemed to go on for miles. Otti said to turn into the first two rows and stop, reach to the side of the seat, and lower a lever so that the shovels of the cultivator dug into the ground on each side of two rows of corn. The shovels did a great job of digging up the weeds between the rows and at the same time put a ridge of dirt on each side of the cornstalk. After we made a complete round, which seemed to take forever to get from one end to the other, Otti got off and said that I was to keep doing what I was doing until he came after me for lunch. This was the total amount of on-the-job training I received that first day. Everything went along super, drove down the row, turned at the end, drove back the other direction, turned, and went back down another set of rows one after the other. After several hours and at the end of the field, I turned and started down another row. There appeared something that was terribly wrong. Where there was usually a long straight row of corn in front of me, there was now a very vacant long row of plowed-up earth with the stalks that should be standing up tall and straight now were completely unearthed and lying flat. Oh man, it suddenly dawned on me that I had missed my turn last time around, and instead of going over two rows, I had gone over one row. When the corn planter originally put the seed corn into the ground, it did it two rows at a time. They were always perfectly in line one with the other. By getting on the wrong row at the end of the field, I had plowed the weeds beside one row and plowed up the cornstalks on the other row. Not much a person could do about the row that was nowhere to be seen. Lesson learned was to be certain to look behind the tractor every time it made a turn at the end of the field to verify being on the correct row. Otti never did say anything about the missing row during the summer I worked there but can be pretty certain that, when he harvested the following fall, it may have entered his mind as to just what in the world happened to the one row that was missing each and every stalk.

Keeping in mind the small amount of prior experience this farmhand brought to the job and not having been given direct instructions from the hiring farmer, I would deem the first few days as being pretty successful. Did not plow up any more corn; lunch was precisely at twelve o'clock noon, and certainly, Mrs. Roth was an excellent cook. The lunch menu we had each day was outstanding and ample, so I really enjoyed all the food placed before us. After lunch, Otti would sit in the parlor and read the newspaper until one o'clock, and then we would be back at work at one o'clock and one without fail. While he was sitting and reading, I usually headed out the back door and sat under the big shade tree with the two dogs lying in the grass beside me. If it was a really hot day, the dogs and I would go to the cattle barn and sit a bale of hay in the alleyway where there was always a breeze blowing. This spot seemed to be about twenty degrees cooler than outside in the sun.

It comes to mind a strange thing that happened one afternoon while I was plowing corn on the straight rows. I was looking back over my shoulder frequently to verify I was plowing weeds and not plowing cornstalks. As I turned my head to look forward, there appeared a black dot coming over the hood of the tractor. Out of nowhere and fast as a bullet, the tiny dot hit me just above my glasses and square between my eyes. It hit a hard blow, and the moment it hit stung with a vengeance. By the time I stopped the tractor, the pain was spreading across my face and forehead. I became instantly sick and dizzy headed all within a half minute. Stood leaning against the tractor tire throwing up for about ten minutes. Got back on the tractor and slowly headed for the house. By the time I parked the tractor, my eyes were beginning to swell shut. Otti appeared and took me into the house where Mrs. Roth put an ice pack over the sting, which felt better instantly. Sat under the big tree in the yard for about an hour with the ice pack, got up, took the tractor back to the field, and plowed the rest of the afternoon. Watched closely every time I circled the area where the angry dot hit me, but no further complications occurred. Eyes were half-swollen shut for the next two days, but there was no more pain, nor did I ever know what hit me. I do know, however, that whatever hit me was very little and carried a mean wallop.

Another task that I remember as being one that totally destroyed my mind was introduced to me on the third day of work. Otti took me to another field of corn that was just past the feedlots. This corn was planted on the side of a hill. This hill had been terraced for water runoff control years before. Instead of straight rows, the corn was planted with the terraces, which made each row weave and meander in all directions at the same time. If he showed me once where to turn, he showed me a half-dozen times, and each time I was on the wrong row. This in turn had the same effect that occurred when I missed a row when it was planted straight, which left one row lying flat. After about thirty minutes of going around in circles and thirty minutes of removing cornstalks, Otti figured that this was way beyond a thirteen-year-old's understanding. I totally agreed with him at this point. He decided that we should go to the hayfield and mow clover instead of plow up corn. He put me on a little Ford tractor with a sickle mower and, after going one round himself, turned the job over to me. What a relief, no more mind-boggling terraces and now on a tractor that my feet touched the pedals while sitting. Life took a turn for the better. It was almost a pleasure to work with a piece of equipment that kind of fit my size. It was surprising how much faster a day went by when a person could sit and work without the stress of which cornrow not to plow up.

For the most part, the rest of the summer was pretty uneventful. Friday mornings were spent in the corn bin with the Oliver 88 attached by a running belt to a corn grinder. Otti and I used a scoop shovel to throw ear corn into the hopper that augured the ears into the grinder. When it came out of the grinder, it was in the form of a rough meal powder that then dumped into the high-sided grain wagon. When the wagon was full to the top, we moved it into the feedlot beside the feeder troughs. Each morning as soon as I arrived, I scooped the ground corn into the feeder bunks where forty or more head of fattening steers would eat until the troughs were clean. Otti fed them at night, but I knew that come Friday morning the first thing we would be doing was back into the corn bin until the wagon was filled. What with the roar of the tractor and the roar of the grinder, anyone in the grain bin could be certain that, when the grinding was complete, your ears would be ringing for the next couple of hours.

Many days were spent mowing hay, and after it cured for a couple of days, my job was to run the rake over the field to windrow the grass into a long trail. Otti came behind me with a baler that picked up the windrow of hay, packed it into a bale, and tied it together with two strings of binder twine. One of his brothers would ride the wagon that was hooked to the back of the baler. As the completed bale came out of the machine, it was pushed up a ramp that delivered the bale to be stacked on the back of the wagon. There were two crews needed during the hay season, one to rake and bale and one to unload the wagons and stack the bales in the barn. I tried to be the one raking most of the time because the crew working inside the barn was uncomfortably hot and dusty. Many days, we were working the hay at one of the farms and then move over to the next until the hay barns were stacked full of bales ready for the coming winter. In the three barns, we would usually have three to four thousand bales when it was completed.

Finally, the day that I had looked forward to for the entire summer finally arrived. This would be the last day that I would be working for Otti and collected my final paycheck. It so happened that the next day was the first day of the Audrain County Fair in Mexico, so the best two things that could happen was going to happen within a twenty-four-hour period. Otti thanked me for helping out that summer and told Dad that I had done a good job, and if I wanted to work next summer, just let him know. Next day, we headed into town, and Mom accompanied me to the Missouri Brokerage Clothing Store. For the first time, I picked out and paid for school clothes with my own hard-earned money. From there, we went to the county fair, but you can be certain that what money I spent on rides and cotton candy was thought through completely before laying the coins down. Spending money took on a totally new meaning now that my sweat was on each and every dollar.

The Day We Moved to a New Home

After the summer working with Otti Roth and well into the middle of fall, we were told that Ralph Bridgford was going to sell the farm we had lived on for the past eleven years to his daughter. She was married to my uncle Mike who was my dad's younger brother. Dad found a farm for sale located on Santa Fe Lane about five miles from Santa Fe that was in an estate. It had about eighty acres with a little farmhouse and a big red barn. This would have been almost perfect for our family of four as Mary was married and in Germany with her husband, Lavern, who was enlisted in the army. I would have been fourteen and was a freshman at Paris High School. This would have been twice as close to Paris, so it would have been an ideal location. As a freshman, I was involved in FFA, played on the freshman basketball team, and attended nearly every function held at the school. Too young to drive, it fell upon Dad to come get me nearly every night of the week. Driving from Santa Fe to pick me up after having worked all day scooping corn on the hammer mill was a lot of miles and very tiring, but not one time did I ever hear a word complaining about me being a bother with such a schedule. I remember going with Dad on his days off around the county talking to anyone he knew that had or may have money. At that time, no one was able to lend him the amount needed for a down payment, so we were forced to give up the idea of buying the farm. A few days later, we got a call from Tuck Mitchell, a businessman in Paris, who said that he had purchased a farm and homestead west of Santa Fe and needed a sharecropper to move in and work the parcel. Next thing we knew, there were about fifteen family members and neighbors backed up to the door of our old farm home and loaded up all our possessions and were headed across country to the next house to be called home. This place was about two miles from the farm Dad tried to buy but couldn't, so it was in an ideal location. That afternoon, the trucks returned and loaded up all the cattle in one truck and all the hogs in the second truck. Within five hours, the crew took care of our living two miles from Santa Fe to now living eight miles from Paris. It was easy to remember the entire move as it was raining in the morning, and that afternoon turned cold and covered the trucks with a thin sheet of ice. The loading of cattle was really a terrible ordeal as they did not have anything solid underfoot to steady themselves when going up the shoot into the truck. When loaded, it only took seconds for the truck floor to be covered with a mixture of cow manure and ice. At any one time, there would be one or two cows down and the other cows falling over them. I thought at the time that this was really bad, and it looked like there was going to be several broken legs and bones before this trip ended. The trip of fifteen miles seemed to be one of the longest short trips we would ever make. When they arrived at the new farm and the loading shoot was in place, the first ones came down the plank going like gang busters. When all the upright cattle were unloaded, it was the task of about half a dozen men to assist the ones down to get into an upright position. A wonder to behold; when all the cattle were on the ground, all of them were walking without any serious injuries. A few days later, one of the yearling heifers died from what must have been internal injuries, but all in all, it was one very lucky hauling experience. All of the hogs made it without any problem. By the time the help had gone home to do their own chores, we found most of the boxes were unpacked and beds were in place and made ready for sleep. Life was almost ready to begin anew. Dad went after the tractor and field equipment the next week and loaded the cultivators, disk, and plow on the hay frame wagon and drove it across country to our new place. The new house was also a two-story home but was much newer and in a lot better condition than the house we moved from. We all had private sleeping quarters and even a spare bedroom in case Mary came home and needed a room to sleep. Highlight of the place was an indoor toilet and running water for the kitchen. Usually, the pump would work for a couple of days, and then Dad would spend an hour or so replacing gaskets and priming the pump. Once repaired, it was a great improvement over the outhouse and well pump we had been using for so many years.

This place was totally different from the farm south of Santa Fe. We had been used to walking out the front door and seeing either rolling fields and pastures or thick woodlots with a mass of trees. This place was the exact opposite. Walk out any door and you only saw flat barren pastures and plowed fields. There were few trees, and if there was any, they were sparsely clumped together and way off in the distance. This was at the very edge of prairie land that ran in each direction for miles. Acres and acres of plowed or stubble fields were on all sides of the house except the north side. Here was a two-story barn, several fenced-in corrals, and a henhouse inside a large chicken yard. Just beside the east side of the house was a big garden that covered at least an acre or more. It was not as large as what we left but easily big enough to continue gardening and would supply fresh vegetables for the family.

Eighth Grade Graduation on the
steps of Paris High School April 1956
Class of four Santa Fe Elementary

Baptism at Gene Clines pond outside of Molina early May 1958. Water temp. about 50 degrees. Like to froze to death.

KW Senior year 1960 Stuffed donkey represented high magazine sales for the week for FFA fund raising. No idea why I had books, never did homework for entire four years!!!!

First thing Dad did when the weather broke was take his hay wagon apart and build a complete new bed. He purchased a one-fourth-inch electric drill, which was by my standards a huge piece of machinery. It was all I could do to pick it up, so there was no way it could be held level to drill a hole. It was my job to hold the electric cord off the ground while the drilling was being done. Having learned the hard way about electricity and electric cords, I held it up with a stick, so at no time did flesh and skin touch the cord itself. That was in the year 1956, and today I have that same drill in my workshop and have even loaned it to my son for some heavy metal drilling.

Come spring, we cleaned off the garden plot, plowed it up with the new John Deere tractor, and made the soil ready for planting after last frost. Having made money selling beans door-to-door in Mexico at a very early age and presently having a bike that was total junk, the bright idea of raising and selling watermelons came to my mind. Talked Dad into plowing a big spot at the end of the chicken yard, stretched a wire from fence to fence to keep the chickens out, worked the ground out smooth, and got ready to plant twenty-five hills of black diamond melons. Having heard that chicken manure is really good fertilizer and having an ample supply in the henhouse left by the previous family, I cleaned out and carried several buckets. If it was good to spread it on top and plow it in, then by putting an ample amount in each melon hill should really help produce a bumper crop. Figured if a little was good, then a lot would be all that much better. In the back of my mind, all that was left to do was pick out the new bicycle and wait for the harvest to happen. In about ten days, there were little plants covering the entire mounds. In about a month, I was proud of the vines that appeared and spread across the entire melon patch. Leaves the size of a straw hat and blooms the size of an adult's open hand appeared everywhere. At this point, it looked like there would be enough melons from this patch to buy a new bike and have enough surplus money to buy all new fishing gear. In a few days, melons the size of a baseball was setting on.

MAY 1958

OCT 1957

MAY 1958

MAR 1959

There must have been thousands of them or at least hundreds. Success was about to be mine. In another three days, the melons were the size of a basketball. At this rate, they should be thirty- and forty-pound black diamond melons within the next three weeks, give or take a week. With a little imagination and daydreaming, I figured, at one dollar each, this patch should make me a very wealthy young farmer. Whoa, what is the problem? A week later, the melons are still the size of a basketball. A week later, they still have not gotten any bigger than they were two weeks before. By now, they should be a dark green on the outside and red ripe on the inside. Picked one up and slammed it down on the ground. Peeled it open expecting to find black seeds and red ripe juicy center. Instead, I found a pale sickening-looking light pink with little white seeds. This was nothing like they looked in my dreams and Henry Fields seed catalog. When I cut open a melon, I was supposed to hear the deep rumble of a ripe melon being torn into. No such sound appeared. Picked up another one and was greeted with the same dingy, not even close to red pink inside. Almost overnight, the vines turned from leaves that were green and standing tall to a slightly yellow sick-looking slightly wilted drooping configuration of what used to be my new bike. There was literally a wagonload of melons covering the entire plot, and each was identical in size and color, and none of them was supposed to look like what I was seeing right now. One afternoon,

Mr. Smith, a neighbor to the north, came over, and as he and Dad were leaning on the yard fence, he looked at my prized patch and in passing asked if I had used chicken manure on the ground before planting. I told him I had buried a scoop of manure under each hill, and he said something to the effect of what I should have done was put about one-fourth cup or less and that the plants had gone to vine and bloom. The excess nitrogen had burned up the melons before they had a chance to grow. Now my chore was to find a way to get rid of a half ton of undersized totally green melons. I decided to throw them into the pig lot as it was well-known that hogs loved melon rinds. The answer to my problem was feed the pigs. Wrong! They would not even touch the melons. After many hours of busting the things to a messy pulp with a baseball bat, I took down the fence between the henhouse and the magic patch. This made fifty old hens very happy to be able to scratch and peck through the slick mess. So ended the dream of a new bike, and so began the lesson learned about counting your watermelons before they ripen.

Memorable Moments Flashback
Rites of Manhood: Owning a BB Gun

A BB gun was a piece of equipment all boys either wanted to own or did own by the time they turned ten years old. My first encounter with a Daisy BB gun rifle was when cousin Donnie had his down by the river after one of the Willingham Sunday picnics. The older guys were shooting at a couple of floating cans that they had thrown into the river. They soon tired of this and moved on to more interesting adventures. They laid the gun against a tree and walked away. I looked around, and there was no one within sight and no one to tell me to keep my hands off the BB gun. The most natural thing to do was take control and shoots those cans. I would guess my age was about seven years old. I could not cock the lever by myself without putting the gunstock between my feet and, with all my strength, got the lever to click. Aimed the barrel at the end of the can and pulled the trigger. Suddenly, pain shot through my hand and up my arm like I had been shot. What I did not know was that the lever had to be closed back against the rifle stock before pulling the trigger. If not, the air pressure of the discharge made the lever close with a wham, which it had just done. It whacked the fingers on my right hand, which was a lot like striking all your fingers with a hammer. Would have let out a scream and cried for my mama but knew I would have more to worry about if they knew I had used a gun without permission.

Placed the gun back just as I found it and quietly walked away with a very quiet set of sobs. It was very lonely being left alone with no one to share my pain. This concluded my seven-year-old memory of why a kid should have someone give him instructions on how to use a gun even if it is only a BB gun.

Second Farm Job with Kendrick Brothers

Several days after Mr. Smith solved my mystery of why the melons made no melons, Dad and I were replacing the front porch flooring and steps. Over the years of rain blowing over the porch and many coats of paint being chipped and rotted, the wood was beyond repair. The complete floor was in such bad condition it was like walking on marshmallows each step you took. As we were working, a pickup truck came down the road and turned into our parking area just off the front porch. A man stepped out of the truck, put on a cap, and preceded toward where we were working. Dark tanned, about six feet tall, walked along rapidly as if to get to where he was going in a hurry. He had a cigar about the size of a hot dog bun clamped in his left teeth. Introduced himself as Everet Kendrick and said that he was our neighbor to the west. He mentioned that Dad may know his father, Warren Kendrick, that owned a farm on the flats of Young's Creek. Dad knew Warren and mentioned that they had ground corn for his dad and Uncle Henry many times before. Almost word for word what was said by Otti Roth a year before I heard Everet Kendrick say. He said that they seriously needed to hire a hand to help with farmwork and was wondering if Dad's son would be available to help out. So happens my bank account was about down to zip or slightly less, so I spoke up immediately and asked when do I start.

Everet said that they paid six dollars a day and did not work on Sundays except when the planting and harvest season was in full

If a baby is born into a family that has a mother and a father and they are to him special for the rest of his life, watches over him, teaches him, cares for him and loves him unconditional, it can be said that this child is one of the luckest kids on the face of the earth. In my case, I had three sets of parents that met this total criteria. All three sets of my parents, original and acquired, had my back from day one and remained so until each of them were called by the Good Lord to leave this earth. I truly looked upon my original parents as being two of the greatest people in America. At the same time I later in life was blessed with being a part of the Kendrick family, started out as a hired worker and was instantly accepted into their clan without any reservations or questions. It can be truly stated that when any one of these people passed away I felt then and do now that I lost my dearest and best friends. Rest in peace Clyde and Olive, Jay and Ruth , Dorothy and Everet. I will never forget either of you until the day I leave this earth.

Blessed with Three Sets of Parents

Jay and Ruth Kendrick

Dorothy and Everet Kendrick

swing. If I was interested, then I could start tomorrow. It was a lot less scary this time than before because now I knew what money would buy and that farmwork came about naturally and was not all that difficult. I was really looking forward to tomorrow so that six dollars days would begin. First day on the job, we were plowing, disking, harrowing, and planting with three tractors. May I mention that they were three huge tractors that would cover hundreds of acres in a short period of time. Everet and his brother, Jay, were partners, each working from four oclock AM until about eleven o'clock in the evening, sleep a couple of hours, and be back on the tractor before dawn the next day. This schedule we followed whenever it was planting or harvesting season. All other times, we started at seven o'clock in the morning and quit at five o'clock in the afternoon. I was expected to work my full day but was never required to try and keep up with my bosses. Occasionally, they did ask if I would work another four hours for a half-day pay. Being very fond of payday and dollars, I always stayed with them but hit the road home at the end of the extended workday. I fully remember that no one worked any harder than Everet and Jay, and for sure, nobody ever went through a box of cigars as quickly and as often as the two of them. Jay had a habit of smoking the cigar down to about three inches from the end then cut off the burned portion and chewed the remainder. I was always told that people who chewed tobacco never had a problem with worms, so I was certain that Jay's gut was clear of intestinal worms.

Day after day, my schedule remained pretty much the same. Arrive at the shed at Everet's place at seven o'clock in the morning, and when entering the shed door either, Jay or Everet would say what my work for the day would be. Nearly 90 percent of the time, it had to do with getting on one of the tractors and heading toward a field that needed either to be disc, plowed, mowed, cultivated, or raked. I had the choice of three tractors to work that day, and without a doubt, it was the International that was my number one choice. The reason for this was because it was the newest, the most comfortable, the most powerful, and, last but not least, the tractor had a radio on it. It was amazing how much the radio mounted on the right fender made the long and dusty day go by so much faster. Without the radio, the only sound you heard for hours on end was the roar of a huge engine. This did nothing to assist a rider to stay awake and beware of what dangers could happen instantly when one's mind wondered. The best station was out of Fulton, Missouri, with a show named *Rom's Ranch* that came on at one o'clock in the afternoon and lasted the rest of the afternoon. This station played pure country music and played the best recordings available at the time. It played song after song of what I had decided was the best country music ever created. The other station was out of Mexico, Missouri, which was also country, but they had a bad habit of playing a song and then spent several minutes talking and doing advertisements when they could have been playing music. With this station in the morning and Fulton in the afternoon, I heard the same songs many times over and soon knew all the words and lyrics by heart. It totally removed the agony of driving a tractor very, very slow when plowing mile-long rows of twelve-inch corn day after day. Good thing there were a few neighbors for mile around because with the radio at full blast and my singing along rang out across the flat fields for hours on end. My singing must have been pure misery for all those that were within hearing distance.

The highlight of everyday working for the Kendrick brothers happened each and every day at high noon. No matter which part of the farms I was working or what I was doing, a truck picked me up at eleven fifty in the morning. Every other day, lunch was served at either Jay's house or Everet's and was served at precisely twelve o'clock. When we pulled into Everet's driveway, there hanging on the wooden fence across the front yard were four little kids peering over the top board waiting for their daddy and his hired hand to arrive. The littlest one was less than two, and the oldest one was about six. There was a four-kids welcoming party with bright eyes and big smiles waiting for the hired hand to show up. They were always in perfect order. First was the oldest a girl named Donna; second on the rail was Dane, and then came David, and the last that had to peek through the boards because he was so little was Dennis. Lunch was ready the moment we walked into the kitchen, so by the time we all washed our hands and sat down, the food was on the table. With a two-liner prayer from one of the little ones, lunch was served. After their plates were cleaned or mostly cleaned, we all five went outside and played for the next half hour or so. Usually, we were in the sandbox building whatever, and other times we played tag or hide-and-go-seek, but it was usually a very active thirty minutes no matter what they chose to do. One slight problem occurred when we were playing in the sandbox because Dennis was still in diapers. Back in those days, it was cloth diapers, which after about an hour became very wet and with the sand all around was a combination of wet diaper and wet sand. All was well until Dennis would decide to crawl onto my lap and sit with me while we moved the sand around. When Everet appeared ready to deliver me back to the tractor, I found that the reminder of Little Dennis went with me. It usually took several minutes in the sun for my jeans to return to dry, so I had a reminder of the past play period with the Kendrick kids. I knew full well that the same scene would greet me hanging on the fence in a couple of days. The same procedure happened at Jay's house every other day, except in his kitchen were two little kids. They were several years younger than their cousins but would be waiting inside the kitchen door for us to arrive. Debbie, the oldest girl, would grin at me and then run behind her mother's dress and peer around, smiling as if she were very bashful. After a few minutes, she would bring out some toys, and we would play on the floor until lunch was ready. Her little brother, Dickie, was barely a toddler and was in a roll-around walker, so he spent his time trying to play but usually ended up banging into or running over his little sister. Their third child was born after I finished working on the farm, so I was never around that little one. Her name was Robin.

I would have to say that the meals served at those two houses were among some of the best food I was ever served.

They both were farmer's wives and had farmer parents, so they had become master chefs taught by their mothers at a very early age. Without a doubt, each and every meal I shared with the Kendrick families was some of the best country cooking ever served. Another memory of eating farm fresh food was the many times I was sent to Jay and Everet's father and uncle's farm down on the old homeplace.

Henry and Warren were the first-generation brothers that farmed together for sixty years. They had two separate pieces of land side by side about two miles east of where Jay and Everet settled and built. Henry was retired, and Warren worked the homeplace by himself. When he needed help, he would call the boys, and the next day, either one or all of us would go to his farm early in the morning. Depending on what he needed, all may work at it, but usually, they would leave me with instructions to return to Everet's whenever the work was completed. It may take one day, or when it took several days, I would drive each morning to Warren's place and spend the day. Warren was in his early eighties but still worked a twelve-hour workday every day but Sunday. His place was rather isolated with their original house built on the banks of Young's Creek where his father before him worked the land. They overlooked a creek that meandered through the farm from one side to the other. Bottomland fields were great land for growing hay and cover crops, so my job usually was to mow or rake the hayfields. When the hay crop was cured and raked, one of the sons would bring over his baler and bale all the fields. One summer, I had the bottom land mowed, cured, and raked; so Everet met us at the field with the baler. He spent several hours baling and leaving the bales in the field. We had planned to return the next day and load the bales in the barn, but that night, a front came in and dropped several inches of rain in a short period of time. This caused the river to overflow its banks, which flooded the hayfield, and all the bales were either underwater or partially underwater. When the river receded, we walked the field stacking three bales at a time leaning against each other. It was the practice at the time to remove the wet bales and fill ditches with them because they were soaked through and would rot and mold inside. Warren asked if I thought my dad would be able to help out the next day as it was the weekend, and of course, Dad said he would. We showed up next morning prepared to haul the rotting hay to a ditch. When we arrived, Warren met us and instructed us to stack them in the barn nearest to the cattle pasture. Dad asked in a polite way if he didn't think this was a bad idea as they were already starting to smell moldy and all were starting to heat inside and may burn down his barn if they got hot enough. Warren said that was no problem. The old cows would eat whatever they could find when the winter snows fell, so that would be good hay about then. Dad and I started loading the wagon but soon found that the bales were so heavy with soaked water that it took two of us on the same bale to lift it. We then stacked them in the barn about ten high and kept asking Warren if he thought this was a good idea. Several days later, I was back at the barn to help him with another chore. When I passed the barn, you could smell it a half mile down the road. It was for sure spoiled and heating something terrible. I placed my hand between two of the bales on the south side of the barn, and it was so hot it would have burned my skin had it been left a second longer. Marvel of all marvels, it did not burn down, and just like Warren said, the ole cows ate it and were glad to have something in their bellies when the snow fell.

Warren's wife was always working in the garden. Her sister, Sarah, who was slightly mentally handicapped, lived with them, and wherever Ada worked, her sister was also there working. They both were outstanding gardeners and, like the old days, had rows of every vegetable imaginable harvested and canned. When lunch was ready, Warren would come by on his tractor, and we would head for the house. There were four places set at the table, and each and every day, there was enough food on the table to feed no less than a half-dozen hired hands. There were placed before us one or two meats with potatoes and gravy, no less than four fresh vegetables, homemade bread, fresh churned butter, several kinds of jams and jellies, and at the end of the meal a choice of cake, pie, or cookies. It was truly a chore to remove yourself from the lunch table and return to the tractor after having put away that amount of food. Never did seem to bother Warren; he went directly back to work and did not stop until quitting time that evening. An amazing thing I saw him do over and over was to build himself a smoke. He was constantly holding a cigarette either in his hand or between his lips, and smoke would roll. When I said build a smoke, that was totally what he was doing. He took a single paper from a holder in his pocket, cupped the paper with his thumb and finger, took out a pouch of Bull Durham tobacco, and filled the paper with a portion of loose tobacco. He then curled the paper over the tobacco and adjusted the contents with both hands before licking the seam from end to end. He pulled the string tight on the pouch with his teeth and one hand, replaced the pouch in his breast pocket, struck a kitchen match all in one smooth motion, and light the end of the cigarette. I saw him do this numerous times and did not even stop the tractor to get all this done. Must have watched him do this a dozen times and never failed to totally amaze me how easy he made it look.

Back at the Main Farm

The long hours and lack of excitement while going around and around on a tractor did kind of get on your nerves. However, very few days went by that something unforeseen or unusual didn't happen to break the monotony. One day while raking straw to be baled and being about half asleep because there was no radio on the Allis, suddenly there was a huge bumblebee flying around my head. In moments, there were two bumblebees flying around my head, and then there were dozens of the insects dive-bombing me from all directions. The roar of the tractor was causing them to zero in on the muffler exhaust. They then started paying attention to who was sitting on the seat just to the rear of the muffler. I shoved the gear lever into neutral and bailed off the tractor hitting the ground with both feet digging into the dirt to get away. My saving grace was that I did not shut off the engine. The vibration of the motor kept them circling the tractor hood instead of coming after me. I spent little time putting a great deal of distance between me and the flying brigade circling the tractor. After several minutes, the bees started to leave and eventually disappeared back into the underground hive. I walked carefully and slowly to the rear of the rake to see if all was safe. The tractor and rake had gone directly over the top of the entrance to the hive. There was a hole about the size of a tennis ball with half-dozen or more yellow-and-black insects guarding the entrance. They appeared to be ready to become airborne to protect their factory if the need arose. I placed my hat as close to where the hole was located but far enough away I felt would be safe. Carefully got back on the tractor, made sure the rake was in neutral, and slowly drove away making as little noise as possible. Caught up with Jay in the work shed and told him of my adventure. Without any hesitation, he picked up a gallon can of gasoline and walked directly to where my hat was located in the middle of the field. He poured a dab of gas in the hole, threw a match into the hole, and stepped back. That ended the problem with that particular set of insects. Amazing fact, I did not receive a single sting, which was unusual when that many bumblebees were flying around my head at one time.

Another episode occurred when the seventeen-year locust made their appearance. One morning when the sun had dried the dew on the grass, there appeared several flying insects about the size of a hummingbird. They, like the bumblebees, were attracted to the roar of the tractor. One appeared then another until suddenly the tractor was covered with the flying insects. Knowing full well that locust could not sting and knowing that no harm could come from them being around the tractor by the thousands, it was nevertheless very unsettling to have dozens of them landing on my shirt and pants. By the time I made it around the field and pulled up beside the wooded area, the blame things were crawling up my collar and clinging onto the skin on the side of my neck. Not that it hurt a great deal, but when the claws of several locust dig into raw flesh, it did make a person pay heed and slap in the direction of where the insect was clinging. The real misery was making the turn at the end of the field where the forest began so that the roar of the muffler shook the overhanging leaves. This made those that were hanging above my head turn loose and fly like a swarm that covered the entire tractor. When they were at their peak numbers and all were making the shrill squawking noise, it literally made your ears ring; it was so loud. The saving grace was that they only lasted about ten days or two weeks, and after they laid their eggs at the base of a tree, they quickly died off. They disappeared almost as suddenly as they appeared several days later.

When planting was complete and when the little plants and weeds were between germination and cultivating, there was a chore that must be completed. The wheat was harvested and safely stored in bins, so now was the time to bale and move wheat straw from the field to the storage sheds located at Elmer's Refectories outside of Mexico. After the combine had removed the grain from the stalk, the leftover stems were deposited on the ground behind the machine. Jay and Everet had a contract with the brick plant in Mexico to buy all the straw that was available. The plant manufactured firebricks and delivered them over the entire United States by train. The straw was used to pack around the brick columns to prevent them from shifting and destroying part of the cargo during shipment. We used a snub-nosed Chevy truck with a thirty-by-twelve-foot flatbed that when loaded held one hundred twenty-five wheat straw bales. Everet would bring out the baler and start baling while Jay and I would come behind him with the truck and pick up the bales and load them on the flatbed. The trick was to get the bales stacked on the flatbed, which was about head high to me. This made it impossible for me to throw bales head high onto the truck bed. The saving grace was a machine called a Snowco bale loader. It attached to the side of the truck with a bracket on the front bumper. With two guys work- ing, me in the driver's seat and Jay on the flatbed, we could follow behind Everet until the one hundred twenty-five bales were loaded and stacked. The loader had a front built into a V, so as I drove forward, a bale would enter the V and strike a plate attached to a trip lever, which then triggered an arm with teeth on each arm that grabbed the bale on each end. As the truck moved forward, a wheel running on the earth surface reeled in a cable, which in turn made the arm swing up and over the flatbed. At a predetermined point, the cable struck a trip lever causing the arm to snap open releasing the bale. The thicker the number of bales was lying on the ground, the faster they flew through the air. This made the job of the stacker one of rapid succession and repeated grab, stack, and step back before the next one came flying by. There was a perfect speed that must be attained so that all could go in order. Too slow and the bale fell over the side; too fast and the bales came rapidly and went flying over the opposite side. What with the heat of the day and having returned to the field after a heavy lunch, I occasionally found myself slightly sleepy behind the steering wheel. As I controlled the speed of the truck and going down the long rows of straw for an hour or so, one may slightly forget about the good speed and vary the action of the loader to some degree. Without the good speed being exact and the sixty-pound bales flying through the air in a hazardous manner, often there came from the back of the truck a voice that was Jay saying something about slowing down. The tone of his voice was unmistakably saying that something was wrong and to correct it immediately. Several times, my driving almost knocked the stacker off the stack, and that was for sure not to be taken lightly. After the truck was loaded with one hundred twenty-five bales, we three got in the truck cab and made the twenty-two-mile trip into Mexico. When we arrived, Everet would back the truck into the nearest Quonset hut that was approximately one hundred yards long and tall enough to take a twenty-five-bale high stack. My job was to throw the bales off the truck; Everet grabbed the strings and then climbed up five or six bales where Jay would take it and continue to the top. My job was rather easy if the stack was below the level of the load, but once past this, I was forced to carry the bales up a half-dozen steps to where Everet was waiting. Inside the metal building, the dust would become very thick. You can imagine the increase in temperature with no air moving while working close to the metal roof during the midafternoon in July. Such a relief to see the last bale of straw placed high upon the pile. It actually seemed cold when we stepped into the open air. Even with the temperature outside at ninety degrees, the comfort level increased dramatically. We sat in the shade for about fifteen minutes drinking from an ice jug until our body temperature reached a safe level. At this point, we loaded into the cab and headed back to the wheat field to retrieve another load.

In usual days' work, we made six or eight loads until either the straw was gone or the huts were full from top to top and side to side.

One hot and totally miserable afternoon when the temperature was approaching ninety-five degrees and after we had moved several loads of straw to the hut, Everet mentioned that maybe we should stop for the afternoon and head down to his dad's river with the fish seine and get a mess of catfish. Now that was a great idea, but it did enter my mind that it was illegal to catch fish with a seine, a law recently passed by the Conservation Commission for the state of Missouri. When they said that they would pay my fine if we got caught, it suddenly became a great idea once again. Any idea was better than loading more straw on a hot July afternoon. They got the seine out of the rafters in the work shed, and away to Warren's river we did go. With Everet on one pole and Jay on the other and me crawling along behind the net releasing the rock snags, we covered about two hundred yards and had not felt one hit on the floating seine. After dragging nearly the entire water hole from riffle to riffle, it seemed that this was going to be a dry run. We approached a huge tree on the right bank that had fallen into the river maybe a decade ago and was hung up just before the riffle. Jay took his end around the tree to the left, and Everet circled to the right when, all of a sudden, the net and floats went bonkers with fish hitting the seine from all directions. Within thirty minutes, we had captured half a gunny sack of fish and could have filled it full had we wished. Stopped back at Warren's house and spent the next hour dressing fish and then spent another hour taking fresh fish to all the neighbors. The next day at Everet's lunch table, we had a huge fish fry. Trouble was we spent most of the lunch hour deboning fish, so the kids had their share. Believe me, they really took a liking to fresh fried catfish.

Thinking back to some of the interesting stories about working for the Kendrick brothers, there were too many to mention. One that stands out as most memorable and for sure the most stressful was the trip we made to Central Illinois to sell soybeans. We spent an entire day loading soybeans from two steel bins into two separate tandem grain trucks. When the Kendrick boys loaded grain, you could be certain that they were loaded to within one inch of the rack top. It was a well-known fact that the chances of getting stopped at a weight station manned by highway patrol along the main highway were at a high percentage. Another fact was when the grain beds were filled to the brim, the load on the axels left little doubt that they were overloaded. I figured tomorrow the two would take off to Illinois, and I would probably be left behind with instructions to mow terraces or disk stubble or repair fence, but never in my wildest dreams did I think that I would be driving one of the trucks. At the time, I just turned sixteen and held a driver's license for about six months. For sure, I did not have a chauffeur's license that was required to drive a commercial vehicle or truck. Not only that but you had to be eighteen years old to even apply for such a permit, which was way in the future for this kid. As I left home early that morning, all was well in my world. Utmost in my thoughts was, at the end of the day, I would have another seven dollars in my paycheck, so what worry could make the day a threat? That feeling came to an abrupt halt when I made the turn into the driveway and headed toward Everet's house. Sitting bumper to bumper were the two loaded trucks just like we left them at the end of the workday yesterday. Today there was an extra truck standing in line. The second thing I noticed was the fact that all three were sitting low on their axels, which left little doubt that all were loaded and loaded full. With a heavy sinking sensation in my stomach, I parked my car beside the machine shed and slowly walked around the corner where Jay was filling the gas tank on the last truck in line. They both were grinning from ear to ear and looking directly at me. The feeling of preceding doom began to put a heavy load on my shoulders. Everet was first to speak and said something to the effect that they had decided to borrow their dad's truck and take all three loads to Illinois at the same time. They both agreed that I probably should drive the snub-nosed Chevy as I had been driving it around the fields and gravel roads, so I was probably most familiar with it. All that I could come up with as an intelligent remark was "Are you sure you want me to drive that loaded monster truck with no more than a new beginner's license and no chauffeur's permit? What about the highway patrol between here and the one-hundred-fifty-mile trip over hills and curves halfway across Illinois? What if I get stopped and they find everything about me is against the law?" They both just grinned and said that the farm would take care of anything that happened, so not too worry, everything would be just fine. All I needed to do was stay between the other two trucks and make sure to keep the gears low enough to pull up and out of the many hills between here and the Missouri border. Looking back after some fifty-five years later, I guess the trip was really not all that bad, but at the time, it seemed every car that approached and every car that passed me looked like a patrol car. It was all just my imagination, and it was running wild the entire long drawn-out trip. After about three hours and four hundred seventy-five shifting of gears, we pulled into the elevator. I was first to open the door and get out of the cab and stand on solid ground. What a great relief to not be behind the steering wheel of a snub-nosed Chevy. After unloading all three trucks, we started back down the road headed for home with no load and a completely different outlook on life. Now if I got stopped, at least the truck was not overloaded, so a large part of me being against the law was eliminated. Stopped for lunch at Monroe City and made it back to the farm in really good time. I can say without a doubt that my mind and body were very tired from the stress. When we pulled into the driveway, one of my hardest days of work had come to an end. Never did the gravel road of Mrs. Elliott's country home ever look as good as it did at the end of that long and worrisome trip to Illinois. To his dying day, Everet told anyone that would listen about the day Kennie hauled freight across state lines. I guess he realized how stressful that trip was for a kid that should not have been driving any farther than into town, let alone taking a snub-nosed Chevy overloaded and crossing state lines.

I realize that fishing stories have pretty well saturated my stories, so I suppose one more will not overload any nonfishing readers. This happened one day in the middle of the week when I was plowing corn the second time around in the field south of Everet's house. In the very center of the field was a puddle of water that covered approximately a half acre and was totally hidden by cattails that lined the bank. The cattails were about four feet tall and taller, so the entire pond was hidden from sight unless you were sitting on a tractor seat looking over the top. It had probably been there for half a century or longer and appeared that nobody had paid any attention to its presence for most of those years. After passing it on the tractor for the fifth time, I suddenly realized that it was about time to stop and take a bathroom break. Turned off the motor and dismounted from the tractor about thirty feet from the nearest cattails. We were far enough away from humanity there were no sounds other than the grasshoppers chirping, dozens of peeper frogs, and the red-winged blackbirds trilling their songs among the cattails. Suddenly, there was from within the wall of cattails a huge explosion of water from the surface of the little pond. Making my way to the far side of the puddle, I found a break in the cattails made by critters of the night moving to and from the pond's edge. I stood only inches from the edge of the water looking over a surface that was like glass with not a ripple to break up the mirrorlike effect. As I stood there motionless, another explosion occurred in the middle of the circle of water. The sun shining down reflected off the side of a leaping bass that looked like a minor submarine that surfaced and then disappeared underwater with spray thrown in all directions. What was quiet water with a dragonfly hovering over the surface was changed to a huge wave and no fly left to hover. Returning to the open field, I located several grasshoppers of various sizes returned to the water's edge and threw them into the water one at a time. The moment they made a move to get back to the pond's edge, the entire surface exploded as if a dozen M80s had gone off underwater. Looked at my watch and saw that it was two thirty in the afternoon, and knowing that I worked until six o'clock in the evening, there was little doubt in my mind where I would be at six two in the evening. It just happened my tackle box and fishing gear was in the trunk of my '56 Ford and ready to see what could be caught out of that great fishing hole that looked like a mud puddle. At quitting time, I parked the tractor in the machine shed, made a dash for the car, and within minutes was throwing a red plastic worm across the pond. When the worm hit the top of the water, there was an instant slam that let me know that on the other end of that line was one of the biggest bass I had ever seen, let alone ever caught. After thirty minutes and a half-dozen battles, I had on the stringer enough huge bass that it was all I could do to raise it. After several minutes of standing and admiring the most beautiful fish I had ever seen, I slowly removed each one from the stringer and released them one by one back to their quiet and peaceful little puddle. Could hardly wait to get home and tell Dad about my recent find and terrific catch. Made a mistake by telling my story to Everet the next morning. He could hardly believe that there was any fish in that little pond, let alone a trophy bass. I should have kept my mouth shut about my little secret pond because, as it happened, those fish became dinner for the Kendrick family in the very near future. Next time I made a trip to the little pond, all I caught was some nice-sized bluegill, but not one single solitary prized bass was available. So ended a once-in-a-lifetime experience of having caught the big fish and didn't even have a picture to prove my story to be true.

Short Description of the Kendrick Clan

Another benefit of working for the Kendrick brothers was the variety of people I met that were a part of their family. Having mentioned Warren many times previously, it should be said that his brothers were cast from the same mold. Each was a product of Warren's parents, and all followed the same genetic bloodline and lifestyle. One brother was Boone, and then came Henry or may have been opposite in age, but all were cut from the same die. They all were born on the old homeplace that Warren moved onto when his parents passed away. Although each was totally different one from the other, they were still an almost exact duplicate of each other. Boone lived on a farm just west of Everet's farm about two miles. This was where he and his wife, Sadie, set up housekeeping and lived their entire life. Sadie was a schoolteacher with about forty years plus experience and raised one daughter. I met her several times but never was around the family, so I was not as familiar as I with Everet and Jay. Boone was a trapper, a hunter, a fisherman, and last but not least a small-time farmer. He had a particular problem of being almost totally deaf and could not hear thunder unless it was very close. Whenever around Boone, he usually stood in the background and read lips, occasionally smiling and nodding his head. Henry, on the other hand, was a much more sophisticated and outgoing individual. He had partnered with brother Warren for half a century and did at one time do part of the farming on the homeplace. Somewhere along the way, he tended to use most of his time on the road or visiting in

Santa Fe. This left Warren to do all the work but seemed that he gave half the money to his brother no matter how little labor was returned. Henry lived in a really modern up-to-date house, had well-manicured pastures, fresh painted barns and machine sheds, and usually wore a nice Western jacket and boots along with a classy Stetson hat. His wife was one of the neatest people that I have ever met; in fact, she was the only one I ever met that was shorter than me. She was definitely a little person but one of the busiest women I have ever known. Her kitchen was specially built to accommodate her height and had several little wooden stools placed around for her to stand on when working. If I was working for the two brothers for a period of more than one day, then a day at lunch was spent with Henry and his wife. She may have been a tiny lady, but you should believe that she was a very accomplished cook, and we ate well any time we sat down to her table. They had one daughter named Joy, but she was several years older and had married and left home long before I was on the scene. What I remember about Henry was that he seldom was around when work was needed to be done. He did, however, do a lot of driving around in his truck checking on anyone that was working. One day when Everet was combining on his dad's lespedeza field, the job of waiting for the hopper to fill was my task. When full, he would stop, which was the signal for me to crank up the snub-nosed Chevy and drive beside the combine and wait until the hopper was empty. I would then return to the top of the hill and await the next stop of the combine. This would usually take anywhere from forty-five minutes to an hour before I was needed again. That meant a lot of spare time to while away. This was mostly accomplished by taking the .270 Remington rifle out of the back window and sneak down the hill to the river bottom. At this location, you would find a colony of groundhogs had set up housekeeping. They dug deep and long burrows underground, and wherever they had established an entrance, there was a mound of dirt. This field was extremely fertile soil being river bottom and had received top soil upstream for many centuries. It was seeded in alfalfa hay, which made very high-quality hay but at the same time was first choice for vegetarians, such as the groundhog. They had destroyed at least ten acres of prime alfalfa and were digging farther out each year. This was where I could earn my pay even when sitting around for the better part of two days. I would lie on my stomach behind one of the mounds and wait until one of the critters felt safe enough to leave the hole and stand upright on a mound entrance. Each time we were working in the area, we could eliminate a dozen or more, which helped slow down the population. We all knew that for every one we killed, there was at least two more to take their place. I shot a couple of boxes of high-powered rifle shells, which gave me a purpose other than sitting in the truck all that time listening to bobwhite and meadowlark birds singing. It did take my mind off how boring waiting can be when sitting for hours in a one-hundred-acre field by myself and Mother Nature. There was another gun kept in the glove box. It was a pearl-handled .22 pistol with a case of long rifle shells. Usually, I had a tobacco can in the floorboard of the truck, so by throwing it out on the ground and emptying the chamber, I got pretty good at making it dance until I ran out of ammo. Everet did not say not to use all the shells, but I did notice that several days and hundreds of shells later, it was not in the glove compartment. Must have needed it somewhere else but never did see it again. Behind the seat was an automatic .22 rifle that made a very good squirrel gun if anybody wanted to shoot squirrels. One afternoon, I was sitting under a huge walnut tree, got out the rifle, and was checking it out. At that moment, Henry drove up as I was picking out a specific walnut and trying to knock it out with a .22 slug. Seemed the more I shot, the less I hit. Henry walked up and asked if I was squirrel hunting and had I hit anything. I told him I thought the sights must be off a little as it did not seem to be shooting straight. He took the gun, looked at the barrel, filled the stock with several rounds, shouldered the rifle, and proceeded to empty the chamber.

Out of fifteen shots blew fourteen walnuts into smithereens. Did not make any difference if the sight was off as he never used it; he just pointed and pulled the trigger, and a walnut disappeared. It was a sight to see, and all I could do was stand there looking up where there used to be a tree loaded with walnuts. He said something about guess the sights were OK, turned, walked away, got in his truck, and drove off. He may not have been the hardest worker around, but he sure was a crack shot with a rifle.

Having worked for the Kendrick brothers for several months off and on during the school years and summer months, I could easily write dozens more pages about working hard, learning, and growing day by day. It was some of the most educational times of my life being taught by some of the hardest working, most honest, and most patient people a teenager could be around. Jay and Everet taught me how to be a worker, but more than that, they taught me about conservation, about tending the land we depend upon, about work ethics, about equipment preservation and repair, and about what to expect through living a life of honor and loyalty to God and country. Through the days of being around these men and women, I learned to appreciate what independence and cooperation with others can develop. To this day, I look upon the Kendrick families as being my very own clan minus the bloodline. I can truly say that the only persons that I hold more dearly than the Kendrick clan would be my very own mom and dad. At the same time, I claim all these individuals as having been responsible for my lifeline as to who I am in this world today.

As the curtain closes on the first sixteen years of a country boys life the task of living and re-living the life of the kid draws to a close. There was definitely dozens more moments of flashback that was not addressed and many, many stories that failed to be reported. I feel that the purpose of this novel has been fulfilled by reporting the true stories of a child that lived through the toddler stage, grew stronger and wiser through adolescence and entered adulthood ever so slightly and lived to tell about it. The difference between the city boy and the country boy story of life is two worlds apart but somewhere in the years of the adult they both will entwine and grow together to include the same adult standards and beliefs. Thank you Lord for letting me be a country boy, it was an experience of a lifetime.

About the Author

Ken Willingham's plans were to write life stories of his grandfather and father from the turn of the century until adulthood. He never got around to it, so when they passed away and he turned seventy-five, it became very clear that he would be the next to go. Ken surmised that he would be the only one to write about his childhood and what life was like before the new inventions began. As Ken did not have electricity until he was twelve years old, he has dozens of stories about life, entertainment, and dangers a child faces on the family farm. Having had education in a one-room school (he was salutatorian of the eighth grade; there were four of us), been raised in a town of less than one hundred inhabitants, and been working since age eight led him to have experiences that are mostly unbelievable for a child. Ken's book is 100 percent true; everything and every tale is what he actually experienced and happened just like it says.